D0343753

The Hour of One

M^r. T. P. COOKE, *as the* FLYING DUTCHMAN.

The Hour of One

SIX GOTHIC MELODRAMAS

EDITED AND INTRODUCED BY

STEPHEN WISCHHUSEN

GORDON FRASER

LONDON 1975

First published 1975 by
The Gordon Fraser Gallery Ltd, London and Bedford

ISBN 0 900406 63 1

Set in Monotype Fournier
Printed in Great Britain by
Fletcher & Son Ltd, Norwich
Designed by Peter Guy

Contents

List of Illustrations

FOR ROSS

THE THEATRE ROYAL, COVENT GARDEN, 1828

Introduction

The word 'gothic' in its literary sense conjures up a world of ruined castles and awesome landscapes, inhabited by ghouls, demons and phantoms, culled not only from the lower forms of human life, but also in surprisingly large numbers from the landed gentry, to live a life of necromancy and magic, only to have their machinations thwarted at innumerable eleventh hours by the might of righteousness. That this world, now witnessed by many on cinema screens and television, evolved and flourished nearly two hundred years ago may appear strange, but as an entertainment form, gothic drama reigned supreme over the English stage during the latter part of the eighteenth and early nineteenth centuries. Its appeal, like its celluloid successor today, was to the masses—the middle and lower middle classes who went to the theatres; those whose morals would not allow them into places of entertainment read almost the self-same thing in novel form as rapidly as the books appeared on the circulating libraries' shelves.

In novel form, perhaps the first gothic story in English literature was Walpole's *Castle of Otranto*, published in 1764. Theatrically speaking, the form's première could be said to have been in 1797 with the first presentation of Lewis's *The Castle Spectre*. Like so much in the genre, the inspiration for this play came from the Continent; in this case, the foundation is said to have been Schiller's *Die Rauber*. Another famous play of the time, Holcroft's *Tale of Mystery*, based on a play by the French dramatist Pixérécourt, is often cited as the first 'melodrama', but all the facts prove that Lewis's work is the earlier; though, to be fair, while *The Castle Spectre* is *in* the idiom, it is Holcroft's work that is actually described on its title-page as being a 'melodrama'.

While the gothic theme was well used by dramatists, its span of popular life was only some thirty years, most of the plays having been written before 1825. Its rivals in the melodramatic form had much longer periods of success, in particular the nautical melodrama—*Blackey'd Susan* was still being performed in London (at the Bedford, Camden Town) in the 1950s. However, the heritage laid down by these plays still lives on, and if the characters in the plays were colourful, so too were some of the authors.

With his play *The Vampire* (1820) James Robinson Planché introduced a new form of trap-door into the English stage—the 'Vampire Trap'. However, Planché was not merely a writer and technical innovator but was also a serious student of art and it was these studies which led him to make changes in both costume and stage design. Until 1823 it was usual for plays to be acted in contemporary costume and it was Planché who designed and supervised the costumes for John Kemble's revival of *King John* in 1823 making this the

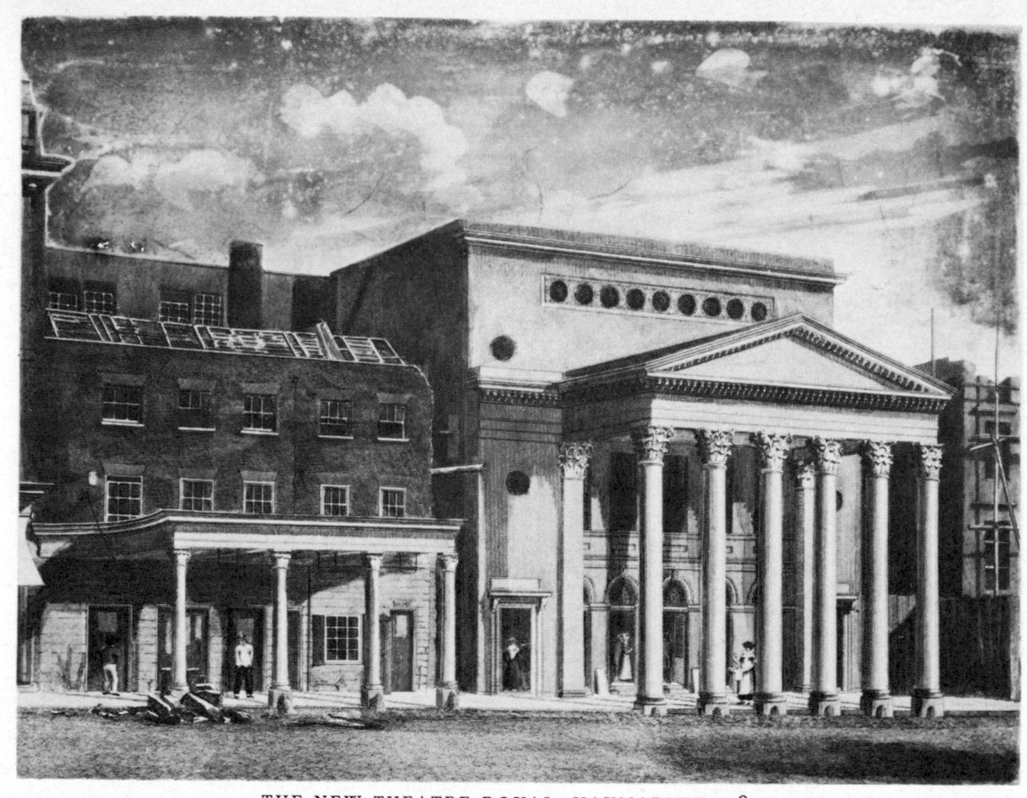

THE NEW THEATRE ROYAL, HAYMARKET, 1821

first recorded attempt at historical accuracy in a Shakespearean play.

M. G. Lewis, author of *The Castle Spectre*, perhaps the most literally coherent of the plays here, had won fame, and a nickname, with the publication of his novel *The Monk* in 1796. In *The Castle Spectre* he was hardly original in his themes, borrowing not only from Schiller, as aforesaid, but also from the German writer, August Kotzebue. Kotzebue, who died in 1819, had a far reaching influence on writers everywhere in the nineteenth century. He wrote over two hundred plays, and at one time was more popular in Germany than Schiller himself. In Britain, Sheridan was not above borrowing from his work and his *Pizarro* was taken from the German master's *Die Spanier in Peru*.

The aim of gothic drama was to divert and entertain, not to instruct and it will be obvious that there are literary shortcomings in the texts of the plays printed here. The emphasis was on the action and spectacle, not the dialogue. Ducrow, the great equestrian actor said once during rehearsals, 'Cut the cackle and let's get to the 'orses.' The fact that on this occasion he was talking about his own particular version of *Hamlet* makes little difference and his attitude was echoed by most of the popular theatres of the day.

THE THEATRES

During the hey-day of gothic drama, that is between the years 1792 and 1825, there were in London only three theatres licensed to perform legitimate drama. Licensed is perhaps not the precise word, for these three theatres—Drury Lane, Covent Garden and, in summer months when the two others were closed, the Haymarket—were Theatres Royal in the truest sense. They had been granted letters patent by royal charter and were opened by the monarch's decree, not by that of the Lord Chamberlain. The other theatres in the capital were licensed only for burlettas. Legally, any piece which had five songs in each act was a burletta, so the minor theatres, as these others were called, found that they could present almost any of the works in the repertoires of the patent theatres as long as they inserted the right number of musical interpolations. Towards the end of the period in question the two major theatres had become so large, through rebuilding schemes, that the audiences in the farther parts of the house could not hear the speech and so a broader style of playing was developed which effectively rendered the fare on offer at the patent houses no different from that obtainable at the minor playhouses.

Of the two major patent theatres, Drury Lane was the elder. Its charter had been granted by Charles II in 1662 and the theatre had first opened its doors in May 1663. To give an idea of the size of this first theatre, the whole of it occupied the area used for the stage in the present (1975) building. However, this first theatre was not the one which was in use during the period under review for there had been two remodelling schemes and it is the third building, opened in

THE NEW THEATRE ROYAL, DRURY LANE, 1812

1794, that concerns us here. At this time the theatre was under the management of John Philip Kemble and the first play in the new theatre, given on 21 April, was *Macbeth* with Kemble and his sister, Mrs Siddons, in the leading roles. During the epilogue the audience was informed of the virtual fire-resistance of the building and the first recorded lowering of a safety curtain took place. The curtain was then beaten upon by a man with a hammer to show its strength. Unfortunately this iron curtain was no salvation, for, most of the rest of the interior having been made of wood, the theatre burned down in 1809, to be replaced by a fourth, and despite constant alterations, still standing, theatre which opened in 1812. The new theatre had a a capacity of 3,060 and was the scene of many innovations including, in 1817, the installation of gas lighting. The colonnade in Russell Street was added in 1831 using the columns taken from the Regent Street Arcade. The present interior of the theatre dates from 1921.

Covent Garden Theatre too had been beset by fire. The first building opened under the management of John Rich in 1732 and was still in use until August 1808 when it burned down. The capacity of this original theatre was 1,879. The new building, which lasted until 1856, was nearly twice the size and had room for 3,000 spectators—just under the capacity of the rival house at Drury Lane. In 1803 the theatre was under the management of Kemble, who had quit Drury Lane after a disagreement with Sheridan. The second building was destroyed by fire in 1856. The third building stands today though it has been subjected to alterations since its opening in 1858.

The third patent house was the Theatre Royal, Haymarket, though its patent was not granted until 1766. It had been known as the 'Little Theatre in the Hay-Market' when it opened in 1720 and was on a site immediately north of the present building. The Haymarket Theatre had been built at a cost of £1,500 by a carpenter named John Potter on the site of the King's Head Inn. During its early years it was the London home of French companies, the first recorded performance having taken place under the patronage of the second Duke of Montague on 29 December 1720. Acrobats and dancers subsequently used the building and by 1730 Henry Fielding was providing most of the dramatic fare, being so successful with his satirical plays that in 1736 he took over the management of the theatre. Fielding's satires were so scathing and far-reaching in effect that they were responsible for triggering off the chain of events that led to the Licensing Act of 1737 which not only reinforced the monopoly of the major theatres but brought censorship to the English stage. The Haymarket was forced to close and remained derelict for some years until Samuel Foote, an actor who had worked with Macklin, took it on. Foote had set his heart on getting a royal patent for his little theatre and eventually this was granted him, though in rather tragic circumstances, as part compensation for a cruel joke played

THE ROYAL COBURG THEATRE, 1818

on him by Lord Mexborough and the Duke of York who had seated him on an unmanageable horse from which he was thrown and had to have a leg amputated. The patent, however, was only for the summer months and was to last only for Foote's lifetime. The theatre eventually passed to George Colman the younger and then to his brother-in-law, David Morris, who quit the old building in 1820 and built the present theatre to a design by Nash in 1821. The Haymarket was always rather an old-fashioned theatre: it was the last to use candles for lighting, and among the last to have a large forestage and proscenium doors. Apart from the exterior, which is virtually unchanged from Nash's design, the theatre now retains very little of its regency atmosphere having been reconstructed in 1879 and 1904.

Of the many minor theatres that were in operation in the nineteenth century, we are concerned here with only three: the Lyceum, the Coburg and the Surrey.

The Lyceum was opened as a place of public entertainment in 1765 by Dr Arnold and plans were made for the building of a theatre adjoining the property in about 1795. Through the opposition of the patent theatres, Arnold was unable to obtain a licence for his new venture and the building was used by circuses and panorama shows until 1802 when Madame Tussaud used it for the first London exhibition of her wax-works. The building and conversion of the actual theatre was completed in 1809 by Arnold's son Samuel whose success came later that year when the Drury Lane company, homeless after their own theatre had been destroyed by fire, took it over and the Lyceum became known as the 'Theatre Royal, English Opera House'. When the Drury Lane company returned to their own theatre, Arnold managed to keep their licence for the summer months and produced an excellent repertory of plays and operas at the Lyceum. The theatre was burned down in 1830 and re-opened in 1834 with the frontage which still stands in Wellington Street. What remains now of the Lyceum has nothing to do with the theatre in which Irving played, for apart from this imposing entrance in Wellington Street, the present building is the 1904 reconstruction.

In its early days one of the most infamous of the minor theatres was the Royal Coburg. Now, as the 'Old Vic' it must be one of the most famous theatres in the world. The Coburg was named after Prince Leopold and Princess Charlotte who were the first subscribers to its building fund. The stones used for the foundations were gleaned from material used for the old Savoy Palace which had just (1816) been demolished to make way for the construction of Waterloo Bridge. Kean played there in 1831 but generally the gentry stayed away—they were unwilling to cross to the 'Surrey-side' of the Thames although at one time the playbills advertised the fact that the theatre provided armed guards against the footpads lurking on the bridge! The theatre, forced to rely on the rough elements of the South Bank population for its audiences, staged sensational melodramas of a type which would

FRONT OF OLD DRURY LANE THEATRE

have certain appeal. The very fact that these lurid plays originated south of the Thames gave rise to the term 'transpontine melodrama' which, by the middle of the nineteenth century was a derogatory term applied to sensational plays wherever they were performed.

Attempts were always being made to raise the status of the theatre and its redecoration scheme of 1820 included the provision of a curtain containing sixty-three pieces of mirror-glass which reflected the whole audience. In 1883, after further redecorations, it became known as the Royal Victoria Theatre; further reconstructions took place and the Old Vic became a music hall until it closed in the early part of 1880. Later that year the freehold was bought by Emma Cons, a social reformer and the first woman member of the London County Council. The theatre re-opened on Boxing Day 1880 as a temperance amusement hall and prospered as a cheap and respectable place for family entertainment. The management passed to Lilian Bayliss, Emma Con's niece, in 1912. Minor repairs were carried out in 1927 and the theatre was reconstructed in 1950 to rectify the war damage which had kept it closed since 1941. Further reconstructions took place in 1963, when the Old Vic became the temporary home of the National Theatre.

The last of the minor theatres with which we are concerned was, in age and tradition, almost as old as the earliest of the patent houses. The Surrey Theatre in Blackfriars Road reached many peaks of success during 152 years of its life. The original theatre had opened in 1782 and was built at a cost of £15,000. It had been constructed as an amphitheatre —in this sense meaning an auditorium which had a circus ring in front of its orthodox stage, thus enabling equestrian displays to be performed. In this form it was known as the Royal Circus, set up by Charles Dibdin and Charles Hughes as a rival to Astley's Royal Amphitheatre. Fire destroyed the building twice, in 1799 and 1805, and after the second fire the site was acquired by Robert Elliston, the actor, who turned the Royal Circus into a legitimate theatre in 1809. In a bid to get round the monopoly ostensibly enjoyed by the patent theatres Elliston introduced a ballet into each production. He progressed until he was a manager of Drury Lane, but his ambitious productions, though successful and well-acclaimed, forced him into bankruptcy and by 1826 he was penniless. Not daunted by this, he had paid off his debts by 1827 and was back in management at the Surrey and it was here in 1829 that he produced Jerrold's *Blackey'd Susan*, one of the most famous plays of the nineteenth century. *Jonathan Bradford* was another of the Surrey's successes and by 1848 it was for this sort of rough-house drama that the theatre had become famous. The great Conquest family ran the house from 1881 to 1903 and it became a music hall in 1904. After a period of decline the building was used as a cinema until 1924 when it finally closed, remaining empty for some years until 1935 when it was bought for an extension to the Royal Ophthalmic Hospital. The building was subsequently demolished.

Geo. Jones del.

I Stow. sculp

INTERIOR OF THE LITTLE THEATRE, HAYMARKET, 1815

Playgoing in London and elsewhere today is comparatively easy. Bookings may be made for almost all parts of the house by telephone, post or personal application and there is little difficulty in finding out what fare is being offered as all national newspapers carry the advertisements and, depending on the audience being sought, other forms of advertising including posters on the Underground and television commercials are often employed. At the beginning of the period of our earliest play, while finding out what was on may have presented no real problem, securing places for any part of the theatre except the boxes, on any night except a benefit night, was impossible.

To begin to comprehend playgoing in the late eighteenth and early nineteenth centuries it is essential to understand that the demarcation of the seating then bore little resemblance to that which we know today. Stalls, dress and upper circles, were not in being and 'boxes' did not have precisely today's meaning. The illustration of the interior of Covent Garden in 1794 well shows the typical form of seating of the time. It will be seen that the area occupied by our stalls was then taken up by the pit—continuous, backless, benches, running straight across the auditorium. The term 'pit' is still used in some provincial theatres today, slightly modified perhaps to pit stalls which is in fact a technical impossibility and contradiction in terms. Behind, and encircling, the pit was the first tier of boxes. Again, reference to the illustration of the Covent Garden interior shows that the seating in the boxes was similar to that in the pit. The backless benches were arranged in two or three rows and were hinged at one end to permit access to the front bench. Each row in each box was capable of accommodating perhaps three or four persons. In some theatres there was a second tier of boxes above the first with one or two galleries above that. The galleries contained similar benches to those in the pit.

It will be seen therefore that it was impossible to reserve a seat in the pit or gallery as 'seats' did not exist and there was no practical way of identifying a particular part of a bench. The number of spectators contained in these parts of theatre could vary enormously. While on a quiet night it was possible to enjoy the play in relative comfort, on a successful night a zealous management would squeeze in as many people as possible. There is an apocryphal story of one particular theatre's attendants encouraging people to 'push along' so much that the people on the end would fall off the bench and have to go round again, thus causing more pushing, and more falling off. Though the story may not be true it does give an idea of the discomfort endured during a visit to a popular play.

Between ten in the morning and four in the afternoon seats in the boxes for the evening performance could be reserved at the theatre in what was known variously as the 'Box Keeper's Office' or, because of the book in which the assignments were made, the 'Box Book Keeper's Office';

INTERIOR OF THE THEATRE ROYAL, COVENT GARDEN, 1794-1808

hence our 'Box Office' of today. On arrival at the theatre in the evening, our box seat patron would check the plan on display in the lobby to see in which box his place was allocated. The keeper of each box was furnished with a list of those who should be in that box and the places would generally be kept until the end of the first act of the main piece.

To be sure of a place in either the pit or the galleries those intending to see the evening's entertainment in full had to be at the theatre at least an hour before the advertised time of the performance. At this time the doors to the various parts would be opened and there would be a general rush to the pay boxes which were situated at the auditorium end of the entrance corridors. In exchange for the fee the patron would be given a metal check which would be surrendered to a check-taker for scrutiny and retention for subsequent tallying with the receipts. Paper tickets did not come in to general use until 1884, though benefit nights were an exception. These were given periodically through the season and, after paying the house expenses, candles, wages, advertising costs, etc., the nett money was the property of the artist who would 'benefit'. Tickets for benefits were printed on paper or card and, as a precaution against forgery, were often signed by the artist. These tickets were available in limited supply from the theatre, and also from the various coffee-houses, the artist's home, and occasionally—but especially for the Opera—from banking halls.

An evening's entertainment would usually have three items on the bill: perhaps a comedy or a burlesque as a 'curtain raiser', the main piece, and the after-piece. It was usual, too, to have a second price of admission, i.e. cheaper admission after the first act of the main piece. In the early years of our period performances could start as early as 6.30 pm and still not be expected to end until nearly midnight. By 1831, Leigh Hunt among others was complaining of the late hours at which performances would end and he praised Madame Vestris at the Olympic for terminating the programme at 11.00 pm, a move which he hoped would be adopted by other managements. However, the practice of curtain raisers and after-pieces continuned until the end of the nineteenth century and was certainly in use during Wyndham's management of the Criterion.

Notice of the entertainment on offer at the various theatres would be made in the London morning papers. Intending patrons would also see about the town the 'Big Bills' which were pasted up daily, performances at most theatres being on a repertory basis. These 'Big Bills' varied in size from crown (ten-by-fifteen inches) through variants to double-crown (twenty-by-thirty inches) which in those days was usually posted broadside instead of in the upright position used today. Quite a common size was the long narrow bill, more favoured towards the end of the nineteenth century, thirty or so inches high and only ten inches wide; its name, 'Long Tom', survives in use on one of the major theatre circuits as that of the long sheet on which advance

INTERIOR OF THE ROYAL COBURG THEATRE, 1818

bookings are detailed. In addition to the details of the day's programme the 'Big Bills' would also carry announcements of some of the attractions on offer for the rest of the week.

Inside the theatre, the playbill itself would be sold. This was a smaller (ten-by-eight inches or thirteen-by-eight inches) version of the 'Big Bill' displayed outside and would be sold by the so-called fruit, or orange, women. These, like their counterparts today, were generally not under the direction of the theatre management but would be controlled by a supervisor (now a catering company) who purchased the sale concession for a set fee each season. Programmes as we know them did not come into general use until the 1870s.

The copy for the 'Big Bill' would be prepared the night before the performance by the prompter. The position of being solely prompter for a production today is virtually unknown but in the eighteenth and nineteenth centuries it was a post of utmost importance. It was the prompter who took the morning rehearsals of stock pieces, who saw to it that the regulations governing back-stage life were adhered to, and it was he who administered the fines levied on the actors for any misdemeanours committed within the theatre. Working under the prompter would be a copyist whose job it would be to copy the parts from the author's manuscript if the play was a new one which had not yet been published, and a call-boy who would call the members of the cast from their dressing rooms as their entrance cues approached. Sometimes in the patent theatres, and almost regularly in the smaller ones, the prompter would also appear in the plays, necessitating the regular engagement of an under-prompter who might also fulfil the position of copyist.

The actual numbers employed in the running of a large theatre in the early nineteenth century are indicated in the following list prepared by the actor O. Smith:

> Stage Manager, Pantomime Director, Ballet and Chorus Master, Prompter, Under-Prompter, Copyists, Music Copyists, and Assistant Director of the Musical Department, Leader of the Band, Repititeur, Musicians, Scene Painters and occasional assistants, colour grinder, Property Master and assistants, Carpenters, Scene-Shifters, Master Tailor and Keeper of the Gentleman's Wardrobe, Keeper of the Ladies' Wardrobe and assistants, Treasurer, Under-Treasurer, House Keeper, Bill Inspector, Money Takers, Check-Takers, Lamplighters, Firemen, Porters, Watch-Men, Dressers, Cleaners.

In addition to these there would be the acting company, chorus singers and occasional supernumeraries.

The importance of the prompter during this period is well illustrated in the following verses from the reminiscences of O'Keefe, a popular actor and author of the time, in which the prompter's duties are laid down:

The play received, by manager 'tis cast;
Aloud in green-room to performers read,
Each keeps his eye upon his part—nought said.

E. Burney, Pinx^t

J. Stow Sc^t

THE PROSCENIUM of the ENGLISH OPERA HOUSE in the STRAND, (LATE LYCEUM.)
as it appeared on the Evening of the 21st. March 1817, with Walker's Exhibition of the Eidouranian.

Rehearsals call'd, and, from the first to last,
The prompter on the stage at table sits;
He vers'd in works of great and little wits,
What safe and dangerous can with art contrast.

Thro' dressing rooms is heard the warning call,
'First music gentlemen; first music, ladies:'
'Third Music!' that's the notice to appal;
Like summons from Lord Mayor, or buffing cadies:
The call-boy is this herald's appellation.
The curtain up, the prompter takes his station.

'Tis not alone with art to throw the word,
If actors in their parts should make a stand;
To prompter many duties more belong,
Than biding at the wing with book in hand.
Off their go-off, come-on, he points the sides,
By margin letters of P.S. O.P.

Stage properties, stage business, music, band,
Of stage arena the prompter keeps the key.
He writes the playbills out, pens paragraphs,
Marks forfeits down for every stage neglect.
The audience gone, he, ere the lights are out,
Of all new scenes tries every new effect:
And, from eleven o'clock, perhaps till three,
He in his duties all that time must spend;
And then from six to twelve o'clock at night,
Upon the stage the Prompter must attend.

Gradually through the period a more logical way of directing the plays was introduced. Hitherto, besides the prompter's presiding over rehearsals of stock plays, the author of a new play, his friends and the exponents of the various roles would each have their say as to how the piece should be done.

The appearance of the legend 'The action of the Melodrama under the direction of Mr T. P. Cooke' on the bill of the English Opera House for 19 August 1820 may not be the first time such a credit was given, but it is the first I have seen, and it is interesting to conjecture why Cooke should have done it. Perhaps it was because he was so successful in melodramatic roles that his name appearing as director as well as among the players would be an assurance of a high standard. It is odd that not more mention has been made of Cooke's talents as a director. It is apparent that he was successful in this line for, among other plays, he is credited with the direction of the 'melodramatic business' of the Adelphi's first production of their version of *The Flying Dutchman* in 1827. Cooke is not alone in having combined the arts of director and actor for his contemporary, Farley, is credited on the bill at Covent Garden in 1829 with the direction of the action of the first performance of *The Devil's Elixir*.

I have spoken of a 'curtain-raiser', and the part the curtain played during the evening's entertainment is most important: once up, it would not come down during the action of a piece. The scenes were changed in full view of the audience, and divisions between the acts were denoted by the lowering

DRURY LANE THEATRE FROM THE STAGE, 1804

of a specially painted 'Act Drop'—so-called because, unlike the scenes which were usually slid in from the side in grooves on and above the stage, the 'Act Drop' was dropped in (unrolled) from above. Flys, that part of the theatre above the stage where scenery can be hoisted up (flown) out of sight came in to general use much later. The nineteenth century theatre curtain was almost invariably green.* According to Richard Southern it took as its commonest form that of the 'french valance' in which a series of lines descended at the back through rows of rings. When the lines were pulled the curtain rose vertically in a series of bunching, shallow festoons.† It is odd that green was the chosen colour, for though it crops up in theatrical parlance often—we have green-rooms, where the Company meet and music-hall people talk of going 'on the green' when they go on stage—it is considered to be an unlucky colour in theatrical superstition. Perhaps this comes from the old tradition of laying a green baize cloth on the stage, during the eighteenth and early nineteenth centuries, to denote that a tragedy was to be given. However, green it was, and green it stayed, until 1880, when there is the first recorded instance of the curtain's being red, and used to hide scene changes, during Irving's revival of *The Corsican Brothers*.

* The only London theatre now to have a green curtain is Wyndham's in Charing Cross Road, the curtain here has been restored to its fully ornate and swagged 1899 condition.

† *Oxford Companion to the Theatre* p. 223.

The practice of not letting the curtain's lowering interrupt the action of the play meant that the plot could be presented continuously, almost cinematically, and as the gothic drama in particular relied upon action and effect as much as language, it is interesting to note how similar to silent film scenarios many of the old scripts are. The stage directions of Act IV, Scene II of Lewis's *Castle Spectre* ably illustrate this point:

> The folding doors unclose, and the oratory is seen illuminated. In its centre stands a tall female figure, her white and flowing garments spotted with blood; her veil is thrown back and discovers a pale and melancholy countenance; her eyes are lifted upwards, her arms extended towards heaven, and a large wound appears on her bosom. Angela sinks upon her knees with her eyes riveted upon the figure, which for some moment remains motionless. At length the spectre advances slowly to a soft and plaintive strain: she stops opposite to Reginald's picture and gazes upon it in silence. She then turns, approaches Angela, seems to invoke a blessing upon her, points to the picture, and returns to the oratory. The music ceases. Angela rises with a wild look, and follows the vision, extending her arm towards it. The spectre waves her hand, as bidding her farewell. Instantly the organ's swell is heard: a full chorus of female voices chant "Jubilante". A blaze of light flashes through the oratory, and the folding doors close with a loud noise. Angela falls motionless on the floor.

rawn by Thos. H. Shepherd. Engraved by Thos. Dale

THE SURREY THEATRE, BLACKFRIARS ROAD, 1828

Lighting the stage for these gothic dramas was important too, but it must be remembered that for most of the period under review all lighting was provided by candles or oil. The 'floats', footlights made up of wicks threaded through a cork float resting in a trough of oil, were the main stage lighting from the front. These were in a trap and could be raised or lowered through the stage. Extra lighting was placed behind the wings and, as the main action generally took place on the fore-stage, the auditorium chandeliers lit the action as well. Gas lighting was introduced in 1817, first in the auditoriums, then, at the Lyceum first of all, on the stage itself. This had varying success in its initial stages and caused twice as many theatre fires in its first decade than had been known previously. Certainly gas lighting made the stage brighter, as indeed it had to as the action retreated from the fore-stage and moved more and more behind the proscenium. At a later date, with newer forms of control, gas gave subtle effects which Irving at least preferred to electricity. Gas had the advantage over the earlier forms of lighting that it could be dimmed and more easily controlled; also, coloured scrims could be applied which would give a general tone to the stage picture.

Melodramatic characters had to be clearly identifiable. Right had to triumph over wrong, and the participants on each side were known to the audiences by their style of playing almost as soon as they had made their first entrance. As melodrama was more the mainstay of the minor theatres, an example of one in performance told by Charles Dickens in *Sketches by Boz*, will be of interest. This was witnessed at a very minor theatre, a booth in fact, at Greenwich Fair, but the technique was the same:

> A Change of performance takes place every day at the fair, but the story of the tragedy is always pretty much the same. There is a rightful heir, who loves a young lady, and is beloved by her; and the wrongful heir who loves her too, and isn't beloved by her; and the wrongful heir gets hold of the rightful heir and throws him in to a dungeon just to kill him off when convenient, for which purpose he hires a couple of assassins—a good one and a bad one—who—the moment they are alone, get up a little murder on their own account, the good one killing the bad one and the bad one wounding the good one. Then the rightful heir is discovered in prison, carefully holding a long chain in his hands, and seated despondingly in a large arm-chair; and the young lady comes in to two bars of soft music and embraces the rightful heir; and then the wrongful heir comes in to two bars of quick music (technically called a 'hurry') and goes on in the most shocking manner, and calling the rightful heir 'Ar-recreant—ar-wretch' in a very loud voice, which answers the double purpose of displaying his passion, and preventing the sound being deadened by the sawdust. The interest becomes intense; the wrongful heir draws his sword and rushes on the rightful heir; a blue smoke is seen, a gong is heard, and a tall

Elevation of the Principal
FRONT of the **ROYAL COBURG THEATRE**, *Building under the Patronage of Their Serene and Royal Highnesses Prince Leopold, and Princess Charlotte*
Designed by I.T. Serres.
Director of the Decorative and Scenery Department at the Theatre and
Published by him as the Act directs at his Study in Covent Garden Chambers 1st Jan. 1817.

white figure (who has been all this time behind the arm-chair covered over with a table cloth) slowly rises to the tune of 'Oft in the Stilly Night'. This is no other than the ghost of the rightful heir's father who was killed by the wrongful heir's father, at the sight of which the wrongful heir becomes apoplectic and is literally 'struck all of aheap', the stage not being large enough to admit of his falling down at full length. Then the good assassin staggers in and says that he was hired in conjunction with the bad assassin, by the wrongful heir, to kill the rightful heir; and he's killed a good many men in his time, but he's very sorry for it, and won't do so any more—a promise which he immediately redeems by dying off-hand without any nonsense about it. Then the rightful heir throws down his chain; and two men, a sailor, and a young woman (the tenantry of the rightful heir) come in and the ghost makes dumb motions to them, which they, by supernatural inference understand—for no-one else can; and the ghost (who can't do anything without blue fire) blesses the rightful heir and the young lady by half-suffocating them with smoke, and then a muffin bell rings and the curtain drops.'

Stage directions in these plays are complicated to follow. It is hoped that the following reproduction giving the relative positions, taken from an original edition will be of help, and also the quotation from the prefaces to the plays stating that 'The reader is supposed to be on stage facing the audience.' The prompt side (PS) is actor's left, opposite prompt (OP) being therefore the actor's right. The directions for second entrance, upper entrance, and variants of these denote how far up or down stage the entrance was to be made.

STAGE DIRECTIONS.

The Conductors of this Work print no Plays but those which they have seen acted. The *Stage Directions* are given from their own personal observations, during the most recent performances.

The instant a *Character* appears upon the Stage, the point of *Entrance*, as well as every subsequent change of *Position*, till its *Exit*, is noted, with a fidelity which may, in all cases, be relied on; the object being, to establish this Work as a *Standard Guide to the Stage business*, as now conducted on the London boards.

EXITS and ENTRANCES.

R. means *Right*; L. *Left*; R. D. *Right Door*; L. D. *Left Door*; S. E. *Second Entrance*; U. E. *Upper Entrance*; M. D. *Middle Door.*

RELATIVE POSITIONS.

R. means *Right*; L. *Left*; C. *Centre*; R. C. *Right of Centre*; L.C. *Left of Centre.* The following view of the Stage with Five Peformers in front, will, it is presumed, fully demonstrate the *Relative Positions.*

*** *The Reader is supposed to be on the Stage facing the Audience.*

NINTH TIME.

Theatre Royal, Drury-Lane,

This preſent WEDNESDAY DECEMBER 27, 1797,
Their Majeſties Servants will perform a new Drama in 5 acts called

The CASTLE-SPECTRE.

With New Dreſſes, Scenery, and Decorations, *by Lewis*
The Characters by
Mr. BARRYMORE,
Mr. WROUGHTON,
Mr. KEMBLE,
Mr. PALMER,
Mr. BANNISTER, Jun.
Mr. AICKIN, Mr. DOWTON,
Mr. TRUEMAN, Mr. DAVIS,
Mr. WENTWORTH, Mr. GIBBON,
Mr. PACKER, Mr. WATHEN,
Mrs. JORDAN,
Mrs. WALCOT,
The Prologue to be ſpoken by Mr. WROUGHTON,
And the Epilogue by Mrs. JORDAN.
The Scenery deſigned by the late Mr. GREENWOOD, and Executed by his SON,
Mr. PUGH, and Others.
After which a Farce called The

IRISH WIDOW.

Sir Patrick O'Neale, Mr. R PALMER, Whittle, Mr. DOWTON,
Nephew, Mr. HOLLAND, Bates, Mr. MADDOCKS,
Keckſey, Mr SUETT, Thomas, Mr. HOLLINSWORTH.
Widow Brady, with the Epilogue Song, Miſs BIGGS,
To which will be added (15th. time) a New Muſical Entertainment called

A TRIP to the NORE.

With New Scenery, and Machinery.
The Muſic partly New and partly Compiled; with an introductory Full Piece.
The Characters by
Mr. SUETT, Mr BANNISTER, Jun.
With a New Song call'd a Salt Eel for Mynheer, by Permiſſion of Mr. DIBDIN.
Mr. HOLLINGSWORTH, Mr. DIGNUM,
Mr. WEWITZER, Mr. SEDGWICK,
Mr. DAVIS, Mr. GRIMALDI,
Mrs. BLAND,
Mrs. WALCOT, Miſs TIDSWELL.
In the courſe of the Piece a View of

GREENWICH HOSPITAL,

And an Exact Repreſentation of
The DEPARTURE of the ROYAL YATCH,
To conclude with a View of
The BRITISH FLEET,
And the
DUTCH PRIZES.

Printed by C. LOWNDES next the Stage-Door *Vivant Rex et Regina!*

The New Drama of The CASTLE-SPECTRE being received with unbounded marks of univerſal approbation—Thoſe Ladies and Gentlemen who have been diſappointed of places, are reſpectfully informed that the 10th. and 11th nights will be To-morrow, and Friday. After The CASTLE-SPECTRE, To-morrow; The Muſical Entertainment of the DESERTER.

☞ A New Comedy is in Rehearſal.

R. Cruikshank, Del. White, Sc.

The Castle Spectre.

Angela sinks upon her knees, with her eyes rivetted upon the figure, which for some moments remain motionless.

Act IV. Scene 2.

THE CASTLE SPECTRE.

A DRAMATIC ROMANCE,

In Five Acts,

BY M. G. LEWIS.

PRINTED FROM THE ACTING COPY, WITH REMARKS, BIOGRAPHICAL AND CRITICAL,

To which are added,

A DESCRIPTION OF THE COSTUME,—CAST OF THE CHARACTERS, ENTRANCES AND EXITS,—RELATIVE POSITIONS OF THE PERFORMERS ON THE STAGE,—AND THE WHOLE OF THE STAGE BUSINESS.

As now performed at the

THEATRES ROYAL, LONDON.

EMBELLISHED WITH A FINE WOOD ENGRAVING

By Mr. White, from a Drawing taken in the Theatre, by Mr. R. Cruikshank.

LONDON:

JOHN CUMBERLAND, 19, LUDGATE HILL.

Costume.

EARL OSMOND.—Yellow tunic, trimmed with silver spangles and buttons; purple velvet belt, white pantaloons spangled, short blue velvet robe trimmed with fur only, open sleeves. Second dress.—Handsome satin morning-gown.

PERCY.—Slate-coloured shirt tunic, trimmed with black galloon, flesh pantaloons. Second dress.—Green old English suit, with puffs trimmed, steel breastplate, long scarlet satin sash, leather belts; black velvet hat, white feathers, gauntlets, russet boots, ruff.

KENRIC.—Brown velvet shape, puffed with blue, cloak of the same, brown stockings.

HASSAN.—White body with sleeves looped up, trowsers of same, black leggings and arms, black velvet flys, silver buttons, sandals.

SAIB.
MULEY. } Ditto.

ALARIC.—Not quite so good.

MOTLEY.—Touchstone's dress.

FATHER PHILIP.—Friar's grey gown, with Falstaff's belly, a cord round the waist, flesh stockings and sandals.

ALLAN.—An old English dress, drab trimmed with black.

HAROLD.—Blue tunic with yellow binding, blue stockings, short breeches.

EDRIC.—Blue Flushing great coat, blue trowsers, striped Guernsey shirt, blue cap, fishing stockings and boots.

REGINALD.—Brown tunic and pantaloons, with a loose torn cloak or drapery, flesh legs and arms, old sandals, the whole dress much torn.

SOLDIERS.—Green tunics with scarlet bindings, and stockings, boots, and breastplates.

ANGELA.—Handsome embroidered white satin dress.

ALICE.—Black open gown trimmed with point lace, red stuff petticoat, black hood, high heel'd shoes, with buckles.

SPECTRE.—Plain white muslin dress, white head dress, or binding under chin, light loose gauze drapery.

Cast of the Characters as performed at the Theatres Royal.

	As originally acted.	Drury Lane.	Covent Garden.
Osmond	Mr. Barrymore.	Mr. Rae.	Mr. Young.
Reginald	Mr. Wroughton.	Mr. Pope.	Mr. Murray.
Percy	Mr. Kemble.	Mr. Barnard.	Mr. Abbott.
Father Philip	Mr. Palmer.	Mr. Gattie.	Mr. Egerton.
Motley	Mr. Bannister, jun.	Mr. Harley.	Mr. Blanchard.
Kenric	Mr. Aickin.	Mr. Carr.	Mr. Claremont.
Saib	Mr. Truman.	Mr. Coveney.	Mr. Treby.
Hassan	Mr. Dowton.	Mr. Penley.	Mr. Slader.
Muley	Mr. Davis.	Mr. Smith.	Mr. Jefferies.
Alaric	Mr. Wentworth.	Mr. Evans.	Mr. Louis.
Allan	Mr. Packer.	Mr. Maddocks.	
Edric	Mr. Wathen.	Mr. Minton.	Mr. Atkins.
Harold	Mr. Gibbon.	Mr. Buxton.	
Angela	Mrs. Jordan.	Mrs. Robinson.	Miss Bristow.
Alice	Mrs. Walcot.	Mrs. Sparks.	Mrs. Kennedy.
Evelina	Mrs. Powell.	Mrs. Knight.	Mrs. Powell.

STAGE DIRECTIONS.

The Conductors of this Work print no Plays but those which they have seen acted. The *Stage Directions* are given from their own personal observations, during the most recent performances.

EXITS and ENTRANCES.

R. means *Right;* L. *Left;* R. D. *Right Door;* L. D. *Left Door;* S. E. *Second Entrance;* U. E. *Upper Entrance;* M. D. *Middle Door.*

RELATIVE POSITIONS.

R. means *Right;* L. *Left;* C. *Centre;* R. C. *Right of Centre;* L.C. *Left of Centre.*

*** *The Reader is supposed to be on the Stage facing the Audience.*

R. RC. C. LC. L.

PROLOGUE.

Spoken by Mr. Wroughton.

Far from the haunts of men, of vice the foe,
The moon-struck child of genius and of woe,
Versed in each magic spell and dear to fame,
A fair enchantress dwells, Romance her name.
She loathes the sun, or blazing taper's light.
The moon-beam'd landscape and tempestuous night,
Alone she loves; and oft, with glimmering lamp,
Near graves new open'd, or 'midst dungeons damp,
Drear forests, ruin'd aisles, and haunted towers,
Forlorn she roves, and raves away the hours!
Anon, when storms howl loud, and lash the deep,
Desperate she climbs the sea-rock's beetling steep;
There wildly strikes her harp's fantastic strings,
Tells to the moon how grief her bosom wrings;
And while her strange song chants fictitious ills,
In wounded hearts Oblivion's balm distils.
A youth, who yet has liv'd enough to know
That life has thorns, and taste the cup of woe,
As late near Conway's time-bowed towers he stray'd,
Invok'd this bright enthusiast's magic aid.
His prayer was heard. With arms and bosom bare,
Eyes flashing fire, loose robes, and streaming hair,
Her heart all anguish, and her soul all flame,
Swift as her thoughts, the lovely maniac came!
High heav'd her breasts, with struggling passions rent,
As prest to give some fear-fraught mystery vent:
And oft, with anxious glance and altered face,
Trembling with terror, she relaxed her pace,

And stopt! and listened!—then with hurried tread
Onwards again she rushed, yet backwards bent her head,
As if from murderous swords or following fiends she fled.
Soon as near Conway's walls her footsteps drew,
She bade the youth their ancient state renew.
Eager he sped, the fallen towers to rear:
'Twas done, and Fancy bore the fabric here.
Next, choosing from great Shakspeare's comic school;
The gossip crone, gross friar, and gibing fool—
These, with a virgin fair and lover brave,
To our young author's care the enchantress gave;
But charged him, 'ere he bless'd the brave and fair,
To lay the exulting villain's bosom bare;
And, by the torments of his conscience, shew,
That prosperous vice is but triumphant woe!
The pleasing task, congenial to his soul,
Oft from his own sad thoughts our author stole:
Blest be his labours, if with like success
They soothe their sorrows whom I now address.
Beneath this dome, should some afflicted breast
Mourn slighted talents, or desert opprest,
False friendship, hopeless love, or faith betray'd,
Our author will esteem each toil o'er-paid,
If, while his muse exerts her livelier vein,
Or tells imagin'd woes in plaintive strain,
Her flights and fancies make one smile appear
On the pale cheek, where trickled late a tear;
Or if *her* fabled sorrows steal one groan,
Which else her hearers would have given their own.

THE CASTLE SPECTRE.

ACT I.

SCENE I.—*A Grove.*

Enter FATHER PHILIP *and* MOTLEY, *through Gate*, L. U. E.

F. Phil. NEVER tell me!—I repeat it, you are a fellow of a very scandalous course of life! But what principally offends me is, that you pervert the minds of the maids, and keep kissing and smuggling all the pretty girls you meet. Oh! fye! fye! [*Crosses to* R.

Mot. I kiss and smuggle them? St. Francis forbid! Lord love you, father, 'tis they who kiss and smuggle me. I protest, I do what I can to preserve my modesty; and I wish that the Archbishop Dunstan had heard the lecture upon chastity which I read last night to the dairy-maid in the dark! he'd have been quite edified. But yet what does talking signify? The eloquence of my lips is counteracted by the lustre of my eyes; and really the little devils are so tender, and so troublesome, that I'm half angry with nature for having made me so very bewitching.

F. Phil. Nonsense! nonsense!

Mot. Put yourself in my place:—suppose that a sweet, smiling rogue, just sixteen, with rosy cheeks, sparkling eyes, pouting lips, &c.—

F. Phil. Oh, fye! fye! fye!—To hear such licentious discourse brings the tears into my eyes!

Mot. I believe you, father; for I see the water is running over at your mouth; which puts me in mind, my good father, that there are some little points which might be altered in you still better than in myself: such as intemperance, gluttony—

F. Phil. Gluttony! Oh! abominable falsehood!

Mot. Plain matter of fact!—Why, will any man pretend to say that you came honestly by that enormous belly, that tremendous tomb of fish, flesh, and fowl? And, for incontinence, you must allow, yourself, that you are unequalled.

F. Phil. I!—I!—

Mot. You! you!—May I ask what was your business in the beech grove the other evening, when I caught you with buxom Margery, the miller's pretty wife? Was it quite necessary to lay your heads together so close?

F. Phil. Perfectly necessary: I was whispering in her ear wholesome advice.

Mot. Indeed? Faith then she took your advice as kindly as it was given, and exactly in the same way too: you gave it with your lips, and she took it with hers.—Well done, father Philip!

F. Phil. Son, son, you give your tongue too great a license.

Mot. Nay, father, be not angry: fools, you know, are privileged persons.

F. Phil. I know they are very useless ones; and in short, master Motley, to be plain with you, of all fools I think you the worst; and for fools of all kinds I've an insuperable aversion.

Mot. Really? Then you have one good quality at least, and I cannot but admire such a total want of self-love! [*Bell rings*, L.] But, hark! there goes the dinner-bell—away to table, father.—Depend upon 't, the servants will rather eat part of their dinner unblessed, than stay till your stomach comes like Jonas's whale, and swallows up the whole.

F. Phil. Well, well, fool; I am going; but first let me explain to you, that my bulk proceeds from no indulgence of voracious appetite. No, son, no—little sustenance do I take; but St. Cuthbert's blessing is upon me, and that little prospers with me most marvellously. Verily, the saint has given me rather too plentiful an increase, and my legs are scarce able to support the weight of his bounties.

[*Exit through gate*, L. U. E.

Mot. He looks like an overgrown turtle, waddling upon its hind fins! Yet, at bottom, 'tis a good fellow enough, warm hearted, benevolent, friendly, and sincere; but no more intended by nature to be a monk, than I to be a maid of honour to the queen of Sheba. [*Going*, L. U. E.

Enter PERCY, R.

Per. I cannot be mistaken—In spite of his dress, his

features are too well known to me! Hist! Gilbert! Gilbert!

Mot. (L.) Gilbert? Oh lord, that's I!—Who calls?

Per. Have you forgotten me?

Mot. Truly, sir, that would be no easy matter; I never forgot in my life what I never knew.

Per. (R.) Have ten years altered me so much that you cannot—

Mot. Hey!—can it be—Pardon me, my dear lord Percy.—In truth, you may well forgive my having forgotten your name, for at first I didn't very well remember my own However, to prevent further mistakes, I must inform you that he who in your father's service was Gilbert the knave, is Motley the fool in the service of Earl Osmond.

Per. Of Earl Osmond?—This is fortunate. Gilbert, you may be of use to me; and if the attachment which as a boy you professed for me still exists—

Mot. It does, with ardour unabated, for I'm not so unjust as to attribute to you my expulsion from Alnwick castle: but now, sir, may I ask, what brings you to Wales?

Per. A woman whom I adore.

Mot. Yes, I guessed that the business was about a petticoat. And this woman is—

Per. (R.) The orphan ward of a villager, without friends, without family, without fortune!

Mot. (L.) Great points in her favour, I must confess. And which of these excellent qualities won your heart?

Per. I hope I had better reasons for bestowing it on her. No, Gilbert; I loved her for a person beautiful without art and graceful without affectation, for a heart tender without weakness, and noble without pride. I saw her at once beloved and reverenced by her village companions; they looked on her as a being of a superior order: and I felt, that she who gave such dignity to the cottage maid, must needs add new lustre to the coronet of the Percies.

Mot. From which I am to understand that you mean to marry this rustic?

Per. Could I mean otherwise I should blush for myself.

Mot. Yet, surely, the baseness of her origin—

Per. Can to me be no objection: in giving her my hand I raise her to my station, not debase myself to hers; nor ever, while gazing on the beauty of a rose, did I think it less fair because planted by a peasant.

Mot. Bravo!—And what says your good grumbling father to this?

Per. Alas! he has long slept in the grave.

Mot. Then he's quiet at last! Well, heaven grant him that peace above, which he suffered nobody to enjoy below. But his death having left you master of your actions, what obstacle now prevents your marriage?

Per. You shall hear.—Fearful lest my rank should influence this lovely girl's affections, and induce her to bestow her hand on the noble, while she refused her heart to the man, I assumed a peasant's habit, and presented myself as Edwy, the low-born and the poor. In this character I gained her heart, and resolved to hail as Countess of Northumberland, the betrothed of Edwy the low-born and the poor! Judge, then, how great must have been my disappointment, when, on entering her guardian's cottage with this design, he informed me, that the unknown, who sixteen years before had confided her to his care, had reclaimed her on that very morning, and conveyed her—no one knew whither.

Mot. That was unlucky.

Per. However, in spite of his precautions, I have traced the stranger's course, and find him to be Kenric, a dependant upon Earl Osmond.

Mot. Surely, 'tis not Lady Angela, who—

Per. The very same! Speak, my good fellow! do you know her?

Mot. Not by your description; for here she's understood to be the daughter of Sir Malcolm Mowbray, my master's deceased friend. And what is your present intention!

Per. To demand her of the earl in marriage.

Mot. Oh! that will never do: for, in the first place, you'll not be able to get a sight of him. I've now lived with him five long years, and till Angela's arrival, never witnessed a guest in the castle. Oh! 'tis the most melancholy mansion! And as to the earl, he's the very antidote to mirth. He always walks with his arms folded, his brows bent, his eyes lowering on you with a gloomy scowl: he never smiles; and to laugh in his presence would be treason. He looks at no one—speaks to no one. None dare approach him, except Kenrick and his four blacks—all others are ordered to avoid him; and whenever he quits his room, ding! dong! goes a great bell, and away run the servants like so many scared rabbits.

Per. Strange!—And what reasons can he have for—

Mot. Oh! reasons in plenty. You must know, there's an ugly story respecting the last owners of this castle. Osmond's brother, his wife, and infant child were murdered by banditti, as it was said: unluckily, the only servant who escaped the slaughter, deposed, that he recognised among the assassins a black still in the service of Earl Osmond. The truth of this assertion was never known, for the servant was found dead in his bed the next morning.

Per. Good heavens!

Mot. Since that time no sound of joy has been heard in Conway Castle. Osmond instantly became gloomy and ferocious; he now never utters a sound except a sigh, has broken every tie of society, and keeps his gates barred unceasingly against the stranger.

Per. Yet Angela is admitted.—But, no doubt, affection for her father—

Mot. Why, no; I rather think that affection for her father's child—

Per. How?

Mot. If I've any knowledge in love, the earl feels it for his fair ward; but the lady will tell you more of this, if I can procure for you an interview.

Per. The very request which—

Mot. 'Tis no easy matter, I promise you; but I'll do my best. In the mean while, wait for me in yonder fishing-hut—its owner's name is Edric;—tell him that I sent you, and he will give you a reteat.

Per. Farewell, then, and remember that whatever reward—

Mot. Dear master, to mention a reward insults me. You have already shewn me kindness: and when 'tis in my power to be of use to you, to need the inducement of a second favour, would prove me a scoundrel undeserving of the first. [*Exit*, L. U. E.

Per. How warm is this good fellow's attachment! Yet our barons complain that the great can have no friends! If they have none, let their own pride bear the blame. Instead of looking with scorn on those whom a smile would attract, and a favour bind for ever, how many firm friends might our nobles gain, if they would but reflect that their vassals are men as they are, and have hearts whose feelings can be grateful as their own! [*Exit*, R.

SCENE II.—*The Castle-Hall.*

Enter SAIB, L *and* HASSAN, R.

Saib. Now, Hassan, what success ?

Has. (R.) My search has been fruitless. In vain have I paced the river's banks, and pierced the grove's deepest recesses. Nor glen nor thicket have I passed unexplored, yet found no stranger to whom Kenric's description could apply.

Saib. (L.) Saw you no one ?

Has. A troop of horsemen passed me as I left the wood.

Saib. Horsemen, say you ?—Then Kenric may be right. Earl Percy has discovered Angela's abode, and lurks near the castle, in hopes of carrying her off.

Has. His hopes then will be vain. Osmond's vigilance will not easily be eluded—sharpened by those powerful motives, love and fear.

Saib. His love, I know; but should he lose Angela, what has he to fear ?

Has. If Percy gains her—every thing ! Supported by such wealth and power, dangerous would be her claim to these domains, should her birth be discovered. Of this our lord is aware; nor did he sooner hear that Northumberland loved her, than he hastened to remove her from Allan's care.

Saib. Think you the lady perceives that our master loves her ?

Has. I know she does not. Absorbed in her own passion for Percy, on Osmond she bestows no thought, and, while roving through these pompous halls and chambers, sighs for the Cheviot-hills, and Allan's humble cottage.

Saib. But as she still believes Percy to be a low-born swain, when Osmond lays his coronet at her feet, will she reject his rank and splendour ?

Has. If she loves well, she will. Saib, I too have loved! I have known how painful it was to leave her on whom my heart hung; how incapable was all else to supply her loss! I have exchanged want for plenty, fatigue for rest, a wretched hut for a splendid palace. But am I happier ? Oh no! Still do I regret my native land, and the partners of my poverty. Then toil was sweet to me, for I laboured for Samba! then repose ever blessed my bed of leaves, for there by my side lay Samba sleeping.

Saib. This from you, Hassan ?—Did love ever find a place in your flinty bosom ?

Has. Did it? Oh, Saib! my heart once was gentle, once was good! But sorrows have broken it, insults have made it hard! I have been dragged from my native land, from a wife who was every thing to me, to whom I was every thing! Twenty years have elapsed since these Christians tore me away; they trampled upon my heart, mocked my despair, and, when in frantic terms I raved of Samba, laughed, and wondered how a negro's soul could feel! [*Crosses to* L.] In that moment, when the last point of Africa faded from my view, when as I stood on the vessel's deck, I felt that all I loved was to me lost for ever, in that bitter moment did I banish humanity from my breast. I tore from my arm the bracelet of Samba's hair; I gave to the sea the precious token, and while the high waves swift bore it from me, vowed, aloud, endless hatred to mankind. I have kept my oath, I *will* kept it ! [*Crosses to* R.

Saib. (L.) Ill-starred Hassan ! your wrongs have indeed been great.

Has. (R.) To remember them unmans me.—Farewell! I must to Kenric. Hold!—Look, where he comes from Osmond's chamber !

Saib. And seemingly in wrath.

Has. His conferences with the earl of late have had no other end. The period of his favour is arrived.

Saib. Not of his favour merely, Hassan.

Has. How ? Mean you that—

Saib. Silence! He's here!

Enter KENRIC, R.

Ken. (R.) Osmond, I will bear your ingratitude no longer.—Now, Hassan, found you the man described ?

Has. (C.) Nor any that resembled him.

Ken. Yet, that I saw Percy, I am convinced. As I crossed him in the wood, his eye met mine. He started as he had seen a basilisk, and fled with rapidity. But I will submit no longer to this painful dependance. To-morrow, for the last time, will I summon him to perform his promise: if he refuses, I will bid him farewell for ever, and, by my absence, free him from a restraint equally irksome to myself and him.

Saib. (L.) Will you so, Kenric ?—Be speedy then, or you will be too late.

Ken. Too late! And wherefore ?

Saib. You will soon receive the reward of your services.

Ken. Ha! know you what the reward will be ?

Saib. I guess, but may not tell.

Ken. Is it a secret?

Saib. Can you keep one?

Ken. Faithfully!

Saib. As faithfully can I.—Come, Hassan. [*Exeunt*, L.

Ken. What meant the slave? Those doubtful expressions—Ha! should the earl intend me false—Kenric! Kenric! how is thy nature changed! There was a time when fear was a stranger to my bosom—when, guiltless myself, I dreaded not art in others. Now, where'er I turn me, danger appears to lurk; and I suspect treachery in every breast, because my own heart hides it. [*Exit*, L.

Enter Father PHILIP, *followed by* ALICE, R.

F. Phil. Nonsense!—You silly woman, what you say is not possible.

Alice. (R.) I never said it was possible. I only said it was true; and that if ever I heard music, I heard it last night.

F. Phil. (L.) Perhaps the fool was singing to the servants.

Alice. The fool, indeed? Oh! fye! fye! How dare you call my lady's ghost a fool?

F. Phil. Your lady's ghost!—You silly old woman!

Alice. Yes, father, yes; I repeat it, I heard the guitar, lying upon the oratory table, play the very air which the lady Evelina used to sing while rocking her little daughter's cradle. She warbled it so sweetly, and ever at the close it went— [*Singing*.

"Lullaby! lullaby! hush thee, my dear!
Thy father is coming and soon will be here."

F. Phil. Nonsense! Nonsense!—Why, prithee, Alice, do you think that your lady's ghost would get up at night only to sing Lullaby for your amusement? Besides, how should a spirit, which is nothing but air, play upon an instrument of material wood and wire?

Alice. How can I tell?—Why, I know very well that men are made; but if you desired me to make a man, I vow and protest I shouldn't know how to set about it. I can only say, that, last night, I heard the ghost of my murdered lady—

F. Phil. Playing upon the spirit of a cracked guitar! Alice! Alice! these fears are ridiculous! The idea of ghosts is a vulgar prejudice. However, the next time you are afraid of a ghost, remember and make use of the receipt

which I shall now give you; and instead of calling for a priest to lay the spirits of other people in the Red-Sea, call for a bottle of red wine, to raise your own. Probatum est. [*Exit*, L.

Alice. Wine, indeed!—I believe he thinks I like drinking as well as himself. No, no! let the toping old friar take his bottle of wine; I shall confine myself to plain cherry-brandy.

Enter ANGELA, R.

Ang. I am weary of wandering from room to room; in vain do I change the scene, discontent is every where.—There was a time when music could delight my ear, and nature could charm my eye! when as the dawn unveiled the landscape, each object it disclosed to me looked pleasant and fair; and while the last sun-beams yet lingered on the western sky, I could pour forth a prayer of gratitude, and thank my good angels for a day unclouded by sorrow!—Now all is gone, all lost, all faded! [*Aside*.

Alice. Lady!

Ang. Perhaps he wanders on those mountains! Perhaps at this moment he thinks upon me! Perhaps then he sighs, and murmurs to himself, "The flowers, the rivulets, the birds, every object reminds me of my well-beloved; but what shall remind her of Edwy?"—Oh! that will my heart, Edwy; I need no other remembrancer. [*Aside*.

Alice. (L.) Lady! Lady Angela! She minds me no more than a post!

Ang. (R.) Oh! are you there, good Alice? What would you with me?

Alice. Only ask how your ladyship rested?

Ang. Ill! very ill!

Alice. Lack-a-day! and yet you sleep in the best bed!

Ang. True, good Alice! but my heart's anguish strewed thorns upon my couch of down.

Alice. Marry, I'm not surpris'd that you rested ill in the cedar-room. Those noises so near you—

Ang. What noises? I heard none.

Alice. How?—When the clock struck one, heard you no music!

Ang. Music?—None.—Not that I——Stay! now I remember that while I sat alone in my chamber this morning—

Alice. Well, lady, well!

Ang. Methought I heard some one singing; it seemed as if the words run thus—[*Singing*.]

"Lullaby! lullaby! hush thee, my dear!"

Alice. [*Screaming.*] The very words!—It was the ghost, lady! it was the ghost!

Ang. The ghost, Alice! I protest I thought it had been you.

Alice. Me, lady!—Lord, when did you hear this singing?

Ang. Not five minutes ago, while you were talking with father Philip.

Alice. The Lord be thanked!—then it was not the ghost. It was I, lady! it was I!—And have you heard no other singing since you came to the castle?

Ang. None.—But why that question?

Alice. Because, lady——But perhaps you may be frightened?

Ang. No, no!—Proceed, I entreat you.

Alice. Why, then, they do say, that the chamber in which you sleep is haunted. You may have observed two folding doors, which are ever kept locked: they lead to the oratory, in which the Lady Evelina passed most of her time, while my lord was engaged in the Scottish wars. She would sit there, good soul! hour after hour, playing on the lute, and singing airs so sweet, so sad, that many a time and oft have I wept to hear her. Ah! when I kissed her hand at the castle-gate, little did I suspect that her fate would have been so wretched!

Ang. And what was her fate?

Alice. A sad one, lady! Impatient to embrace her lord, after a year's absence, the countess set out to meet him on his return from Scotland, accompanied by a few domestics and her infant daughter, then scarce a twelvemonth old. But, as she returned with her husband, robbers surprised the party scarce a mile from the castle; and since that time no news has been received of the earl, of the countess, the servants, or the child.

Ang. Dreadful! Were not their corpses found?

Alice. Never! The only domestic who escaped, pointed out the scene of action; and as it proved to be on the river's banks, doubtless the assassins plunged the bodies into the stream.

Ang. Strange; And did Earl Osmond then become owner of this castle?—Alice! was he ever suspected of—

Alice. Speak lower, lady! It was said so, I own: but for my own part I never believed it. To my certain knowledge, Osmond loved the lady Evelina too well to hurt her; and when he heard of her death, he wept, and sobbed as if his heart were breaking. Nay, 'tis certain that he proposed to her before marriage and would have made her his wife, only that she liked his brother better. But I hope you're not alarmed by what I mentioned of the cedar-room?

Ang. No, truly, Alice; from good spirits I have nothing to fear, and heaven and my innocence will protect me against bad.

Alice. My very sentiments, I protest: But heaven forgive me; while I stand gossiping here, I warrant all goes wrong in the kitchen! [*Crosses,* R.] Your pardon, lady: I must away! I must away! [*Exit,* R.

Ang. [*Musing.*] Osmond was his brother's heir——His strange demeanour!—Yes, in that gloomy brow is written a volume of villany! Heavenly powers! an assassin then is master of my fate!—An assassin too who—I dare not bend my thoughts that way!—Oh! would I had never entered these castle walls!—had never exchanged for fearful pomp the security of my pleasures—the tranquillity of my soul!

Return, return, sweet Peace! and o'er my breast
Spread thy bright wings, distil thy balmy rest;
And teach my steps thy realms among to rove;
Wealth and the world resigned, nought mine but love.

[*Exit,* R.

END OF ACT I.

ACT II.

SCENE I.—*The Armory. Suits of Armour are arranged on both sides upon Pedestals, with the names of their possessors written under each.*

Enter MOTLEY, *peeping,* L.

Mot. The coast is clear!—Hist! Hist!—You may enter.

Enter PERCY, L.

Per. Loiter not here. Quick, my good fellow! Conduct me to Angela!

Mot. (R.) Softly, softly! A little caution is needful; and I promise you just now I'm not upon roses.

Per. (L.) If such are your fears, why not lead me at once to Angela? Are we not more exposed in this open hall?

Mot. Be contented, and leave all to me: I will contrive matters so that Osmond shall have you before his eyes, and be no jot the wiser. [*Takes down some armour.*] But you must make up your mind to play a statue for an hour or two.

Per. How?

Mot. [*Putting armour on Percy.*] Nay, 'tis absolutely necessary—Quick! The late earl's servants are fully persuaded that his ghost wanders every night through the long galleries, and parades the old towers and dreary halls which abound in this melancholy mansion. He is supposed to be dressed in complete armour; and that which you wear at present was formerly his. Now, hear my plan.—The earl prepares to hold a conference with the lady Angela—even now I heard her summoned to attend him in the armory: placed upon this pedestal you may listen to their discourse unobserved, and thus form a proper judgment both of your mistress and her guardian As soon as it grows dark, I will conduct you to Angela's apartments: the obscurity will then shelter you from discovery, and even should you be observed, you will pass for earl Reginald's spectre.

Per. I do not dislike your plan: but tell me, Gilbert, do you believe this tale of the apparition?

Mot. Oh! heaven forbid! Not a word of it. Had I minded all the strange things related of this castle, I should have died of fright in the first half-hour. Why, they say, that earl Hubert rides every night round the castle on a white horse; that the ghost of lady Bertha haunts the west pinnacle of the chapel tower; and that lord Hildebrand, who was condemned for treason some sixty years ago, may be seen in the great hall regularly at midnight, playing at foot-ball with his own head! Above all, they say that the spirit of the late countess sits nightly in her oratory, and sings her baby to sleep. However, if it be so—[*Bell sounds thrice.*] Hark! 'tis the earl; quick, to your post! [*Percy ascends the pedestal.*] Farewell—I must get out of his way, but as soon as he quits this chamber, I'll rejoin you. [*Exit*, R.

[*The middle folding-doors are thrown open; Saib, Hassan, Muley, and Alaric enter, preceding earl Osmond, who walks with his arms folded, and his eyes bent upon the ground. Saib advances to a sofa, into which, after making a few turns through the room, Osmond throws himself. He motions to his attendants, and they withdraw* (M. D.) *He appears lost in thought; then suddenly rises, and again traverses the room with disordered steps.*]

Osm. I will not sacrifice my happiness to hers! No, Angela, you ask of me too much. Since the moment when I pierced her heart, deprived of whom life became odious; since my soul was stained with his blood who loved me, with hers whom I loved, no form has been grateful to my eye, no voice spoken pleasure to my soul, save Angela's—save only Angela's! Mine she is, mine she shall be, though Reginald's bleeding ghost flit before me, and thunder in my ear—"Hold! Hold!"—Peace, stormy heart! She comes!

Enter ANGELA, R.

Osm. (L.) [*In a softened voice.*] Come hither, Angela. Wherefore so sad? That downcast eye, that listless air, neither suit your age or fortunes. The treasures of India are lavished to adorn your person; yet still do I see you, forgetting what you are, look back with regret to what you were!

Ang. (R.) Oh! my good lord, esteem me not ungrateful! I acknowledge your bounties—but they have not made me happy. I still linger in thought near those scenes where I passed the blessed period of infancy; I still thirst for those simple pleasures which habit has made so dear. The birds which my own hands reared, and the flowers which my own hands planted; the banks on which I rested when fatigued, the wild tangled wood which supplied me with strawberries, and the village church where I prayed to be virtuous, while I yet knew of vice and virtue but the name, all have acquired rights to my memory and my love!

Osm. Absurd!

Ang. While I saw you, Cheviot Hills, I was happy, oh! how happy! At morn when I left my bed, light were my spirits, and gay as the zephyrs of summer; and when at night my head again pressed my pillow, I whispered to myself, "Happy has been to-day, and to-morrow will be as happy!" Then sweet was my sleep; and my dreams were of those whom I loved dearest.

Osm. Romantic enthusiast! These thoughts did well for the village maid, but disgrace the daughter of Sir Malcolm Mowbray. hear me, Angela; an English baron loves you, a nobleman than whom our island boasts few more potent. 'Tis to him that your hand is destined, 'tis on him that your heart must be bestowed.

Ang. I cannot dispose of that which has long been another's—My heart is Edwy's.

Osm. Edwy's? A peasant's?

Ang. For the obscurity of his birth chance must be blamed; the merit of his virtues belongs wholly to himself.

Osm. By Heaven you seem to think that poverty is a virtue!

Ang. Sir, I think 'tis a misfortune, not a crime: and when in spite of nature's injustice, and the frowns of a prejudiced and illiberal world, I see some low-born but illustrious spirit prove itself superior to the station which it fills, I hail it with pleasure, with admiration, with respect! Such a spirit I found in Edwy, and finding loved! He has my plighted faith; he received it on the last evening which I passed in Northumberland, as we sat on a low bench before old Allan's cottage. It was a heavenly night, sweet and tranquil, as the loves of angels. A gentle breeze whispered among the honeysuckles which bloomed above us, and the full moon tinged with her silver light the distant towers of Alnwic. It was then, that for the first time I gave him my hand, and I swore that I never would give it but to him! It was then, that for the first time he pressed his lips to mine, and I swore that my lips should never be pressed by another!

Osm. Girl! Girl! you drive me to distraction!

Ang. You alarm me, my lord! Permit me to retire.

[*Going; Osmond detains her violently by the arm.*

Osm. Stay!—[*In a softer tone.*] Angela! I love you.

Ang. [*Starting.*] My lord!

Osm. [*Passionately.*] Love you to madness!—Nay, strive not to escape: remain and hear me! I offer you my hand; if you accept it, mistress of these fair and rich domains, your days shall glide away in happiness and honour; but if you refuse and scorn my offer, force shall this instant—

Ang. Force? Oh no!—You dare not be so base!

Osm. Reflect on your situation, Angela; you are in my power—remember it, and be wise!

Ang. If you have a generous mind, that will be my surest safeguard. Be it my plea, Osmond, when thus I sue to you for mercy, for protection! look on me with pity, Osmond! 'Tis the daughter of the man you loved, 'tis a creature, friendless, wretched, and forlorn, who kneels before you, who flies to you for refuge!—True, I am in your power; then save me, respect me, treat me not cruelly; for—I am in your power!

Osm. I will hear no more. Will you accept my offer?

Ang. Osmond, I conjure you—

Osm. Answer my question!

Ang. Mercy! Mercy!

Osm. Will you be mine?—Speak! Speak!

Ang. [*After a moment's pause, rises, and pronounces with firmness.*] Never, so help me Heaven!

Osm. [*Seizing her.*] Your fate then is decided!

[*Angela shrieks.*

Per. [*In a hollow voice.*]—Hold!

Osm. [*Starts, but still grasps Angela's arm.*] Ha! what was that?

Ang. [*Struggling to escape.*] Heard you not a voice?

Osm. [*Gazing upon Percy.*] It came from hence—From Reginald!—Was it not a delusion? Did indeed his spirit —[*Relapsing into his former passion.*] Well be it so! though his ghost should rush between us, thus would I clasp her! What sight is this! [*At the moment that he again seizes Angela, Percy extends his truncheon with a menacing gesture, and descends from the pedestal. Osmond releases Angela, who immediately rushes from the chamber* R. D., *while Percy advances a few steps and remains gazing on the Earl steadfastly.*] I know that shield!—that helmet!—Speak to me, dreadful vision! Tax me with my crimes! Tell me, that you come—Stay! Speak! [*Following Percy, who, when he reaches the door, through which Angela escaped, turns, and signs to him with his hand.—Osmond starts back in terror.*] He forbids my following! He leaves me! The door closes—[*In a sudden burst of passion, and drawing his sword.*] Hell, and fiends! I'll follow him, though lightnings blast me!

[*He rushes distractedly from the chamber,* R. D.

SCENE II.—*The Castle Hall.*

Enter ALICE, (R.)

Alice. Here's rudeness! here's ill-breeding! On my conscience, this house grows worse and worse every day!

Enter MOTLEY, (L.)

Mot. (L.) What can he have done with himself? How now, dame Alice, what has happened to you? You look angry.

Alice. (R.) By my troth, fool, I've little reason to look pleased. To be frightened out of my wits by night, and thumped and bumped about by day, is not likely to put one in the best humour.

Mot. Poor soul! And who has been thumping and bumping you?

Alice. Who has? You should rather ask who has not—Why only hear: As I was just now going along the narrow passage which leads to the armoury—singing to myself, and thinking of nothing—I met lady Angela flying away, as if for dear life! So I dropped her a courtesy, but might as well have spared my pains. Without minding me any more than if I had been a dog or a cat, she pushed me on one side; and before I could recover my balance, somebody else, who came bouncing by me, gave me t'other thump—and there I lay sprawling upon the floor. However, I tumbled with all possible decency.

Mot. Somebody else! What, somebody else?

Alice. I know not—but he seemed to be in armour.

Mot. In armour? Pray, Alice, looked he like a ghost?

Alice. What he looked like, I cannot say; but I'm sure he didn't feel like one: however, you've not heard the worst. While I was sprawling upon the ground, my lord comes tearing along the passage; the first thing he did was to stumble against me—away went his heels—over he came—and, in the twinkling of an eye, there lay his lordship! As soon as he got up again—Mercy! how he stormed!—He snatched me up—called me an ugly old witch—shook the breath out of my body—then clapped me on the ground again, and bounced away after the other two!

Mot. My mind misgives me! But what can this mean, Alice?

Alice. The meaning I neither know, or care about; but this I know—I'll stay no longer in a house where I'm treated so disrespectfully. "My lady!" says I, "Out of my way!" says she, and pushes me on one side. "My lord!" says I, "You be damn'd," says he, and pushes me on t'other!—I protest I never was so ill used, even when I was a young woman! [*Exit*, L.

Mot. Should earl Percy be discovered—the very thought gives me a crick in my neck! At any rate I had better inquire whether— [*Going*, R.

Enter FATHER PHILIP, *hastily*, R.

F. Phil. (R.) [*Stopping him.*] Get out of the house!—That's your way!

Mot. (L.) Why, what's the meaning—

F. Phil. Don't stand prating here, but do as I bid you!

Mot. But first tell me—

F. Phil. I can only tell you to get out of the house.—Kenric has discovered earl Percy. You are known to have introduced him—the Africans are in search of you: If you are found, you will be hung out of hand. Fly then to Edric's cottage—hide yourself there! Hark!—Some one comes! Away! away! ere it is too late!— [*Pushing him out.*

Mot. [*Confused.*] But earl Percy—but Angela—

F. Phil. Leave them to me! You shall hear from me soon. Only take care of yourself, and fly with all diligence! Away! [*Exit Motley*, L.

So, so, he's off, and now I've time to take breath. I've not moved so nimbly for the last twenty years; and, in truth, I'm at present but ill calculated for velocity of motion. However, my exertions have not been thrown away: I've saved this poor knave from Osmond's vengeance; and should my plan for the lady's release succeed—poor little soul! To see how she took on, when Percy was torn from her! Well, well, she shall be rescued from her tyrant. The movable panels—the subterraneous passages—the secret springs, well known to me—Oh! I cannot fail of success; but, in order to secure it, I'll finally arrange my ideas in the buttery. Whenever I've any great design in hand, I always ask advice of a flagon of ale, and mature my plan over a cold venison-pasty. [*Exit*, R.

SCENE III.—*A spacious Chamber; on one side is a Couch; the other a Table, which is placed under an arched and lofty Window* R. *in flat.*

Enter OSMOND, M. D. *followed by* SAIB, HASSAN, MULEY, *and* ALARIC, *who conduct* PERCY, *disarmed.*

Osm. This, sir, is your prison: but, doubtless, your confinement will not continue long. The moment which gives me Angela's hand, shall restore you to liberty; and till that moment arrives, farewell.

Per. Stay, sir, and hear me! By what authority presume you to call me captive? Have you forgotten that you speak to Northumberland's earl?

Osm. Well may I forget him, who could so far forge himself. Was it worthy of Northumberland's earl to steal disguised into my castle, and plot with my servant to rob me of my most precious treasure?

Per. Mine was that treasure; you deprived me of it basely, and I was justified in striving to regain my own.

Osm. Earl, nothing can justify unworthy means. If you were wronged, why sought you not your right with your sword's point? I then should have esteemed you a noble foe, and as such would have treated you: but you have stooped to paltry artifice, and attacked me like some midnight ruffian, privately, and in disguise. By this I am authorized to forget your station, and make your penance as degrading as your offence was base.

Per. If such are indeed your sentiments, prove them now. Restore my sword, unsheath your own, and be Angela, the conqueror's reward!

Osm. No, earl Percy! I am not so rash a gamester as to suffer that cast to be recalled, by which the stake is mine already. Angela is in my power.

Per. Insulting coward.

Osm. Be calm, earl Percy! You forget yourself. That I am no coward, my sword has proved in the fields of Scotland. My sword shall again prove it, if, when you are restored to liberty, you still question the courage of my heart! Angela once mine, repeat your defiance, nor doubt my answering.

Per. Angela thine? That she shall never be. There are angels above who favour virtue, and the hour of retribution must one day arrive.

[*Throws himself upon the couch.*

Osm. But long ere the arrival of that hour, shall Angela have been my bride, and now farewell lord Percy. —Muley, and Saib!

Both. My lord?

Osm. To your charge I commit the earl; quit not this apartment, nor suffer him for one moment from your sight.

Saib and Muley. My lord, we shall obey you.

[*Osmond goes off, attended by Hassan and Alaric,* M. D.

Saib. Look, Muley, how bitterly he frowns!

Muley. Now he starts from the sofa! 'Faith, he's in a monstrous fury!

Saib. That may be. When you mean to take in other people, it certainly is provoking to be taken in yourself.

Per. [*After walking a few turns with a disordered air, suddenly stops.*] He is gone to Angela! Gone perhaps, to renew that outrage whose completion my presence alone prevented!

Muley. Now he's in a deep study: marry, if he studies himself out of this tower, he's a cleverer fellow than I take him for.

Per. Were I not Osmond's captive, all might yet be well. Summoning my vassals, who by this time must be near at hand, forcing the castle, and tearing Angela from the arms of her tyrant. Alas! my captivity has rendered this plan impracticable! And are there then no hopes of liberty?

Saib. He fixes his eyes on us.

Per. Might not these fellows—I can but try it. Now stand my friend, thou master-key to human hearts! Aid me, thou potent devil, gold!—Hear me my worthy friends. Come nearer!—My good fellows, you are charged with a disagreeable office, and to obey a tyrant's mandates cannot be pleasant to you: there is something in your looks which has prejudiced me too much in your favour to believe it possible.

Saib. Nay, there certainly is something in our appearance highly prepossessing.

Muley. And I know that you must admire the delicacy of our complexions!

Per. The tincture of your skin, my good fellow, is of little consequence: many a worthy heart beats within a dusky bosom, and I am convinced that such a heart inhabits yours; for your looks tell me that you feel for, and are anxious to relieve my sufferings. See you this purse, my friends?

Muley. It's too far off, and I am short-sighted. If you'll put it a little nearer—

Per. Restore me to liberty!—and not this purse alone, but ten times its value shall be yours.

Saib. To liberty?

Muley. That purse?

Saib. Muley!

Muley. Saib!

Per. You well know, that my wealth and power are equal, not to say superior, to earl Osmond's: release me from my dungeon, and share that power and wealth!

Muley. In truth, my lord, your offers are so generous, and that purse is so tempting—Saib, what say you?

[*Winking to him.*

Saib. The earl speaks so well, and promises so largely, that I own I'm strangely tempted.

Muley. Look you, Saib; will you stand by me?

Saib. [*After a moment's thought.*] I will!

Muley. There's my hand then! My lord, we are your servants!

Per You agree then to release me?

Muley. 'Tis impossible to do otherwise; for I feel that pity, generosity, and every moral feeling, command me to trouble your lordship for that purse.

Per. There it is. And now unlock the door.

Muley. [*Chinking the purse.*] Here it is! And now I'm obliged to you. As for your promises, my lord, pray don't trouble yourself to remember them, as I sha'n't trouble myself to remember mine.

Per. [*Starting.*] Ha! what mean you?

Saib. [*Firmly.*] Earl, that we are faithful!

Per. What! will you not keep your word?

Muley. In good troth, no; we mean to keep nothing—except the purse.

Per. Confusion! To be made the jest of such rascals.

Saib. Earl Percy, we are none, but we should have been, could your gold have bribed us to betray our master. We have but done our duty—you have but gained your just reward; for they who seek to deceive others should ever be deceived themselves.

Per. Silence, fellow!—Leave me to my thoughts!

[*Throwing himself passionately upon the couch.*

Muley. Oh! with all our hearts. We ask no better.

Saib. Muley, we share that purse?

Muley. Undoubtedly. Sit down and examine its contents.—

[*They seat themselves on the floor in the front of the stage.*

Per. How unfortunate, that the only merit of these villains should be fidelity!—

[*Chorus of voices, Singing without, behind window.*]

"Sing Megen-oh! Oh! Megen-Ee!"

Muley. Hark!—What's that?

Saib. I'll see. [*Mounting upon the table.*] This window is so high—

Muley. Here, here! Take this chair.—

[*Saib places the chair upon the table, and thus lifts himself to a level with the window, which he opens.*]

SONG AND CHORUS.

Mot. [*Singing without.*] Sleep you or wake you, lady bright?

Chorus. [*Without.*] Sing Megen-oh! Oh! Megen-Ee!

Mot. Now is the fittest time for flight.

Chorus. Sing Megen-oh! Oh! Megen-Ee!

Mot. Know from your tyrant father's power,
Beneath the window of your tower
A boat now waits to set you free;
Sing Megen-oh! Oh! Megen-Ee!

Chorus. Sing Megen-oh! Oh! Megen-Ee!

Per. [*Who has half-raised himself from the couch during the last part of the song, and listened attentively.*]—Surely, I know that voice!

Muley. Now, what's the matter?

Saib. A boat lies at the foot of the tower, and the fishermen and their wives sing while they draw their nets.

Per. I could not be mistaken; it was Gilbert.

SECOND STANZA.

Mot. Though deep the stream, though high the wall,

Chorus. Sing Megen-oh! Oh! Megen-Ee!

Mot. The danger trust me, love, is small;

Chorus. Sing Megen-oh! Oh! Megen-Ee!

Mot. To spring below then never dread;
My arms to catch you shall be spread;
And far from hence you soon shall be,
Sing Megen-oh! Oh! Megen-Ee!

Chorus.—Sing Megen-oh! Oh! Megen-Ee!

Per. I understand him.

Muley. Prithee, come down, Saib; I long to divide the purse—

Saib. Stay a moment; [*Shutting the window and descending.*] Here I am, and now for the purse—

[*They resume their seats upon the ground; Saib opens the purse, and begins to reckon the gold.*]

Per. Yes, I must brave the danger—I will feign to sleep; and when my gaolers are off their guard, then aid me, blessed Providence! [*Extending himself upon the couch.*

Saib. Hold, Muley!—What if, instead of sharing the purse, we throw for its contents? Here are dice.

Muley. With all my heart; and look—to pass our time the better, here's a bottle of the best sack in the earl's cellar.

Saib. Good! Good!—And now, be this angel the stake! But first, what is our prisoner doing?

Muley. Oh! he sleeps; mind him not. Come, come, throw!

Saib. Here goes—nine!—now to you.

Muley. Nine too!—double the stake.

Saib. Agreed! and the throw is mine. Hark! What noise?

[*During this dialogue, Percy has approached the table in silence: at the moment he prepares to mount it, Saib looks round, and Percy hastily throws himself back on the couch.*]

Muley. Oh!—nothing, nothing!

Saib. Methought I heard the earl—

Muley. Mere fancy!—you see he is sleeping soundly. Come, come; throw!

Saib. There then—eleven!

Muley. That's bad—huzza!—sixes!

Saib. Plague on your fortune!—come, double or quits!

Muley. Be it so, and I throw—zounds;—only five.

Saib. Then I think this hit must be mine—aces, by heavens!

Muley. Ha! ha!—your health, friend!

Per. [*Who has again reached the table, mounted the chair, and opening the window, now stands at it, and signs to the men below.*] They see me, and extend a cloth beneath the window!—'Tis a fearful height!

Saib. Do you mean to empty the bottle?—Come, come—give it me.

Muley. Take it, blunder-head!— [*Saib drinks.*

Per. They encourage me to venture!—Now then, or never! [*Aloud.*] Angels of bliss protect me!—

[*He throws himself from the window.*

Muley and Saib. [*Starting at the noise.*] Hell and furies!

Saib. [*Dashes down the bottle, and climbs to the window hastily, while Muley remains below in an attitude of surprise.*] Escaped! Escaped!

Per. Mot. &c. [*Without.*] Huzza! huzza! huzza.

END OF ACT II.

ACT III.

SCENE I.—*A view of the River Conway, with a Fisherman's Hut,* R. S. E.—*Sun-set.*

Enter ALLAN *and* EDRIC, *from Hut,* R. S. E.

Allan. (L.) Still they come not!—Dear, dear, still they come not!—Ah! these tumults are too much for my old body to bear.

Edr. (R.) Then you should have kept your old body at home. 'Tis a fine thing truly for a man of your age to be galloping about the country after a girl, who, by your own account, is neither your chick nor child!

Allan. Ah! She was more to me! She was my all, Edric, my all!—How could I bear my home when it no longer was the home of Angela?—How could I rest in my cottage at night, when her sweet lips had not kissed me—and murmured, "Father, sleep well!"—She is so good! so gentle!—I was sick once, sick almost to death!—Angela was then my nurse and comforter; she watched me when I slept, and cheered me when I awoke; she rejoiced when I grew better; and when I grew worse, no medicine gave me ease like the tears of pity which fell on my burning cheeks from the eyes of my darling!

Edr. Tears of pity indeed! a little rhubarb would have done you more good by half.—But our people stay a long time; perhaps Motley has been discovered and seized; if so, he will lose his life, the earl his freedom, Angela her lover, and, what's worst of all, I shall lose my boat! I wish I hadn't lent it, for I doubt that Motley's scheme has failed.

Allan. I hope not—oh! I hope not!—Should Percy remain a captive, Angela will be left unprotected in your wicked lord's power—Oh! that will break my poor old wife's heart for certain!

Edr. And if it should break it, a mighty misfortune truly!—Zounds! master Allan, any wife is at best a bad thing; a poor one makes matters yet worse; but when she's old, lord! 'tis the very devil!

Allan. Hark! hark! Do you hear? 'Tis the sound of oars!—They are friends!—Oh! heaven be thanked! the earl is with them.

[*A boat appears,* L. U. E. *with Percy, Motley, and Soldiers, disguised as Fishermen.—They land.*]

Per. [*Springing on shore.*] Once more then I breathe the air of liberty!—Worthy Gilbert, what words can suffice to thank you?

Mot. (R.) None; therefore do not waste your breath in the attempt. You are safe—thanks to St. Peter and the blanket! and your lady's deliverance now demands all your thoughts. Ha! who is that with Edric?

Per. Allan, by all my hopes! Welcome, welcome, good old man? Say, came my vassals with you?

Allan. Three hundred chosen men are within the sound of your bugle. But now, my lord, tell me of Angela: is she well? Did you speak to her? And speaks she sometimes of me?

Per. She is well, my old friend, and I have spoken to her—though but for a moment. But be comforted, good Allan! Should other means fail, I will this very night attack the castle, and compel Osmond to resign his prey.

Allan. Heaven grant that you may succeed! Let me but once see Angela your bride!—Let me but once hear her say the sweet words, "Allan, I am happy!" then I and my old wife will seek our graves, lay us down, and die with pleasure!

Mot. Die with pleasure, you silly old man! you shall do nothing so ridiculous.—You shall live a great many years; and instead of lying down in your grave, we'll tuck you up warm with your old wife in the best down bed of Alnwic. But now let us talk of our affairs, which, if I mistake not, are in the high road to success.

Per. How? Has any intelligence reached you of your ally, the friar?

Mot. You have guessed it. As it passed beneath his window, the pious porpus contrived to drop this letter into the boat. Its contents must needs be of consequence; for I assure you it comes from one of the greatest men in England. Pray examine it, my lord! I never can read when the wind's easterly. [*Motley gives Percy the Letter, who reads to himself.*] Well sir, what says the letter?

Per. Listen.—[*Reads.*] "*I have recognised you in spite of your disguise, and seized the opportunity to advise your exerting yourself solely to obtain earl Percy's liberty. Heed not Angela: I have sure and easy means for procuring her escape; and before the clock strikes two, you may expect me with her at the fisherman's hut. Farewell, and rely upon father Philip!*"—Now, Gilbert, what say you? May the monk's fidelity be trusted?

Mot. His fidelity may undoubtedly; but whether his success will equal his good intentions, is a point which time alone can decide. Should it not—

Per. Then with my faithful vassals will I storm the castle to-morrow. But where are my followers?

Allan. Fearing lest their numbers should excite suspicion, I left them concealed in yonder wood.

Per. Guide me to them.—Edric, for this night I must request the shelter of your hut.

Edr. Willingly, my lord. But my cottage is so humble, your treatment so wretched—

Per. Silence, my good fellow! The hut where good will resides is to me more welcome than a palace, and no food can be so sweet as that which is seasoned with smiles. You give me your best; a monarch could give no more, and it happens not often that men ever give so much. Now farewell for an hour!—Allan, lead on!

[*Exeunt Percy, Allan, &c.* L.

Mot. And in the mean while, friend Edric, I'll lend you a hand in preparing supper.

Edr. Truly the task won't give you much trouble, for times have gone hard with me of late. Our present lord sees no company, gives no entertainments, and thus I sell no fish. Things went better while earl Reginald lived.

Mot. What! you remember him?

Edr. Never shall I forget him, or his sweet lady. Why, I verily believe they possessed all the cardinal virtues!—So pious, so generous, so mild! so kind to the poor—and so fond of fish!

Mot. Fond of fish!—One of the cardinal virtues, of which I never heard before!

Edr. But these thoughts make me sad. Come, master Motley; your lord's supper still swims in the river:—if you'll help to catch it, why do so, and thank you heartily. Can you fish?

Mot. Can I? Who in this world cannot?—I'll assure you, friend Edric, there is no profession more universal than yours; we all spread our nets to catch something or other; and happy are they, in this world of disappointments, who throw out no nets save fishing ones!

[*Retires up the stage, as if going to the boat.*

SCENE II.—*The Castle-Hall.*

Enter KENRIC, L.

Ken. Yonder he stalks, and seems buried in himself!—Now then to attack him while my late service is still fresh upon his memory. Should he reject my petition positively, he shall have good cause to repent his ingratitude. Percy is in the neighbourhood; and that secret, known only to myself, will surely——But, silence!—Look where he comes! [*Exit* L.

Enter OSMOND, R.

Osm. It shall not be! Away with these foreboding terrors, which weigh down my heart!—I will forget the past, I will enjoy the present, and make those raptures again mine, which——Ah! no, no, no!—Conscience, that serpent, winds her folds round the cup of my bliss, and, ere my lips can reach it, her venom is mingled with the draught. And see where he walks, the chief object of my fears!—He advances!

Re-enter KENRIC, L.

Ken. So melancholy, my lord?

Osm. Ay, Kenric, and must be so till Angela is mine. Know that even now she extorted from me a promise, that, till to-morrow, I would leave her unmolested.

Ken. But till to-morrow.

Osm. But till to-morrow?—Oh! in that little space a lover's eye views myriads of dangers! Yet think not, good Kenric, that your late services are undervalued by me, or that I have forgotten those for which I have been long your debtor. When, bewildered by hatred of Reginald, and grief for Evelina's loss, my dagger was placed on the throat of their infant, your hand arrested the blow—Judge then how grateful I must feel, when I behold in Angela her mother's living counterpart.—Worthy Kenric, how can I repay your services?

Ken. These you may easily.—Let me then claim that independence so long promised, and seek for peace in some other climate, since memory forbids me to taste it in this.

Osm. Kenric, ere named, your wish was granted. In a far distant country a retreat is already prepared for you: there may you hush those clamours of conscience, which must reach me, I fear, e'en in the arms of Angela. Are you contented?

Ken. [*Affected.*] My lord!—Gratitude—Amazement—and I doubted—I suspected—Oh! my good lord, how have I wronged your kindness!

Osm. No more—I must not hear you!—[*Aside.*] Shame! shame! that ever my soul should stoop to dissembling with my slave! [*Crosses to* L.

SAIB *enters*, L. *and advances with apprehension.*

Osm. How now?—Why this confusion?—Why do you tremble?—Speak!

Saib. My lord!—The prisoner—

Osm. The prisoner?—Go on! go on!

Saib. [*Kneeling.*] Pardon, my lord, pardon! Our prisoner has escaped!

Osm. Villain! [*Wild with rage he draws his dagger, and rushes upon Saib—Kenric holds his arm.*]

Ken. Hold! hold!—What would you do?

Osm. [*Struggling.*] Unhand me, or by heaven—

Ken. Away! away!—Fly, fellow, and save yourself! [*Exit Saib*, L. *Kenric releasing Osmond.*] Consider, my lord—Haply 'twas not by his keeper's fault that—

Osm. [*Furiously.*] What is't to me by whose? Is not my rival fled? Soon will Northumberland's guards encircle my walls, and force from me—Yet that by heaven they shall not! No! Rather than resign her, my own hand shall give this castle a prey to flames; then, plunging with Angela into the blazing gulf, I'll leave these ruins to tell posterity how desperate was my love, and how dreadful my revenge! [*Going, he stops, and turns to Kenric.*] And you, who dared to rush between me and my resentment—you, who could so well succeed in saving others—now look to yourself! [*Exit*, R.

Ken. Ha! that look—that threat. Yet he seemed so kind, so grateful! He smiled too! Oh! there is ever danger when a villain smiles.

SAIB *enters softly*, L. *looking round him with caution.*

Saib. [*In a low voice.*] Hist! Kenric!

Ken. (R.) How now? What brings—

Saib. (L.) Silence, and hear me! You have saved my life; nor will I be ungrateful. Look at this phial!

Ken. Ha! did the earl—

Saib. Even so: a few drops of this liquor should to-night have flavoured your wine—you would never have drank again! Mark me then—When I offer you a goblet at supper, drop it as by accident. For this night I give you life: use it to quit the castle; for no longer than till to-morrow dare I disobey our lord's commands. Farewell, and fly from Conway—You bear with you my thanks.

[*Exit*, L.

Ken. Can it be possible? Is not all this a dream? Villain! villain! Yes, yes, I must away! But tremble, traitor! A bolt, of which you little think, hangs over, and shall crush you! The keys are still in my possession; Angela shall be the partner of my flight. My prisoner too—Yet hold! May not resentment—may not Reginald's sixteen years' captivity—Oh no! Angela shall be my advocate; and, grateful for her own, for her parent's life preserved, she can, she will obtain my pardon. Yet, should she fail, at least I shall drag down Osmond in my fall, and sweeten death's bitter cup with vengeance.

[*Exit*, L.

SCENE III.—*The Cedar-room, with Folding-doors in the middle, and a large antique Bed; on one side is a Portrait of a Lady, on the other that of a Warrior armed. Both are at full length. After a pause the Female Portrait falls back, and* FATHER PHILIP, *after looking in, advances cautiously.*

F. Phil. [*Closing the panel in Flat*, R.] Thus far I have proceeded without danger, though not without difficulty. Yon narrow passage is by no means calculated for persons of my habit of body. But by my holydame, I begin to suspect that the fool is in the right! I certainly am growing corpulent. And now, how shall I employ myself? Sinner that I am, why did I forget my bottle of sack? The time will pass tediously till Angela comes. And to complete the business, yonder is the haunted oratory. What if the ghost should pop out on me? Blessed St. Bridget, there would be a tête-à-tête! Yet this is a foolish fear: 'tis yet scarce eight o'clock, and your ghosts always keep late hours; yet I don't like the idea of our being such near neighbours. If Alice says true, the apparition just now lives next door to me; but the lord forbid that we should ever be visiting acquaintance!

Osm. [*Without*, L. D.] What, Alice! Alice! I say!

F. Phil. By St. David, 'tis the earl! I'll away as fast as I can. [*Trying to open the* R. *door.*] I can't find the spring. Lord forgive me my sins; Where can I hide my-

self? Ha! the bed! 'Tis the very thing. [*Throws himself into the bed*, L. U. E. *and conceals himself under the clothes.*] Heaven grant that it mayn't break down with me! for, oh! what a fall would be there, my countrymen! They come! [*The* L. *door is unlocked.*

Enter OSMOND, ANGELA, *and* ALICE, L. D.

Osm. [*Entering.*] You have heard my will, lady. Til your hand is mine, you quit not this chamber.

Ang. If then it must be so, welcome my eternal prison! Yet eternal it shall not be. My hero, my guardian-angel is at liberty. Soon shall his horn make these hateful towers tremble, and your fetters be exchanged for the arms of Percy.

Osm. Beware, beware, Angela! Dare not before me—

Ang. Before you! Before the world! Is my attachment a disgrace? No! 'tis my pride; for it's object is deserving. Long ere I knew him, Percy's fame was dear to me. While I still believed him the peasant Edwy, often, in his hearing, have I dwelt upon Northumberland's praise, and chid him that he spoke of our lord so coldly! Judge then, earl Osmond, on my arrival here, how strongly I must have felt the contrast! What peasant names you his benefactor? What beggar has been comforted by your bounty? what sick man preserved by your care? Your breast is unmoved by woe, your ear is deaf to complaint, your doors are barred against the poor and wretched. Not so are the gates of Alnwick Castle; they are open as their owner's heart.

Osm. Insulting girl!—This to my face?

Ang. Nay, never bend your brows! Shall I tremble, because you frown? Shall my eye sink, because anger flashes from yours?—No! that would ill become the bride of Northumberland. [*Crosses*, L.

Osm. Amazement!—Can this be the gentle, timid Angela?

Ang. Wonder you that the worm should turn when you trample it so cruelly? Oh! wonder no more: ere he was torn from me, I clasped Percy to my breast, and my heart caught a spark of that fire which flames in his unceasingly!

Alice. Caught fire, lady!

Osm. Silence, old crone!—I have heard you calmly, Angela; now then hear me. Twelve hours shall be allowed you to reflect upon your situation; till that period is elapsed, this chamber shall be your prison, and Alice, on whose fidelity I can depend, your sole attendant. This term expired, should you still reject my hand, force shall obtain for me what love denies. [*Crosses*, L.] Speak not: I will hear nothing! I swear that to-morrow sees you mine, or undone! and, skies, rain curses on me if I keep not my oath! Mark that, proud girl! mark it, and tremble!

[*Exit*, L.

Ang. Tremble, did he say? Alas! how quickly is my boasted courage vanished! Yet I will not despair; there is a power in heaven, there is a Percy on earth; on them will I rely to save me.

Alice. The first may, lady; but as to the second, he'll be of no use, depend on't. Now might I advise, you'd accept my lord's offer: what matters it whether the man's name be Osmond or Percy? An earl's an earl after all; and though one may be something richer than t'other—

Ang. Oh! silence, Alice!—nor aid my tyrant's designs: rather instruct me how to counteract them;—you have influence in the castle; assist me to escape.

Alice. I help you to escape! Not for the best gown in your ladyship's wardrobe! I tremble at the very idea of my lord's rage; and, besides, had I the will, I've not the power. Kenric keeps the keys; we could not possibly quit the castle without his knowledge; and if the earl threatens to use force with you—Oh gemini! what would he use with me, lady?

Ang. Threatens, Alice! I despise his threats! Ere it pillows Osmond's head, will I plunge this poniard in my bosom.

Alice. Holy fathers!—a dagger!

Ang. Even now, as I wandered through the armoury, my eye was attracted by its glittering handle. Look, Alice! it bears Osmond's name; and the point—

Alice. Is rusty with blood! Take it away, lady! take it away! I never see blood without fainting!

Ang. [*Putting up the dagger.*] This weapon may render me good service. But, ah! what service has it rendered Osmond? Haply 'twas this very poniard which drank his brother's blood—or which pierced the fair breast of Evelina! Said you not, Alice, that this was her portrait?

Alice. I did, lady; and the likeness was counted excellent.

Ang. How fair! how heavenly!

Alice. [*Having locked the folding-doors.*] Ah! 'twas a sad day for me, when I heard of the dear lady's loss! look at the bed, lady:—that very bed was hers. How often have I seen her sleeping in that bed! And, oh! how like an angel she looked when sleeping! I remember, that just after Earl Reginald—Oh! Lord! didn't somebody shake the curtain?

Ang. Absurd! It was the wind.

Alice. I declare it made me tremble!—Well, as I was saying, I remember, just after Earl Reginald had set out for the Scottish wars, going into her room one morning, and hearing her sob most bitterly.—So advancing to the bed-side, as it might be thus—"My lady," says I, with a low courtesy, "Isn't your ladyship well?"—So, with that, she raised her head slowly above the quilt, and, giving me a mournful look—[*Here, unseen by Angela, who is contemplating Reginald's portrait, Father Philip lifts up his head, and gives a deep groan.*]

Alice. The devil! the devil! [*Exit*, L. D.

Ang. [*Turning round.*] How now? [*Father Philip rising from the bed—it breaks under him, and he rolls at Angela's feet.*] Good heavens! a man concealed! [*Attempting to pass him, he detains her by her robe.*]

F. Phil. Stay, daughter, stay! If you run, I can never overtake you!

Ang. Amazement! Father Philip!

F. Phil. The very same; and at present the best friend that you have in the world. Daughter, I came to save you.

Ang. To save me? Speak! Proceed!

F. Phil. Observe this picture; it conceals a spring, whose secret is unknown to all in the castle except myself. Upon touching it, the panel slides back, and a winding passage opens into the marble hall. Thence we must proceed to the vaulted vestibule: a door is there concealed, similar to this; and, after threading the mazes of a subterranean labyrinth, we shall find ourselves in safety on the outside of the castle walls.

Ang. Oh! worthy, worthy father! Quick, let us hasten! let us not lose one moment!

F. Phil. Hold! hold! Not so fast. You forget that between the hall and vestibule we must traverse many chambers much frequented at this early hour. Wait till the castle's inhabitants are asleep. Expect me, without fail, at one.

Ang. Stay yet one moment. Tell me, does Percy—

F. Phil. I have apprized him, that this night will restore you to liberty, and he expects you at the fisherman's cottage. Now, then, farewell, fair daughter!

[*Exit F. Phil. through the sliding panel, closing it after him.*

Ang. Good friar, till one, farewell! This is thy doing, Father of Justice! receive my thanks. Yes, Percy, we shall meet once more—shall meet never again to separate! Those dreams shall be realized—those smiling, golden dreams which floated before us in Allan's happy cottage. I must not expect thee, Friar, before one. Till that hour arrives, will I kneel at the feet of yonder saint, and tell my beads, and pray for morning. [*She kneels.*

[*Soft music, as the scene comes down very slowly.*]

END OF ACT III.

ACT IV.

SCENE I.—*The Castle-Hall. The lamps are lighted.*

Enter FATHER PHILIP, R.

F. Phil. 'Tis near midnight, and the earl is already retired to rest. What if I ventured now to the lady's chamber? Hark! I hear the sound of footsteps!

Enter ALICE, L.

F. Phil. (R.) How, Alice, is it you?

Alice. (L.) So, so! have I found you at last, father? I have been in search of you these four hours!—Oh! I've been so frightened since I saw you, that I wonder I keep my senses!

F. Phil. So do I; for I'm sure they're not worth the trouble. And, pray, what has alarmed you thus? I warrant you've taken an old cloak pinned against the wall for a spectre, or discovered the devil in the shape of a tabby-cat.

Alice. [*Looking round in terror.*] For the love of heaven, father, don't name the devil! or, if you must speak of him, pray mention the good gentleman with proper politeness. I'm sure, for my own part, I had always a great respect for him, and if he hears me, I dare say he'll own as much, for he certainly haunts this castle in the form of my late lady.

F. Phil. Form of a fiddle-stick!—Don't tell me of your—

Alice. Father, on the word of a virgin, I saw him this very evening in Lady Angela's bed!

F. Phil. In Lady Angela's? On my conscience, the devil has an excellent taste! But, Alice! Alice! how dare you trot about the house at this time of night, propagating such abominable falsehoods? One comfort is, that nobody will believe you. Lady Angela's virtue is too well known and I'm persuaded she wouldn't suffer the devil to put a single claw into her bed for the universe.

Alice. How you run on! Lord bless me, she wasn't in bed herself.

F. Phil. Oh! was she not?

Alice. No to be sure: but you shall hear how it happened. We were in the cedar-room together; and while we were talking of this and that, Lady Angela suddenly gave a great scream. I looked round, and what should I see but a tall figure, all in white, extended upon the bed! At the same time I heard a voice, which I knew to be the Countess Evelina's, pronounce in a hollow tone—"Alice! Alice! Alice!" three times. You may be certain that I was frightened enough. I instantly took to my heels; and just as I got with outside of the door, I heard a loud clap of thunder.

F. Phil. Well done, Alice! A very good story, upon my word. It has but one fault—'tis not true.

Alice. Odds my life, father, how can you tell any thing about it? Sure I should know best; for I was there, and you were not. I repeat it—I heard the voice as plain as I hear yours: do you think I've no ears!

F. Phil. Oh! far from it: I think you've uncommonly good ones; for you not only hear what has been said, but what has not. As to this wonderful story of yours, Alice, I don't believe one word of it; I'll be sworn that the voice was no more like your lady's than like mine; and that the devil was no more in the bed than I was. Therefore, take my advice, set your heart at rest, and go quietly to your chamber, as I am now going to mine. Good night. [*Exit*, L.

Alice. There, he's gone!—Dear heart! dear heart! what shall I do now? 'Tis past twelve o'clock, and stay by myself I dare not. I'll e'en wake the laundry-maid, make her sit up in my room all night; and 'tis hard if two women a'n't a match for the best devil in christendom.

[*Exit*, R.

Enter SAIB *and* HASSAN, L.

Saib. The earl then has forgiven me! A moment longer and his pardon would have come too late. Had not Kenric held his hand, by this time I should be at supper with St. Peter.

Has. Your folly well deserved such a reward. Knowing the earl's hasty nature, you should have shunned him till the first storm of passion was past, and circumstances had again made your ministry needful. Anger then would have armed his hand in vain; for interest, the white man's God, would have blunted the point of his dagger.

Saib. I trusted that his gratitude for my past services—

Has. European gratitude? Seek constancy in the winds, fire in ice, darkness in the blaze of sunshine! But seek not gratitude in the breast of an European!

Saib. Then why so attached to Osmond? For what do you value him?

Has. Not for his virtues, but for his vices, Saib; can there for me be a greater cause to love him? Am I not branded with scorn? Am I not marked out for dishonour? Was I not free, and am I not a slave? Was I not once beloved, and am I not now despised? What man, did I tender my service, would accept the negro's friendship? What woman, did I talk of affection, would not turn from the negro with disgust? Yet, in my own dear land, my friendship was courted, my love was returned. I had parents, children, wife! Bitter thought, in one moment all were lost to me! Can I remember this, and not hate these white men? Can I think how cruelly they have wronged me, and not rejoice when I see them suffer? Attached to Osmond, say you?—Saib, I hate him! Yet viewing him as an avenging fiend sent hither to torment his fellows, it glads me that he fills his office so well! Oh! 'tis a thought which I would not barter for empires, to know that in this world he makes others suffer, and will suffer himself for their tortures in the next! [*Crosses*, R.

Saib. (L.) Hassan, I will sleep no more in the lion's den. My resolve is taken: I will away from the castle, and seek, n some other service, that security—

Osm. [*Within*, M. D.] What, hoa! help! lights there! lights!

Has. Hark! Surely 'twas the earl!

OSMOND *rushes in wildly at* M. D.

Osm. (C.) Save me! Save me! They are at hand! Oh! let them not enter! [*Sinks into the arms of Saib.*

Saib. (L.) What can this mean? How violently he trembles?

Has. (R) Speak, my lord! Do you not know us?

Osm. [*Recovering himself.*] Ha! whose voice? Hassan's? And Saib too here? Oh! was it then but a dream? Did I not hear those dreadful, those damning words? Still, still they ring in my ears. Hassan! Hassan! Death must be bliss, in flames or on the rack, compared to what I have this night suffered!

Has. Compose yourself, my lord. Can a mere dream unman you thus?

Osm. A mere dream, say st thou? Hassan, 'twas a dream of such horror! Did such dreams haunt my bitterest foe, I should wish him no severer punishment. Mark you not how the ague of fear still makes my limbs tremble? Roll not my eyes as if still gazing on the spectre? Are not my lips convulsed, as were they yet pressed by the kiss of corruption? Oh! 'twas a sight that might have bleached joy's rosy cheek for ever, and strewed the snows of age upon youth's auburn ringlets! Hark, fellows! Instruments of my guilt, listen to my punishment! Methought I wandered through the low-browed caverns, where repose the reliques of my ancestors! Suddenly a female form glided along the vault; it was Angela! She smiled upon me, and beckoned me to advance. I flew towards her; my arms were already unclosed to clasp her; when, suddenly, her figure changed, her face grew pale, a stream of blood gushed from her bosom! Hassan, 'twas Evelina!

Saib and Has. Evelina!

Osm. Such as when she sank at my feet expiring, while my hand grasped the dagger still crimsoned with her blood! "We meet again this night!" murmured her hollow voice! "Now rush to my arms—but first see what you have made me! Embrace me, my bridegroom! We must never part again!" While speaking, her form withered away: the flesh fell from her bones; her eyes burst from their sockets; a skeleton, loathsome and meagre, clasped me in her mouldering arms!

Saib. Most horrible!

Osm. And now blue dismal flames gleamed along the walls; the tombs were rent asunder; bands of fierce spectres rushed around me in frantic dance; furiously they gnashed their teeth, while they gazed upon me, and shrieked in loud yell "Welcome, thou fratricide! Welcome, thou lost for ever!" Horror burst the bands of sleep; distracted I flew hither: But my feelings—words are too weak, too powerless to express them. [*Crosses*, L.

Saib. (C.) My lord! my lord! this was no idle dream! it was a celestial warning; 'twas your better angel that whispered, "Osmond, repent your former crimes! Commit not new ones!" Remember, that this night should Kenric—

Osm. Kenric? Oh! speak! Drank he the poison?

Saib. Obedient to your orders, I presented it at supper; but ere the cup reached his lips, his favourite dog sprang upon his arm, and the liquor fell to the ground untasted.

Osm. Praised be heaven! Then my soul is lighter by a crime! Kenric shall live, good Saib. What though he quit me, and betray my secrets? Proofs he cannot bring against me, and bare assertions will not be believed. At worst, should his tale be credited, long ere Percy can wrest her from me, shall Angela be mine. [*Crosses*, C.] Hassan, to your vigilance I leave the care of my beloved. Fly to me that instant, should any unbidden footstep approach yon chamber-door. I'll to my couch again. Follow me, Saib, and watch me while I sleep. Then, if you see my limbs convulsed, my teeth clenched, my hair bristling, and cold dews trembling on my brow, seize me—rouse me—snatch me from my bed! I must not dream again. Oh! how I hate thee, sleep! Friend of virtue, oh! how I hate thy coming! [*Exit with Saib, through* M. D.

Has. Yes, thou art sweet, vengeance! Oh! how it joys me when the white man suffers! Yet weak are his pangs, compared to those I felt when torn from thy shores, oh, native Africa! from thy bosom, my faithful Samba!—Oh! when I forget my wrongs, may I forget myself! When I forbear to hate these Christians, God of my fathers, may'st thou hate me!—Ha! Whence that light? A man moves this way with a lamp! How cautiously he steals along! He must be watched. This friendly column will shield me from his regards. Silence! He comes.

[*Retires*, L. S. E.

Enter KENRIC, *softly, with a lamp*, R.

Ken. All is hushed! the castle seems buried in sleep. Now then to Angela! [*Exit*, L.

Has. [*Advancing.*]—It was Kenric!—Still he moves onwards—Now he stops—'Tis at the door of Angela's chamber!—He unlocks it!—He enters!—Away then to the earl: Christian, soon shall we meet again!

[*Exit*, M. D.

SCENE II.—*Angela's Apartment.*

ANGELA *stands by the window, which is open, and through which the moon is seen.*

Ang. Will it never arrive, this tedious lingering hour? Sure an age must have elapsed since the friar left me, and still the bell strikes not one! Hark! Surely I heard—some one unlocks the door!—Oh! should it be the earl! should he not retire ere the monk arrives!—The door opens—How!—Kenric here!—Speak—what would you?

Enter KENRIC, L. *door.*

Ken. Softly, lady!—If overheard, I am lost—and your fate is connected with mine—[*Placing his lamp on the table.*

Ang. What means this mystery?—This midnight visit—

Ken. Is the visit of a friend, of a penitent!—Lady, I must away from the castle: the keys are in my possession: I will make you the companion of my flight, and deliver you safe into the hands of Percy.—But, ere we depart—[*Kneeling.*]—Oh! tell me, lady, will you plead for me with one, who to me alone owes sixteen years of hard captivity?

Ang. Rise, Kenric: I understand you not. Of what captive do you speak!

Ken. Of one, who by me has been most injured, who to you will be most dear. Listen, lady, to my strange narration. I was brought up with Osmond, was the partner of his pleasures, the confidant of his cares. The latter sprung solely from his elder brother, whose birthright he coveted, whose superiority he envied. Yet his aversion burst not forth, till Evelina Neville, rejecting his hand, bestowed hers with her heart on Reginald. Then did Osmond's passion overleap all bounds. He resolved to assassinate his brother when returning from the Scottish wars, carry off the lady, and make himself master of her person by force. This scheme he imparted to me: he flattered, threatened, promised, and I yielded to his seduction!

Ang. Wretched man!

Ken. Condemn me not unheard. 'Tis true, that I followed Osmond to the scene of slaughter, but no blood that day imbrued my hand. It was the earl whose sword struck Reginald to the ground; it was the earl whose dagger was raised to complete his crime, when Evelina threw herself upon her husband's body, and received the weapon in her own.

Ang. Dreadful! dreadful!

Ken. His hopes disappointed by this accident, Osmond's wrath became madness. He gave the word for slaughter, and Reginald's few attendants were butchered on the spot. Scarce could my prayers and arguments save from his wrath his infant niece, whose throat was already gored by his poniard. Angela, yours still wears that mark.

Ang. Mine?—Almighty powers!

Ken. Lady, 'tis true. I concealed in Allan's cottage the heiress of Conway: there were you doomed to languish in obscurity, till, alarmed by the report of his spies that Percy loved you, he caused me to reclaim you from Allan, and resolved, by making you his wife, to give himself a lawful claim to these possessions.

Ang. The monster! Oh! good, good Kenric! and you knelt to me for pardon? You to whom I owe my life! You to whom—

Ken. Hold! oh, hold!—lady, how little do I deserve your thanks!—Oh! listen! listen!—I was the last to quit the bloody spot: sadly was I retiring, when a faint groan struck my ear. I sprang from my horse; I placed my hand on Reginald's heart; it beat beneath the pressure!

[*Here Osmond appears at the door, motions to Saib to retire,* L. *and advances himself unobserved.*]

Ang. It beat! it beat! Cruel, and your dagger—

Ken. Oh! that would have been mercy. No, lady; it struck me, how strong would be my hold over Osmond, while his brother was in my power; and this reflection determined me to preserve him. Having plunged the other bodies in the Conway's flood, I placed the bleeding earl's on my horse before me, and conveyed him still insensible to a retreat, to all except myself a secret. There I tended his wounds carefully, and succeeded in preserving his life.—Lady, Reginald still exists.

[*Here Osmond, with a furious look, draws his dagger, and motions to stab Kenric. A moment's reflection makes him stay his hand, and he returns the weapon into the sheath.*]

Ang. Still exists, say you? My father still exists?

Ken. He does, if a life so wretched can be termed existence. While his swoon lasted, I chained him to his dungeon wall; and no sooner were his wounds healed, than I entered his prison no more. Lady, near sixteen years have passed, since the human voice struck the ear of Reginald!

Ang. Alas! alas!

Ken. But the hour of his release draws near: I discovered this night that Osmond seek's my life, and resolved to throw myself on your mercy. Then tell me, lady, will you plead for me with your father? Think you, he can forgive the author of his sufferings?

Ang. Kenric, you have been guilty—cruel: but restore to me my father, aid us to escape, and all shall be forgiven, all forgot.

Ken. Then follow me in silence; I will guide you to Reginald's dungeon: this key unlocks the castle gates; and ere the cock crows, safe in the arms of Percy—[*Here his eye falls upon Osmond, who has advanced between him and Angela. She shrieks and sinks into a chair.*] Horror!—The earl!—Undone for ever!

Osm. Miscreant!—Within there!

Enter SAIB, HASSAN, *and* MULEY, L. S. E.

Osm. Hence with that traitor! confine him in the western tower!

Ang. [*Starting wildly from her seat.*] Yet speak once more, Kenric; Where is my father? What place conceals him?

Osm. Let him not speak! Away with him!

[*Kenric is forced off by the Africans,* L. D.

Osm. [*Paces the stage with a furious air, while Angela eyes him with terror: at length he stops, and addresses her.*] Nay, stifle not your curses! Why should your lips be silent when your eye speaks? Is there not written on every feature "Vengeance on the assassin! Justice on my mother's murderer?"—But mark me, Angela! Compared to that which soon must be thine, these titles are sweet and lovely. Know'st thou the word parricide, Angela? Know'st thou their pangs who shed the blood of a parent?—Those pangs must be thine to-morrow. This long-concealed captive, this new-found father—

Ang. Your brother, Osmond? your brother?—Surely you cannot, will not—

Osm. Still doubt you, that I both can, and will?—Remember Kenric's tale! Remember, though the first blow failed, the second will strike deeper!—But from whom must Reginald receive that second? Not from his rival brother? not from his inveterate foe!—from his daughter, his unfeeling daughter! 'Tis she, who, refusing me her hand, will place a dagger in mine; 'tis she, whose voice declaring that she hates me, will bid me plunge that dagger in her father's heart!

Ang. Man! man! drive me not mad!

Osm. Then fancy that he lies in some damp solitary dungeon, writhing in death's agonies, his limbs distorted, his eyestrings breaking, his soul burthened with crimes, his last words curses on his unnatural child, who could have saved him, but would not!

Ang. Horrible! horrible!

Osm. Must Reginald die, or will Angela be mine?

Ang. Thine?—She will perish first!

Osm. You have pronounced his sentence, and his blood be on your head!—Farewell!

Ang. [*Detaining him, and throwing herself on her knees.*] Hold! hold! Look with pity on a creature whom your cruelty has bowed to the earth, whose heart you have almost broken, whose brain you have almost turned!—Mercy, Osmond! Oh! mercy! mercy!

Osm. Lovely, lovely suppliant! Why owe to cold consent what force may this instant give me?—It shall be so, and thus—[*Attempting to clasp her in his arms, she starts from the ground suddenly, and draws her dagger with a distracted look.*]

Ang. Away! approach me not! dare not to touch me, or this poniard—

Osm. Foolish girl! let me but say the word, and thou art disarmed that moment. [*Attempting to seize it, his eyes rest upon the hilt, and he starts back with horror.*] By hell, the very poniard which—

Ang. [*In an exulting tone.*] Ha! hast thou found me, villain?—Villain, dost thou know this weapon? Know'st thou whose blood incrusts the point? Murderer, it flowed from the bosom of my mother!

Osm. Within there! help!—[*Hassan and Alaric enter.*] Oh! God in heaven! [*He falls senseless into their arms, and they convey him from the chamber, the door is locked after them.*]

Ang. He faints!—Long may the villain wear thy chains, oblivion!—Long be it ere he wakes to commit new crimes!—[*She remains for some moments prostrate on the ground in silent sorrow. The castle bell strikes "one!" She rises.*]

Hark! the bell! 'Tis the time which the monk appointed He will not tarry. Ha! what was that? Methought the sound of music floated by me! It seemed as if some one had struck the guitar!—I must have been deceived; it was but fancy. [*A plaintive voice sings within, accompanied by a guitar.*]

"Lullaby!—Lullaby!—Hush thee, my dear,
Thy father is coming, and soon will be here!"

Ang. Heavens! The very words which Alice—The door too! It moves! It opens! Guard me, good angels!

[*The folding-doors unclose, and the oratory is seen illuminated. In its centre stands a tall female figure, her white and flowing garments spotted with blood; her veil is thrown back, and discovers a pale and melancholy countenance: her eyes are lifted upwards, her arms extended towards heaven, and a large wound appears upon her bosom. Angela sinks upon her knees, with her eyes rivetted upon the figure, which for some moments remain motionless. At length the spectre advances slowly to a soft and plaintive strain: she stops opposite to Reginald's picture, and gazes upon it in silence. She then turns, approaches Angela, seems to invoke a blessing upon her, points to the picture, and retires to the oratory. The music ceases. Angela rises with a wild look, and follows the vision, extending her arms towards it. The spectre waves her hand, as bidding her farewell. Instantly the organ's swell is heard; a full chorus of female voices chant "Jubilate!" A blaze of light flashes through the oratory, and the folding-doors close with a loud noise. Angela falls motionless on the floor.*]

END OF ACT IV.

ACT V.

SCENE I.—*A view of Conway Castle, by Moonlight.* [*Stage rather dark.*]

Enter ALLAN *and* MOTLEY, L.

Allan. (R.) But should the friar's plot have failed—

Mot. (L.) Failed, and a priest and a petticoat concerned in it—oh no, a plot composed of such good ingredients cannot but succeed. Ugh! would I were again seated by the fisher's hearth: the wind blows cruel sharp and bitter

Allan. For shame, Gilbert; is not my lord equally exposed to its severity.

Mot. Oh, the flame in his bosom keeps him warm, and in a cold night love wraps one up better than a blanket; but that not being my situation, the present object of my desires is a blazing wood fire, and Venus would look to me less lovely than a smoking sack posset. Oh! when I was in love, I managed matters much better; I always paid my addresses by the fire-side, and contrived to urge my soft suit just at dinner-time—then how I filled my fair one's ears with fine speeches, while she filled my trencher with roast beef! Then what figures and tropes came out of my mouth, and what dainties and tid bits went in! 'Twould have done your heart good to hear me talk, and see me eat, and you'd have found it no easy matter to decide whether I'd most wit or appetite.

Allan. And who was the object of this voracious passion?

Mot. A person well calculated to charm both my heart and my stomach; it was a lady of great merit, who did earl Percy's father the honour to superintend his culinary concerns. I was scarce fifteen, when she kindled a flame in my heart, while lighting the kitchen fire. From that moment I thought on nothing but her; my mornings were passed in composing poems on her beauty; my evenings in reciting them in her ear—for nature had equally denied the fair creature and myself the faculty of reading and writing.

Allan. You were successful, I hope.

Mot. Why at length she consented to be mine; when, oh! cruel fortune! taking one night a drop too much—poor dear creature, she never got the better of it—I wept her loss, and composed an elegy upon it, which has been thought, by many persons of great judgment, not totally destitute of taste and sublimity. It began thus:

"Baked be the pies to coals,
Burn, roast meat, burn,
Boil o'er, ye pots—ye spits, forget to turn,
Cindrelia's death—"

Allan. Here comes the earl.

Enter EARL PERCY, R.

Mot. In truth, my lord, you venture too near the castle; should you fall into Osmond's power a second time, your next jump may be into a better world.

Per. Oh, there's no danger, Gilbert; my followers are not far off, and will join me at a moment's warning. Then fear not for me.

Mot. With all my heart; but permit me to fear for myself: we are now within bow-shot of the castle: the archers may think proper to amuse us with a proof of their skill, and were I to feel an arrow quivering in my gizzard, probably I should be much more surprised than pleased. Good my lord, let us back to the fisherman's hut.

Per. Your advice may be wise, Gilbert; but I cannot follow it: see you nothing near yonder tower?

Mot. Yes, certainly. Two persons advance towards us: yet they cannot be our friends, for I see neither the lady's petticoat nor the monk's paunch!

Per. Still they approach, though slowly: one leans on his companion, and seems to move with pain. Let us retire and observe them.

Mot. Away, sir: I'm at your heels.

[*They retire*, R. S. E.

Enter SAIB *conducting* KENRIC, L.

Saib. Nay, yet hold up a while! Now, we are near the fisher's cottage.

Ken. Good Saib, I needs must stop! Enfeebled by Osmond's tortures, my limbs refuse to bear me further!—here lay me down: then fly to Percy, guide him to the dungeon, and, ere 'tis too late, bid him save the father of Angela!

Per. [*To Motley.*] Hark! did you hear?

Saib. Yet, to leave you thus alone!—

Ken. Oh, heed not me! Think that on these few moments depend our safety—Angela's freedom—Reginald's life! You have the master-key! Fly, then; oh, fly to Percy!

[*Percy and Motley come forward*, R. *to Kenric and Saib.*

Per. Said he not Reginald? Speak again, stranger!—What of Reginald?

Saib. Ha! look up, Kenric!—'Tis Percy's self!

Per. and Mot. How! Kenric?

Ken. [*Sinking at Percy's feet.*] Yes, the guilty, penitent Kenric! Oh, surely 'twas Heaven sent you hither!

Know, Earl Percy, that Reginald lives, that Angela is his daughter!

Per. Amazement! And is this known to Osmond?

Ken. Two hours have scarcely passed since he surprised the secret. Tortures compelled me to avow where Reginald was hidden, and he now is in his brother's power. Fly, then, to his aid! Alas! perhaps at this moment his destruction is completed! Perhaps, even now, Osmond's dagger—

Per. Within there! Allan! Harold!

Enter ALLAN, EDRIC, HAROLD, *and Soldiers,* R.

Per. Friends, may I depend on your support?

Har. While we breathe, all will stand by you!

Soldiers. All! All!

Per. Follow me then—away!

Ken. Yet stay one moment! Percy, to this grateful friend have I confided a master-key, which will instantly admit you to the castle, and have described to him the retreat of Reginald! Be he your guide, and hasten—Oh! that pang! [*He faints; Allan and Edric support him.*

Per. Look to him! He sinks! Bear him to your hut, Edric, and there tend his hurts.—[*To Saib.*] Now on, good fellow, and swiftly! Osmoud, despair! I come!
[*Exit, with Saib, Motley, Harold, and Soldiers,* L. U. E. *while Allan and Edric convey away Kenric, still fainting.*

SCENE II.—*A vaulted Chamber.*

Stage still dark.

Enter FATHER PHILIP, R. *with a basket on his arm, and a torch, conducting* ANGELA.

F. Phil. (L.) Thanks to St. Francis, we have as yet passed unobserved! Surely, of all travelling companions, fear is the least agreeable: I couldn't be more fatigued, had I run twenty miles without stopping!

Ang. (R.) Why this delay? Good father, let us proceed.

F. Phil. Ere I can go further, lady, I must needs stop to take breath, and refresh my spirits with a taste of this cordial. [*Taking a bottle from the basket*

Ang. Oh! not now! Wait till we are safe under Percy's protection, and then drink as you list. But not now, father; in pity, not now!

F. Phil. Well, well; be calm, daughter!—Oh! these women! these women! They mind no one's comfort but their own! Now where is the door?

Ang. How tedious seems every moment which I pass within these hated walls!—Ha! yonder comes a light.

F. Phil. So, so—I've found it at last.
[*Touching a spring, a secret door flies open.*

Ang. It moves this way! By all my fears, 'tis Osmond! In, father, in!—Away, for heaven's sake!
[*Exeunt,* L. D. *in flat, closing it after them.*

Enter OSMOND *and* HASSAN *with a torch,* R.

Osm. [*After a pause of gloomy meditation.*] Is all still within the castle?

Has. As the silence of the grave.

Osm. Where are your fellows?

Has. Saib guards the traitor Kenric: Muley and Alaric are buried in sleep.

Osm. Their hands have been stained with blood, and yet can they sleep? Call your companions hither. [*Hassan offers to leave the torch.*] Away with the light! its beams are hateful! [*Exit Hassan,* R.] Yes! this is the place. If Kenric said true, for sixteen years have the vaults beneath me rung with my brother's groans. I dread to unclose the door! How shall I sustain the beams of his eye, when they rest on Evelina's murderer? Ha! at that name my expiring hate revives! Reginald! Reginald! for thee was I sacrificed! Oh! when it strikes a second blow, my poniard thall strike surer!

Enter HASSAN, MULEY, *and* ALARIC, R. *with torches.*

The Africans. [*Together.*] My lord! my lord!

Osm. Now, why this haste?

Has. I tremble to inform you, that Saib has fled the castle. A master-key, which he found upon Kenric, and of which he kept possession, has enabled him to escape.

Osm. Saib, too, gone?—All are false! All forsake me!

Has. Yet more, my lord; he has made his prisoner the companion of his flight.

Osm. [*Starting.*] How? Kenric escaped?

Ala. 'Tis but too certain; doubtless he has fled to Percy.

Osm. To Percy? Ha! Then I must be speedy: my fate hangs on a thread! Friends, I have ever found ye faithful; mark me now! [*Opening the private door.*] Of these two passages, the left conducts to a long chain of dungeons: in one of these my brother still languishes.—

Once already have you seen him bleeding beneath my sword —but he yet exists. My fortune, my love, nay my life, are at stake! Need I say more? [*Each half unsheathes his sword.*] That gesture speaks me understood. On then before, I follow you. [*The Africans pass through the private door: Osmond is advancing towards it, when he suddenly starts back.*] Ha! Why roll these seas of blood before me? Whose mangled corse do they bear to my feet?—Fratricide? Oh! 'tis a dreadful name! Yet how preserve myself and Reginald? It cannot be! We must not breathe the same atmosphere. Fate, thy hand urges me! Fate, thy voice prompts me! Thou hast spoken;—I obey. [*He follows the Africans; the door is closed after him.*]

SCENE III.—*A gloomy subterraneous Dungeon, wide and lofty: the upper part of it has in several places fallen in, and left large Chasms. On one Side are various Passages leading to other Caverns: on the other is an Iron Door with Steps leading to it, and a Wicket in the Middle.* REGINALD, *pale and emaciated, in coarse Garments, his Hair hanging wildly about his Face, and a Chain bound round his Body, lies sleeping upon a Bed of Straw. A Lamp, a small Basket, and a Pitcher, are placed near him. After a few Moments he awakes, and extends his Arms.—The stage nearly dark.*

Reg. My child! My Evelina!—Oh! fly me not, lovely forms!—They are gone, and once more I live to misery. Thou wert kind to me, sleep! Even now, methought I sat in my castle-hall: a maid, lovely as the queen of fairies, hung on my knees, and hailed me by that sweet name, "Father!" Yes I was happy!—Yet frown not on me, therefore, darkness! I am thine again my gloomy bride! —Be not incensed, despair, that I left thee for a moment; I have passed with thee sixteen years! Ah! how many have I still to pass?—Yet fly not my bosom quite, sweet hope! Still speak to me of liberty, of light! Whisper, that once more I shall see the morn break, that again shall my fevered lips drink the pure gale of evening! God, thou knowest that I have borne my sufferings meekly: I have wept for myself, but never cursed my foes; I have sorrowde for thy anger, but never murmured at thy will. Patient have I been; oh! then reward me; let me once again press my daughter in my arms; let me, for one instant, feel again that I clasp to my heart a being who loves me. Speed thou to heaven, prayer of a captive!

[*He sinks upon a stone, with his hands clasped, and his eyes bent steadfastly upon the flame of the lamp.*]

ANGELA *and* FATHER PHILIP *are seen through the Chasms above, passing slowly along, from* R. *to* L.

Ang. Be cautious, father!—Feel you not how the ground trembles beneath us?

F. Phil. Perfectly well; and would give my best breviary to find myself once more on terra-firma. But the outlet cannot be far off: let us proceed.

Ang. Look down upon us, blessed angels! Aid us! Protect us!

F. Phil. Amen, fair daughter! [*They disappear.*

Reg. [*After a pause.*] How wastes my lamp? The hour of Kenric's visit must long be past, and still he comes not. How, if death's hand hath struck him suddenly? My existence unknown—Away from my fancy, dreadful idea! [*Rising, and taking the lamp.*] The breaking of my chain permits me to wander at large through the wide precincts of my prison. Haply the late storm, whose pealing thunders were heard e'en in this abyss, may have rent some friendly chasm: haply some nook yet unexplored—Ah! no, no, no! My hopes are vain, my search will be fruitless. Despair in these dungeons reigns despotic; she mocks my complaints, rejects my prayers, and when I sue for freedom, bids me seek it in the grave!—Death! oh, death! how welcome wilt thou be to me! [*Exit,* R. S. E.

[*The noise is heard of a heavy bar falling; the door opens,* L. U. E.]

Enter FATHER PHILIP *and* ANGELA, L. U. E.

F. Phil. How's this? A door?

Ang. It was barred on the outside.

F. Phil. That we'll forgive, as it wasn't bolted on the in. But I don't recollect—Surely I've not—

Ang. What's the matter?

F. Phil. By my faith, daughter, I suspect that I've missed my way.

Ang. Heaven forbid!

F. Phil. Nay, if 'tis so, I sha'n't be the first man who of two ways has preferred the wrong.

Ang. Provoking! And did I not tell you to choose the right-hand passage!

F. Phil. Truly, did you: and that was the very thing which made me choose the left. Whenever I am in doubt myself, I generally ask a woman's advice. When she's of one way of thinking, I've always found that reason 's on the other. In this instance, perhaps, I have been mistaken: but wait here for one moment, and the fact shall be ascertained. [*Exit*, R. S E.

Ang. How thick and infectious is the air of this cavern! Yet perhaps for sixteen years has my poor father breathed none purer. Hark! Steps are quick advancing! The friar comes, but why in such confusion?

Re-enter FATHER PHILIP, *running* R. S. E.

F. Phil. Help! help! it follows me!

Ang. [*Detaining him.*] What alarms you? Speak!

F. Phil. His ghost! his ghost!—Let me go!—let me go!—let me go!

[*Struggling to escape from Angela, he falls and extinguishes the torch; then hastily rises, and rushes up the stair-case, and closing the door after him*, L. U. E.]

Ang. Father! Father! Stay, for heaven's sake!—He 's gone! I cannot find the door!—— Hark! 'Twas the clank of chains!—A light too! It comes yet nearer!—Save me, ye powers!—What dreadful form! 'Tis here! I faint with terror! [*Sinks almost lifeless against the dungeon's side.*

Re-enter REGINALD, *with a Lamp*, R. S. E.

Reg. [*Placing his lamp upon a pile of stones.*] Why did Kenric enter my prison. Haply, when he heard not my groans at the dungeon door, he thought that my woes were relieved by death! Oh! when will that thought be verified?

Ang. Each sound of his hollow plaintive voice strikes to my heart. Dared I accost him—yet perhaps a maniac—no matter; he suffers, and the accents of pity will sound sweetly in his ears!

Reg. Thou art dead and at rest my wife! Safe in yon skies, no thought of me molests thy quiet. Yet sure I wrong thee! At the hour of death thy spirit shall stand beside me, shall close mine eyes gently, and murmur, "Die, Reginald, and be at peace!"

Ang. (L.) Hark! Heard I not—Pardon, good stranger—

Reg. (R.) [*Starting wildly from his seat.*] 'Tis she! She comes for me! Is the hour at hand, fair vision? Spirit of Evelina, lead on, I follow thee!

[*He extends his arms towards her, staggers a few paces forwards, then sinks exhausted on the ground.*]

Ang. He faints! perhaps expires!—Still, still! See, he revives!

Reg. 'Tis gone! Once more the sport of my bewildered brain! [*Starting up.*] Powers of bliss! Look where it moves again! Oh! say, what art thou? If Evelina, speak, oh, speak!

Ang. Ha! Named he not Evelina? That look! This dungeon too! The emotions which his voice—It is, it must be! Father! oh! Father! Father!

[*Falling upon his bosom.*

Reg. Said you? Meant you? My daughter—my infant, whom I left—Oh! yes, it must be true! My heart which springs towards you, acknowledges my child! [*Embracing her.*] But say how gained you entrance? Has Osmond—

Ang. Oh! that name recalls my terrors! Alas! you see in me a fugitive from his violence, guided by a friendly monk, whom your approach has frightened from me. I was endeavouring to escape: we missed our way, and chance guided us to this dungeon. But this is not a time for explanation. Answer me! Know you the subterraneous passages belonging to this castle?

Reg. Whose entrance is without the walls? I do.

Ang. Then we may yet be saved! Father, we must fly, this moment. Percy, the pride of our English youth, waits for me at the Conway's side. Come then, oh! come! Stay not one moment longer.

[*As she approaches the door, lights appear above*, R. U. E.

Reg. Look! look, my child! The beams of distant torches flash through the gloom!

Osm. [*Above.*] Hassan, guard you the door. Follow me, friends. [*The lights dissappear.*

Ang. Osmond's voice! Undone! Undone! Oh! my father! he comes to seek you, perhaps to—Oh! 'tis a word too dreadful for a daughter's lips!—

Reg. Hark! they come! The gloom of yonder cavern may a while conceal you: fly to it—hide yourself—stir not, I charge you.

Ang. What, leave you? Oh! no, no!

Reg. Dearest, I entreat, I conjure you, fly! Fear not for me!

Ang. Father! Oh! Father!

Reg. Farewell! perhaps for ever! [*He forces Angela into the cavern, then returns hastily, and throws himself on the bed of straw.*] Now then to hear my doom!

Enter OSMOND, L. U. E. *followed by* MULEY *and* ALARIC *with torches.*

Osm. The door unbarred? Softly, my fears were false! Wake, Reginald, and arise!

Reg. You here, Osmond? What brings you to this scene of sorrow? Alas! hope flies while I gaze upon your frowning eye! Have I read its language aright, Osmond?

Osm. Aright if you have read my hatred.

Reg. Have I deserved that hate? See, my brother, the once proud Reginald lies at your feet, for his pride has been humbled by suffering! Hear him adjure you by her ashes, within whose bosom we both have lain, not to stain your hands with the blood of your brother!

Osm. He melts me in my own despite.

Reg. Kenric has told me that my daughter lives! Restore me to her arms; permit us in obscurity to pass our days together! Then shall my last sigh implore upon your head heaven's forgiveness, and Evelina's.

Osm. It shall be so. Rise, Reginald, and hear me! You mentioned even now your daughter: know, she is in my power; know, also, that I love her!

Reg. How?

Osm. She rejects my offers. Your authority can oblige her to accept them. Swear to use it, and this instant will I lead you to her arms. Say will you give the demanded oath?

Reg. I cannot dissemble: Osmond, I never will.

Osm. How?—Reflect that your life—

Reg. Would be valueless, if purchased by my daughter's tears—would be loathsome, if imbittered by my daughter's misery. Osmond, I will not take the oath.

Osm. [*Almost choked with passion.*] 'Tis enough.—[*To the Africans.*] You know your duty! Drag him to yonder cavern! Let me not see him die!

Reg. [*Holding by a fragment of the wall, from which the Africans strive to force him.*] Brother, for pity's sake! for your soul's happiness!

Osm. Obey me, slaves! Away!

ANGELA *rushes in wildly from the Cavern.*

Ang. Hold off!—hurt him not! he is my father!

Osm. Angela here?

Reg. Daughter, what means—

Ang. [*Embracing him.*] You shall live, father! I will sacrifice all to preserve you Here is my hand, Osmond. Osmond, release my father, and solemnly I swear—

Reg. Hold, girl, and first hear me! [*Kneeling.*] God of nature, to thee I call! If e'er on Osmond's bosom a child of mine rests; if e'er she call him husband who pierced her hapless mother's heart, that moment shall a wound, by my own hand inflicted—

Ang. Hold! Oh! hold—end not your oath!

Reg. Swear never to be Osmond's!

Ang. I swear!

Reg. Be repaid by this embrace: [*They embrace.*]

Osm. Be it your last! Tear them asunder! Ha! what noise?

Enter HASSAN, *hastily,* L. U. E.

Has. My lord, all is lost! Percy has surprised the castle, and speeds this way!

Osm. Confusion! Then I must be sudden. Aid me, Hassan!

[*Hassan and Osmond force Angela from her father, who suddenly disengages himself from Muley and Alaric. Osmond, drawing his sword, rushes upon Reginald, who is disarmed, and beaten upon his knees; when at the moment that Osmond lifts his arm to stab him, Evelina's Ghost throws herself between them: Osmond starts back, and drops his sword.*]

Osm. Horror! What form is this?

Ang. Die. [*Disengages herself from Hassan, springs suddenly forwards, and plunges her dagger in Osmond's bosom, who falls with a loud groan, and faints. The Ghost vanishes: Angela and Reginald rush into each other's arms.*]

Enter PERCY, SAIB, HAROLD, &c. L U. E. *pursuing* OSMOND'S *Party. They all stop on seeing him bleeding upon the ground.*

Per. Hold, my brave friends! See where lies the object of our search!

Ang. Percy! Dear Percy!

Per. [*Flying to her.*] Dearest Angela!

Ang. My friend, my guardian angel! Come, Percy, come! embrace my father! Father, embrace the protector of your child!

Per. Do I then behold earl Reginald?

Reg. [*Embracing him.*] The same, brave Percy! Welcome to my heart! Live ever next it.

Ang. Oh, moment that o'erpays my sufferings! And yet—Percy, that wretched man—He perished by my hand!

Muley. Hark! he sighs! There is life still in him.

Ang. Life! then save him! save him! Bear him to his chamber! Look to his wound! Heal it, if possible! At least gain him time to repent his crimes and errors!

[*Osmond is conveyed away: Servants enter with torches, and the Stage becomes light.*]

Per. Though ill deserved by his guilt, your generous pity still is amiable. But say, fair Angela, what have I to hope? Is my love approved by your noble father? Will he—

Reg. Percy, this is no time to talk of love. Let me hasten to my expiring brother, and soften with forgiveness the pangs of death!

Per. Can you forget your sufferings?

Reg. Ah! youth, has he had none? Oh! in his stately chambers, far greater must have been his pangs than mine in this gloomy dungeon; for what gave me comfort was his terror, what gave me hope was his despair. I knew that I was guiltless — knew, that though I suffered in this world, my lot would be happy in that to come.

THE END.

DISPOSITION OF THE CHARACTERS AT THE FALL OF THE CURTAIN.

SOLDIERS, ANGELA, REGINALD, PERCY, SOLDIERS.
R.] [L.

THEATRE ROYAL
BIL LIA
BIL LIA RDS
LYCEUM

THEATRE ROYAL, COVENT GARDEN,

This present SATURDAY, November 13, 1802,

Will be presented (8th time) a NEW COMEDY, called

DELAYS and BLUNDERS.

With New Scenes and Dresses.

The Principal Characters by

Mr. LEWIS,
Mr. MUNDEN,
Mr. FAWCETT,
Mr. MURRAY,
Mr. EMERY,
Mr. SIDDONS,
Mr. DAVENPORT, Mr. SIMMONS, Mr. THOMPSON,
Mrs. LITCHFIELD,
Mrs. H. JOHNSTON,
Mrs. H. SIDDONS,
And Mrs. MATTOCKS.

The PROLOGUE to be spoken by Mr. BRUNTON.

After which will be produced, for the First time, a New Melo-Drame in Two acts, consisting of Speaking, Dancing & Pantomime, called

A TALE OF MYSTERY.

With New Music, Scenes, Dresses, & Decorations.

The OVERTURE and MUSIC composed by Dr. BUSBY.

The Principal Characters by

Mr. H. JOHNSTON,
Mr. MURRAY,
Mr. BLANCHARD,
Mr. FARLEY,
Mr BRUNTON,
Mr. CORY, Mr. SIMMONS,
Mr. CLAREMONT, Mr. BEVERLY,
Mr. CURTIES, Mr. ABBOT, Mr. TRUMAN,
Mrs. GIBBS,
And Mrs. MATTOCKS.

The Dances by

Mr. BOLOGNA, Jun.
Mr. DUBOIS, Mr. KING,
Mess. Klanert, Blurton, Platt, Wilde, L. Bologna, Howell, Lewiss, &c.
and Master BYRNE,
Mesdames Watts, Bologna, Norton, Bologna, Dibdin, Burnet,
And Mrs. WYBROW,
(Her First Appearance this Season)

From the uncommon great demand for Places for the MAN of the WORLD; Mr. COOKE will appear in the Character of Sir Pertinax Macsycophant on Monday next——Lady Rodolpha Lumbercourt by Mrs H. JOHNSTON.

Ladies & Gentlemen who have Places for the succeeding nights of the popular new Comedy of DELAYS & BLUNDERS, are respectfully informed, the 9th, 10th & 11th representations will be on Tuesday, Thursday and Saturday next Week.

In consequence of the extreme overflow from all parts of the Theatre Last night at the Opera of the CABINET, it will be repeated twice more this season, which will be on Wednesday & Friday next—And the Week after will be produced a New Comic Opera in Three acts, called FAMILY QUARRELS. With New Music, Scenes, Dresses & Decorations. The Music entirely New, & composed by Mess. Reeve, Moorehead, Davy & Braham.

E. MACLEISH, Printer, 2, Bow-street, Covent-Garden.

DOLBY'S BRITISH THEATRE.

A TALE OF MYSTERY.

I. R. Cruikshank, Del. *White, Sculpt.*

Bonamo. What mean these cries? What strange proceedings are here?

Selina. They are horrible

Bonamo. Why, my lord, are these daggers drawn against a man under my protection?

ACT I. SCENE I.

Dolby's British Theatre.

A TALE OF MYSTERY,

A MELO-DRAME,

IN TWO ACTS.

BY THOMAS HOLCROFT.

THE MUSIC BY DR. BUSBY.

PRINTED UNDER THE AUTHORITY OF THE MANAGERS, FROM THE PROMPT BOOK.

WITH

NOTES, CRITICAL AND EXPLANATORY.

ALSO

AN AUTHENTIC DESCRIPTION OF THE COSTUME AND THE GENERAL STAGE BUSINESS,

AS PERFORMED AT THE

THEATRES-ROYAL, LONDON.

Embellished with a Wood Engraving, from an original Drawing made expressly for this Work, by Mr. I. R. CRUIKSHANK, and executed by Mr WHITE.

London:

PRINTED AND PUBLISHED BY T. DOLBY, BRITANNIA PRESS, 17, CATHERINE-STREET, STRAND;

And Sold by Messrs. HODGSON and Co. 10, Newgate-Street.

Price Sixpence.

Costume.

BONAMO.—Purple velvet and gold mantle, black trunks, black silk hose, and sword.

ROMALDI.—Purple velvet and gold jacket, light drab and gold pantaloons, russet boots.

STEPHANO.—Drab hat, green plume, blue and gold jacket, white pantaloons, and russet boots.

MONTANO.—Black velvet mantle, black trunks, and black silk hose.

MICHELLI.—Drab rustic dress.

FRANCISCO.—Plain brown dress.

GARDENERS, PEASANTS, &c. Rustics dresses.

SELINA.—White muslin, trimmed with blue satin.

FIAMETTA.—White satin cap, brown stuff gown, trimmed with puce satin.

Cast of the Characters as performed at the Theatre, Royal, Covent Garden, 1824.

Bonamo	Mr. Egerton.
Romaldi	Mr. Cooper.
Stephano	Mr. Baker.
Montano	Mr. Claremont.
Michelli	Mr. Blanchard.
Francisco	Mr. Farley.
Selina	Miss Jones.
Fiametta	Mrs. Davenport

A TALE OF MYSTERY.

ACT I.

SCENE I.—*A Gothic Hall in the House of Bonamo, with two side doors, and folding doors in the back Scene: a table, pen, ink, and paper, chairs. &c. Music.*

Enter SELINA *and* FIAMETTA.

Sel. You seem hurried, Fiametta.

Fiam. Hurried, truly! yes, yes, and you'll be hurried too.

Sel. I?

Fiam. Fine news!

Sel. Of what kind?

Fiam. A very bad kind. The Count Romaldi—

Sel. [*Alarmed.*] What of him?

Fiam. Is coming.

Sel. When?

Fiam. This evening.

Sel. Heavens! what can he want?

Fiam. Want? he wants mischief. We all know he wants you to marry his son, because you're a rich heiress.

Sel. Surely, my uncle will never consent?

Fiam. Your uncle and all Savoy fear him.

Bona. [*Calling without,* L.] Fiametta!

Fiam. I am here, sir.

Bona. But I want you here.

Fiam. Lord, sir, I am busy.

Sel. Go, run to my uncle.

Fiam. It's a shame that he should not think of marrying you to his own son, when he knows how dearly you love each other.

Sel. It is the excellence of my dear uncle's heart that disdains the appearance of self-interest.

Fiam. So, rather than be blamed himself, he'll make you and I and every body miserable! But I'll talk to him.

Bona. [*Without.*] Fiametta, I say.

Fiam. Coming! [*Going.*] He shall hear of it. I'm in the proper cue. He knows I'm right, and I'll not spare him. [*Exit talking*, L.

[*Hunting Music.*]

Enter STEPHANO, M. D. *with his fowling-piece, n and game.*

Sel. (C.) Why are you so late, Stephano? I had a thousand alarms.

Steph. (C.) Forgive me, dear Selina; the pursuit of game led me too far among the mountains.

Sel. Do you know—

Steph. What?

Sel. I almost dread to tell you. Count Romaldi is coming.

Steph. Romaldi!

Sel. I shudder when I recollect the selfishness of his views, and the violence of his character.

Steph. Add, the wickedness of his heart.

[*Music to express contention.*

Enter BONAMO *and* FIAMETTA, L

Fiam. (L. C.) I tell you again, sir, it is uncharitable, it is cruel, it is hard-hearted in you to give any such orders.

Bona. (C.) And I tell you they shall be obeyed. Have not I a right to do as I please in my own house?

Fiam. No, sir, you have no right to do wrong any where.

Steph. (R. C.) What is the dispute, sir?

Fiam. He has ordered me to turn the poor Francisco out of doors; because, forsooth, the house is not large enough to hold this Count Romaldi.

Sel. (R. C.) Think, my dear uncle, how grateful and kind is his heart.

Steph. And that he is a man of fortune.

Bona. Folly and misfortune are twins: nobody can tell one from the other. He has got footing here, and you seem all determined he shall keep it.

Sel. I own I am interested in his favour: his manners are so mild

Steph. His eye so expressive.

Sel. His behaviour so proper.

Fiam. I'll be bound he is of genteel parentage!

Bona. Who told you so?

Fiam Not he, himself, for certain: because, poor creature, he is dumb. But only observe his sorrowful looks. What it is I don't know, but there is something on his mind so—

Bona. You are a fool!

Fiam. Fool or not, I have served you faithfully these three-and-twenty years; so you may turn me out of doors at last, if you please.

Bona. I!

Fiam. Yes; for if you turn Francisco out, I'll never enter them again.

Bona. You certainly know more concerning this man?

Fiam. Since it must be told, I do.

Bona. Then speak.

Fiam. It is quite a tragedy.

Bona. Indeed! let us hear.

Fiam. It is now seven or eight years ago, when, you having sent me to Chambery, I was coming home; it was almost dark; every thing was still; I was winding along the dale, and the rocks were all as it were turning black; of a sudden I heard cries; a man was murdering; I shook from head to foot; presently the cries died away; and I beheld two bloody men, with their daggers in their hands, stealing off under the crags at the foot of the hill. I stood like a stone, for I was frightened out of my wits! So I thought I heard groans; and, afeared as I was, I had the sense to think they must come from the poor murdered creature. So I listened, and followed my ears, and presently I saw this very man——

Sel. Francisco?

Fiam. Weltering in his blood! To be sure I screamed and called loud enough; for what could I do by myself? So presently my cries *was* heard! and honest Michelli, the miller, with his man, came running.

Bona. I now remember the tale. The poor man recovered, and every body praised Michelli.

Fiam. So they ought; he is an honest good soul! What then, sir, can you suppose I thought, when about a week ago, I again saw Francisco's *apparition* standing before me; making signs that he was famished with hunger and thirst. I knew him at once; and he soon bethought himself of me. If you had *seen* his clasped hands, and his thankful looks, and his dumb notes, and his signs of joy at having found me! While I have a morsel he shall never want. I'll hire him a cottage; I'll wait upon him; I'll work for him; so turn him out of doors, if you have the heart.

Steph. Fiametta, you wrong my father.

Bona. I'll hear his story from himself.

Fiam. He can't speak.

Bona. But he can write.

Fiam. I'll warrant him. I'm sure he's a gentleman.

Bona. Bring him here: if he prove himself an honest man, I am his friend.

Fiam. I know that, or you should be no master of mine. [*Exit*, L

Steph. His kind attentions to Selina are singular.

Sel. Every morning I find him waiting for me with fresh gathered flowers; which he offers with such modest yet affectionate looks.

[FIAMETTA *returns with* FRANCISCO, L. *the latter poor in appearance, but clean; with a reserved, placid, and dignified air.*

Bona. Come near, friend. You understand his gestures, Fiametta; so stay where you are.

Fiam. I intend it.

Bona. [*To himself.*] He has a manly form; a benevolent eye! [*Music.*] Sit down, sir. Leave us, my children.

[FRANCISCO *suddenly rises, as* STEPHANO *and* SELINA *offer to go, brings them back, and entreats by signs that they may remain.*

Bona. Since he desires it, stay. There are pen, ink, and paper; when you cannot answer by signs, write; but be strict to the truth. [*Music.*

Fran. [*With dignity, points to heaven and his heart.*

Bona. Who are you?

[FRANCISCO *goes back to a table, sits and writes; and* STEPHANO, *standing behind him, takes up the paper and reads the answers.—Music.*

Fran. "A noble Roman!"

Bona. Your family?—

Fran. [*Gives a sudden sign of* Forbear! *and writes—Music.*] "Must not be known."

Bona. Why? [*Music*

Fran. "It is disgraced."

Bona. By you? [*Music.*

Fran. [*Gesticulates.*]

Fiam. [*Interpreting.*] No, no, no!

Bona. Who made you dumb? [*Music.*

Fran. "The Algerines."

Bona. How came you in their power? [*Music.*

Fran. "By treachery."

Bona. Do you know the traitors? [*Music.*

Fran. [*Gesticulates.*]

Fiam. [*Eagerly.*] He does, he does!

Bona. Who are they?

Fran. "The same who stabbed me among the rocks."

[*Music expressive of horror.*

Bona. Name them.

Fran. [*Gesticulates violently, denoting painful recollection; then writes.*] "Never!"

Bona. Are they known by me?

Fiam. [*Interpreting*] They are! they are!

Bona. Are they rich?

Fran. "Rich and powerful."

Bona. Astonishing! Your refusal to name them gives strange suspicions. [*Goes to* FRANCISCO.] I must know more: tell me all, or quit my house.

[*Music to express disorder.*

Enter PIERO, L.

Pier. Count Romaldi, sir.

Fran. [*Starts up, struck with alarm.*]

Steph. So soon!

Bona. Shew him up.

Pier. He's here. [*Similar music.*

[ROMALDI *suddenly enters, as* FRANCISCO *is attempting to pass the door: they start back at the sight of each other.* ROMALDI *recovers himself; and* FRANCISCO, *in an agony of mind, leaves the room,* L.

Bona. (C.) What is all this! Where is he gone? Call him back, Fiametta!

[*Exeunt* FIAMETTA *and* STEPHANO; *both regarding* ROMALDI *with dislike,* L.

Rom. [L. C. *with forced ease.*] At length, my good friend, I am here. I have long promised myself the pleasure of seeing you. Your hand. How hearty you look! And your lovely niece! Her father's picture.

Bona. Rather her mother's.

Rom. My son will adore her. In two days I expect him here. I have serious business to communicate.

Sel. [*To her uncle.*] Permit me to retire, sir.

Bona. [*Tenderly.*] Go, my child; go.

Sel. [*Aside.*] Grant, oh merciful Heaven, I may not fall a sacrifice to avarice! [*Exit*, L.

Bona. And now your pleasure, Count?

Rom. Nay, I imagine, you can guess my errand. You know my friendship for my son; who, let me tell you, is your great admirer. The care you have bestowed upon your niece, her education, mind, and manners, and the faithful guardian you have been, both of her wealth and person, well deserve praise.

Bona. If I have done my duty, I am greatly fortunate.

Rom. She is a lovely young lady; and you are not ignorant of my son's passion: to which your duty towards your niece must make you a friend. I therefore come, with open frankness, to propose their union.

Bona. And I, with equal candour, must tell you, I can give no answer.

Rom. [*Haughtily affecting surprise.*] No answer!

Bona. Your rank and wealth make the proposal flattering; but there is a question still more serious.

Rom. [*In the same tone.*] What can that be?

Bona. One which my niece only can resolve.

Rom. Inexperience like hers should have no opinion.

Bona. How, my lord! Drag the bride, by force, to that solemn altar, where, in the face of Heaven, she is to declare her choice is free?

Rom. Mere ceremonies.

Bona. Ceremonies! Bethink yourself; lest marriage become a farce, libertinism a thing to laugh at, and adultery itself a finable offence!

Rom. Ay, ay; you are a moralist; a conscientious man. Your son is reported to have designs on Selina.

Bona. My lord!

Rom. No anger: I speak as a friend. Her fortune is tempting; but you disdain to be influenced. The wealth and rank of our family——

Bona. Surpass mine. True; still my niece, I say, must be consulted.

Rom. Indeed! [*Sternly.*] Then my alliance, it seems, is refused?

Bona. By no means; I have neither the right to refuse nor to accept. If Selina——

Re-enter SELINA *with a letter*, L.

Sel. [*Presenting it to* BONAMO, R. C.] From the unfortunate Francisco.

Rom. What, that strange fellow I met as I came in?

Sel. [*Aside.*] He knows his name!

Rom. I forgot to ask how he got admittance here?

Sel. [*With marked displeasure.*] I should hope, my lord, there would always be some charitable door open to the unfortunate!

Rom. [*With courteous resentment.*] I addressed your uncle, lovely lady.

Bona. When you came in, he was relating his adventures, which have been strange.

Rom. [*Retaining himself.*] And are you, my friend, simple enough to believe such tales?

Sel. What tales, my lord?

Bona. The proofs are convincing! the mutilation he has suffered; the wounds he received, not a league from hence; the——

Rom. [*Alarmed.*] Did he name——

Bona. Who? The monsters that gave them?—No; but they are not unknown to him.

Rom. That—that is fortunate.

Bona. I was amazed to learn——

Rom. What?

Bona. That they are rich and powerful. But I forget: the story can have no interest for you.

Rom. [*Eagerly.*] You mistake: I—[*Recollecting himself*]—my feelings are as keen as yours.

Bona. But what has he written? [*Offers to open the letter.*]

Rom. (c) If you will take my advice, you will not read. Doubtless he has more complaints, more tales, more favours to request. Be kind and hospitable; but do not be a dupe.

Bona. Of which, I own, there is danger.

Rom. [*Seizing the letter, which* BONAMO *carelessly holds.*] Then let me guard you against it.

Sel. [*After continually watching and suspecting* ROMALDI, *snatches the letter back*; *while he, remarking her suspicions, is confused.*] This letter, my lord, was given in charge to me; I promised to bring an answer; and I respectfully intreat my uncle will read it.

Bona. Well, well. [*Reads.*] "Friend of humanity, should I remain, the peace of your family might be disturbed. I therefore go; but earnestly intreat you will neither think me capable of falsehood nor ingratitude—Wherever I am, my wishes and my heart will be here.—Farewell." He shall not go.

Rom. (L.C.) Why not? He owns the peace of your family may be disturbed.

Bona. Fly, Selina; tell him I require, I request him to sleep here to-night, that I may speak with him to-morrow.

Rom. [*Aside.*] That must not be.

Sel. Thanks, my dear uncle! you have made me happy. [*Exit in haste,* L.—*Confused music.*

Enter PIERO, L.

Bona. What now, Piero?

Pier. Signior Montano is below.

Rom. [*Alarmed and aside.*] Montano!

Bona. I'm very glad of it, for I wanted his advice. [*To* ROMALDI.] The best of men!

Pier. Please to come up, sir.

Rom. With your permission, I will retire.

Enter MONTANO, L.

Music plays alarmingly, but piano when he enters and while he stays.

Mon. I beg pardon, good sir, but—

[*Music loud and discordant at the moment the eye of* MONTANO *catches the figure of* ROMALDI; *at which* MONTANO *starts with terror and indignation. He then assumes the eye and attitude of menace; which* ROMALDI *returns. The music ceases.*

Mon. Can it be possible!

Rom. [*Returning his threatening looks.*] Sir!

Mon. You here!

Rom. Not having the honour of your acquaintance, I know not why my presence should please or displease you.

Mon. [*After a look of stern contempt at* ROMALDI, *and addressing* BONAMO.] Good night, my friend; I will see you to-morrow. [*Exit, suddenly,* L.

Music.

Bona. [*Calling.*] Nay, but signior! Signior Montano! Are the people all mad? Fiametta!

Fiam. [*Without,* L.] Sir!

Bona. Run, overtake him; and say I must speak with him. [*Music ceases.*] Excuse me for going. [*To* ROMALDI.

Rom. Why in such haste? I have heard of this Montano: a credulous person; a relator of strange stories.

Bona. Signior Montano credulous! There is not in all Savoy a man of sounder understanding. Good night, my lord; I will send your servant: that door leads to your bed-room. Call for whatever you want; the house is at your command.

[*Exit with looks of suspicion,* L.—*Music expressive of terror.*

Rom. What am I to think? How act? The arm of Providence seems raised to strike!—Am I become a coward? shall I betray, rather than defend myself? I am not yet an idiot.

Enter the Count's Servant, MALVOGLIO, L. *who observes his master. Music ceases.*

Mal. Your lordship seems disturbed?

Rom. Francisco is here.

Mal. I saw him.

Rom. [*Both* C.] And did not your blood freeze?

Mal. I was sorry.

Rom. For what?

Mal. That my dagger had missed its aim.

Rom. We are in his power

Mal. He is in ours.

Rom. What are your thoughts?

Mal. What are yours, my lord?

Rom. Guess them.

Mal. Executioners!

Rom. Infamy!

Mal. Racks!

Rom. Maledictions!

Mal. From all which a blow may yet deliver us.

[SELINA, *entering* M. D. *and hiding behind the door, opposite to the chamber of* ROMALDI, *overhears them.*

Rom. 'Tis a damning crime!

Mal. Were it the first.

Rom. Where is he to sleep?

Mal. There! [*Pointing to the chamber opposite to* ROMALDI'S.

Sel. [*Behind the door.*] They mean Francisco! The monsters!

Rom. Obstinate fool! Since he will stay—

Mal. He must die.

Sel. The monsters!

Rom. I heard a noise.

Mal. [*Looking towards the folding doors.*] He's coming.

Rom. Let us retire and concert—

Mal. Then, at midnight—

Rom. When he sleeps—

Mal. He'll wake no more!

[*Exeunt*, L. S. E.

[*The Stage dark: soft and solemn music.* FIAMETTA *enters, with* FRANCISCO *and a lamp, which she places on the table. She regards him with compassion, points to his bed-room, then curtsies with kindness and respect, and retires* M. D. *he returning her kindness. He seats himself as if to write, rises, takes the lamp, looks round with apprehension, goes to the chamber-door of* ROMALDI, *starts away with horror, recovers himself, again places the lamp on the table, and sits down to write. The door of* ROMALDI *opens;* MALVOGLIO *half appears, watching* FRANCISCO; *but as he turns, again retires.*

Enter SELINA, R. *who gently pulls the sleeve of* FRANCISCO; *he starts; but seeing her, is satisfied.*

Music pauses.

Sel. [*In a low voice.*] Dare not to sleep! I will be on the watch! Your life is in danger! [*Exit*, R.

[*Music continues.*

Fran. [*Greatly agitated, draws a pair of pistols, lays them on the table, and seats himself.*

ROMALDI *and* MALVOGLIO *appear*, L. S. E.

[*Music suddenly stops.*

Rom. [*To* MALVOGLIO.] Watch that entrance. [*To* FRANCISCO.] Wretched fool! Why are you here?

[*Music expressive of terror and confusion.*

Fran [*Starts up, seizes his pistols, points them toward* ROMALDI *and* MALVOGLIO, *and commands the former, by signs, to read the paper that lies on the table.*

[*Music ceases.*

Rom. [*Reads.*] "Repent; leave the house. Oblige me not to betray you. Force me not on self defence." Fool! do you pretend to command? [*Throws him a purse.*] We are two. Take that, and fly.

[*Music.*

Fran. [*After a look of compassionate appeal, spurns it from him; and commands them to go.*

[*After which, sudden pause of Music.*

Rom. [*Aside to* MALVOGLIO.] I know him; he will not fire.

[*Music. They draw their daggers; he at first avoids them; at length they each seize him by the arm, and are in the attitude of threatening to strike, when the shrieks of* SELINA, *joining the music, which likewise expresses terror, suddenly brings* BONAMO, STEPHANO, *and Servants, through the folding doors*, M. D.

Sel. Uncle! Stephano! Murder!

[ROMALDI *and* MALVOGLIO, *at hearing the noise behind, quit* FRANCISCO, *and feign to be standing on self-defence——Music ceases.*

Bona. (C.) What mean these cries? What strange proceedings are here?

Sel. They are horrible.

Bona. Why, my lord, are these daggers drawn against a man under my protection!

Rom. Self-defence is a duty. Is not his pistol levelled at my breast?

Bona. [*To* FRANCISCO] Can it be?

Fran. [*Inclines his head.*]

Bona. Do you thus repay hospitality?

Sel. Sir, you are deceived: his life was threatened.

Rom. [*Sternly*] Madam——

Sel. I fear you not! I watched, I overheard you!

Bona. Is this true?

Rom. No.

Sel. By the purity of heaven, yes! Behind that door, I heard the whole; Francisco must quit the house, or be murdered!

Rom. [*To* BONAMO, *sternly*] I expect, sir, my word will not be doubted.

Bona. (C.) My lord, there is one thing of which I cannot doubt: the moment you appeared, terror was spread through my house. Men's minds are troubled at the sight of you: they seem all to avoid you. Good seldom accompanies mystery; I therefore now decidedly reply, to your proposal, that my niece cannot be the wife of your son; and must further add, you oblige me to decline the honour of your present visit.

Rom. [*With haughtiness,* L.] Speak the truth, old man, and own you are glad to find a pretext to colour refusal, and gratify ambition. Selina and Stephano; you want her wealth, and mean in that way to make it secure. But, beware! Dare to pursue your project, and tremble at the consequences! To-morrow, before ten o'clock, send your written consent; or dread what shall be done.

[*Exeunt* ROMALDI *and* MALVOGLIO.—*Music.*

Bona. (L.) Dangerous and haughty man! But his threats are vain; my doubts are removed; Selina shall not be the victim of mean precaution, and cowardly fears. I know your wishes, children. Let us retire. [*To his servants*] Make preparations for rejoicing: early to-morrow, Stephano and Selina shall be affianced.

[*Music of sudden joy while they kneel.*]

Steph. My kind father!

Sel. Dearest, best of guardians! [*Music pauses.*

Bona. Francisco shall partake the common happiness.

Fiam. [R. *as they are all retiring.*] Dear, dear! I sha'n't sleep to night.

[*Exeunt:* BONAMO *expressing friendship to all, which all return;* FRANCISCO *with joy equal to that of the lovers. Cheerful music gradually dying away.*

END OF ACT I.

ACT II.

Joyful Music.

SCENE I.—*A beautiful garden and pleasure grounds, with garlands, festoons, love devices and every preparation for a marriage festival.*

First and Second Gardeners. PIERO *and his companions; all busy.*

Pier. Come, come; bestir yourselves! The company will soon be here.

First Gard. Well; let them come: all is ready.

Pier. It has a nice look, by my fackins!

First Gard. I believe it has! thanks to me.

Pier. Thanks to *you!*

Second Gard. And me.

Pier. And *you*? Here's impudence! I say it is thanks to me.

F. and S. Gard. You, indeed?

Pier. Why, surely, you'll not have the face to pretend to deny my incapacity?

F. Gard. Yours?

S. Gard. Yours?

Pier. Mine! mine!

Enter STEPHANO, R.

Steph. What is the matter, my honest friends?

F. Gard. Why, here's Mr. Piero pretends to dispute his claim to all that has been done,

S. Gard. Yes; and says every thing is owing to his incapacity.

F. Gard. Now I maintain the incapacity was all my own. [*To* STEPH.] Saving and excepting yours, sir.

S. Gard. And mine.

F. Gard. Seeing you gave the first orders.

Pier. But *wasn't* they given to me, sir: Didn't you say to me, Piero, says you——

Steph. [*Interrupting.*] Ay, ay; each man has done his part: all is excellent, and I thank you kindly. Are the villagers invited!

Pier. Invited! They no sooner heard of the wedding than they were half out of their wits! There will be such dancing and sporting! Then the music! Little Nanine, with her hurdy-gurdy; her brother, with the tabor and pipe; the blind fiddler, the lame piper, I and my jew's harp! such a band!

Steph. Bravo: Order every thing for the best.

Pier. But who is to order? Please to tell me that, sir?

Steph. Why, you.

Pier. There; [*To his companions.*] Mind! I am to order! Mark that!

Steph. You shall be major-domo for the day.

Pier. You hear. I am to be—do—drum-major for the day!

Steph. Selina is coming. To your posts. [*Music.*

[*They hurry each to his garland, and conceal themselves by the trees and bushes.*

Enter BONAMO, SELINA, *and* FIAMETTA, R.
Music ceases.

Bona. [*Looking round.*] Vastly well, upon my word!

Sel. [*Tenderly.*] I fear, Stephano, you have slept but little?

Bona. [*Gaily.*] Sleep, indeed! He had something better to think of. Come, come; well breakfast here in the bower. Order it, Fiametta.

Fiam. Directly, sir.

[*She goes, and returns with the servants; aiding them to arrange the breakfast table.*

Bona. How reviving to age is the happiness of the young! And yet—[*Sighs*]—thou hast long been an orphan, Selina; it has no more than doubled thy fortune; which was great at my brother's sudden death. Would thou hadst less wealth, or I more!

Sel. And why, my dear uncle?

Bona. Evil tongues—this Romaldi——

Steph. Forget him.

Sel. Would that were possible! his menace—before ten o'clock—oh! that the hour were over.

Bona. Come, come; we'll not disturb our hearts with fears. To breakfast, and then to the notary. I forgot Francisco; why is he not here?

Sel. Shall I bring him?

Bona. Do you go, Fiametta.

Fiam. Most willingly.

Bona. Come, sit down. [*They seat themselves.*

[*Sweet music.* PIERO *peeps from behind a shrub.* STEPHANO *gives a gentle clap with his hands, and the peasants all rise from heir hiding-places, and suspend their garlands in a picturesque group, over* BONAMO, SELINA, *and* STEPHANO.—*Music ceases.*

Pier. What say you to that now.

Bona. Charming! charming!

Pier. I hope I am not made a major for nothing.

Bona. [*To* FRANCISCO, *who enters with* FIAMETTA.] Come, sir, please to take your seat.

Pier. [*To* STEPH.] Shall the sports begin?

Steph. [*Gives an affirmative sign.*]

Pier. Here! dancers! pipers! strummers! thrummers! to your places. This bench is for the band of music—mount.

[*Dancing commences. In the midst of the rejoicing the clock strikes; the dancing suddenly ceases; the music inspires alarm and dismay.*

Enter MALVOGLIO, R.

[*He stops in the middle of the stage: the company startup;* FRANCISCO, STEPHANO, SELINA, *and* BONAMO, *all express terror. The peasants, alarmed and watching: the whole, during a short pause, forming a picture.*

[MALVOGLIO *then presents a letter to* BONAMO, *with a malignant assurance, and turns away, gratified by the consternation he has occasioned: with which audacious air and feeling, he retires. While* BONAMO *opens the letter and reads with great agitation, music expresses confusion; then ceases.*

Bona. Oh, shame! dishonour! treachery!

Steph. My father!——

Sel. My uncle!

Fiam. What treachery?

Fran. [*Attitude of despair.*]

Bona. No more of love or marriage! no more of sports, rejoicing, and mirth.

Steph. Good Heavens!

Sel. My guardian! my friend! my uncle!

Bona. [*Repelling her.*] I am not your uncle.

Sel. Sir!

Steph. Not?

Bona. She is the child of crime! of adultery.

[*A general surprize: the despair of* FRANCISCO *extreme.*

Steph. 'Tis malice, my father!

Bona. Read.

Steph. The calumny of Romaldi!

Bona. [*Seriously.* Read.]

Steph. [*Reads.*] "Selina is not your brother's daughter. To prove I speak nothing but the truth, I send you the certificate of her baptism."

Bona. 'Tis here—authenticated. Once more read.

Steph. [*Reads*] "May the 11th 1584, at ten o'clock this evening was baptized Selina Bianchi, the daughter of Francisco Bianchi."

Fran. [*Utters a cry, and falls on the seat.*]

Sel. Is it possible! my father!

Fran. [*Open his arms, and Selina falls on his neck.*]

Steph. Amazement!

Bona. Sinful man! not satisfied with having dishonoured my brother, after claiming my pity, would you aid in making me contract a most shameful alliance? Begone! you and the offspring of your guilt.

Steph. Selina is innocent.

Fran. [*Confirms it.*]

Bona. Her father is——a wretch! Once more begone.

Fran. [*During this dialogue had held his daughter in his arms: he now rises with a sense of injury, and is leading her away.*]

Bona. Hold, miserable man,—[*To himself*]—Houseless—pennyless—without bread—without asylum—must she perish because her father has been wicked? [*To* FRANCISCO] Take this purse, conceal your shame, and, when 'tis empty, let me know your hiding place.

Fran. [*Expresses gratitude, but rejects the purse.*]

Sel. [*With affection*] Spare your benefits, sir, till you think we deserve them.

Bona. Poor Selina!

Steph. [*Eagerly*] What say you, sir?

Bona. Nothing—let them begone.

Sel. Stephano! farewell.

Steph. She shall not go! or—I will follow.

Bona. And forsake your father! ungrateful boy! [*To* FRAN.] Begone, I say. Let me never see you more. [*To the Peasants*] Confine that frantic youth.

[*Violent distracted music.*

[STEPHANO *endeavours to force his way to* SELINA: FIAMETTA *passionately embraces her; and by gesture reproaches* BONAMO, *who persists, yet is tormented by doubt.* STEPHANO *escapes, and suddenly hurries* SELINA *forward, to detain her; after violent efforts, they are again forced asunder; and, as they are retiring on opposite sides, with struggles and passion, the Scene closes.*

SCENE II.—*The house of Bonamo.*

BONAMO, STEPHANO, *brought on by the Peasants,* L. *who then leave the room.*

Bona. Disobedient, senseless boy!

Steph. (C.) [*Exhausted.*] Selina! give me back Selina, or take my life!

Bona. (R.) Forbear these complaints.

Steph. She is the woman I love.

Bona. Dare you——

Steph. None but she shall be my wife.

Bona. Your wife!

Steph. To the world's end I'll follow her!

Bona. And quit your father? Now, when age and infirmity bend him to the grave?

Steph. We will return to claim your blessing.

Bona. Stephano! I have loved you like a father, beware of my malediction.

Steph. When a father's malediction is unjust, Heaven is deaf.

Enter FIAMETTA, L. *as if striving to repress her anger.*

Fiam. Very well! It's all very right! But you will see how it will end!

Bona. [*To* STEPH.] I no longer wonder, Count Romaldi should advise me to drive such a wretch from my house.

Fiam. Count Romaldi is himself a wretch.

Bona. Fiametta !——

Fiam. [*Overcome by her passion.*] I say it again : a vile, wicked wretch ! and has written—

Bona. [*Imperiously.*] The truth. The certificate is incontestible,

Fiam. I would not for all the world be guilty of your sins.

Bona. Woman !

Fiam. I don't care for you ; I loved you this morning ; I would have lost my life for you, but you are grown wicked.

Bona. Will you be silent !

Fiam. Is it not wickedness to turn a sweet innocent helpless young creature out of doors ; one who has behaved with such tenderness ; and leave her at last to starve ? Oh, it is abominable !

Bona. Once more, hold your tongue.

Fiam. I won't ! I can't ! Poor Stephano ! And do you think he'll forbear to love her ? If he did, I should hate him ! But he'll make his escape. You may hold him to-day, but he'll be gone to-morrow. He'll overtake and find his dear forlorn Selina ; and they will marry, and live in poverty : but they will work, and eat their morsel with a good conscience ; while you will turn from your dainties with an aching heart !

Bona. For the last time, I warn you.

Fiam. I know the worst : I have worked for you all the prime of my youth ; and now you'll serve me as you have served the innocent, wretched Selina ; you'll turn me out of doors. Do it ! But I'll not go till I've said out my say : so I tell you again, you are a hard-hearted uncle, an unfeeling father, and an unjust master ! Every body will shun you? You will dwindle out a life of misery, and nobody will pity you ; because you don't deserve pity. So now I'll go, as soon as you please. [*Going*, L.

Enter SIGNIOR MONTANO, *hastily*, L.
FIAMETTA *and* STEPHANO *eagerly attentive.*

Mon. What is it I have just heard, my friend? Have you driven away your niece ?

Bona. She is not my niece.

Mon. 'Tis true.

Fiam. (L. C.) How ?

Mon. But where did you learn that ?

Bona. From these papers.

Mon. Who sent them ?

Bona. Count Romaldi.

Mon. Count Romaldi is—a villain.

Fiam. There ! there !

Steph. You hear, sir !

Fiam. I hope I shall be believed another time.

Bona. [*Greatly interested.*] Silence, woman !—By a man like you, such an accusation cannot be made without sufficient proofs.

Mon. You shall have them. Be attentive.

Fiam. I won't breathe ! A word shan't escape my lips. [*They press round* MONTANO.

Mon. (C.) Eight years ago, before I had the honour to know you, returning one evening after visiting my friends, I was leisurely ascending the rock of Arpennaz.

Fiam. So, so ! The rock of Arpennaz ! You hear! But I'll not say a word.

Mon. Two men, wild in their looks, and smeared with blood, passed hastily by me, with every appearance of guilt impressed upon their countenances.

Fiam. The very same ! Eight years ago ! The rock of Arpennaz ! The—

Bona. Silence !

Fiam. I'll not say a word. Tell all, sir ; I am dumb.

Mon. They had not gone a hundred paces before he, who appeared the master, staggered and fell. I hastened to him : he bled much, and I and his servant supported him to my house. They said they had been attacked by banditti, yet their torn clothes, a deep bite, which the master had on the back of his hand, and other hurts appearing to be given by an unarmed man, made me doubt. Their embarrassment increased suspicion, which was confirmed next day by Michelli, the honest miller of Arpennaz ; who, the evening before, near the spot from which I saw these men ascend, had succoured a poor wretch, dreadfully cut and mangled.

Fiam. It's all true ! 'Twas I ! I myself ! My cries made Michelli come ! Eight years—

Bona. Again ?

Fiam. I've done.

Mon. I no longer doubted I had entertained men of blood, and hastened to deliver them up to justice ; but, when I returned, they had flown, having left a purse, and this letter.

Bona. [*Having seen it.*] 'Tis the hand of Romaldi.

Mon. Imagine my surprise and indignation yesterday evening, when I here once more beheld the assassin! I could not disguise my emotion; and I left you with such abruptness to give immediate information. The archers are now in pursuit: I have no doubt they will soon secure him, as they have already secured his accomplice.

Steph. Malvoglio?

Mon. Yes, who has confessed—

Steph. What?

Mon. That the real name of this pretended Romaldi is Bianchi.

Bona. Just heaven! Francisco's brother!

Mon. Whose wife this wicked brother loved. Privately married, and she pregnant, Francisco put her under the protection of his friend here in Savoy.

Steph. My uncle! His sudden death occasioned the mystery.

Mon. But the false Romaldi decoyed Francisco into the power of the Algerines, seized his estates, and, finding he had escaped, attempted to assassinate him.

Fiam. Now are you convinced! He would not 'peach his brother of abomination! [*Raising her clasped hand.*] I told you Francisco was an angel! but, for all you know me so well, I'm not to be believed.

Bona. You are not to be silenced.

Fiam. No; I'm not. Francisco is an angel, Selina is an angel, Stephano is an angel: they shall be married, and all make one family; of which, if you repent, you shall be received into the bosom.

Bona. [*Slowly, earnestly.*] Pray, good woman, hold your tongue.

Fiam. Repent, then! Repent! [*Here distant thunder is heard, and a rising storm perceived.*]

Bona. [*To* Mon. *and* Steph.] I do repent!

Fiam. [*Affectionately*] Then I forgive you. [*Sobs*] I won't turn you away. You're my master again.

[*Kisses his hand, and wipes her eyes.*

Bona. But where shall we find Selina, and—

Fiam. Oh, I know where!

Steph. [*Eagerly*] Do you?

Fiam. Why, could you think that—Follow me! Only follow me. [*Exeunt hastily. Thunder heard, while the Scene changes.* *Music.*

SCENE III.—*The wild mountainous country called the Nant of Arpennaz; with pines and massy rocks. A rude wooden bridge on a small height thrown from rock to rock; a rugged mill-stream a little in the back ground; the miller's house on the right; a steep ascent by a narrow path to the bridge; a stone or bank to sit on, on the right-hand side.—The increasing storm of lightning, thunder, hail, and rain, becomes terrible. Suitable music.*

Enter Romaldi *from the rocks, disguised like a peasant, with terror, pursued, as it were, by the storm.*

Rom. Whither fly? Where shield me from pursuit, and death, and ignominy? My hour is come! The fiends that tempted, now tear me. [*Thunder*] The heavens shoot their fires at me! Save! Spare! Oh spare me! [*Falls on the bank.*

[*Music, Hail, &c. continue; after a pause, he raises his head. More fearful claps of thunder are heard, and he again falls on his face. The storm gradually abates. Pause in the music. A very distant voice is heard.* [Holloa!] *Music continues. He half rises, starts, and runs from side to side, looking and listening. Music ceases. Voice again.* [Holloa!]

Rom. They are after me! Some one points me out! No den, no cave, can hide me! [*Looks the way he came.*] I cannot return that way, I cannot. It is the place of blood! A robbed and wretched brother! 'Tis his blood, by which I am covered! Ay! There! There have I been driven for shelter! Under those very rocks! Oh, that they would open! Cover me, earth! Cover my crimes! Cover my shame! [*Falls motionless again.*

[*Music mournful; then changes to the cheerful pastorale, &c.*

Michelli *is seen coming toward the bridge, which he crosses, stopping to look round and speak; then speaks as he descends by the rugged narrow path, and then in the front of the stage.*

Mich. [*On the bridge*] 'Tis a fearful storm! One's very heart shrinks! It makes a poor mortal think of his sins—and his danger.

Rom. [*Rises, after listening*] Danger! What?—Is it me? [*Listening*]

Mich. [*Descending*] Every thunder clap seems to flash vengeance in his face!

Rom. I am known; or must be!—Shall I yield; or shall I——[*Points his pistol at* MICHELLI, *then shrinks*] More murder!

Mich. [*In the front of the stage*] At such terrible times, a clear conscience is better than kingdoms of gold mines.

Rom. [*In hesitation whether he shall or shall not murder*] How to act?

Mich. [*Perceiving* ROMALDI, *who conceals his pistol*] Now, friend.

Rom. Now, miller!

Mich. [*Observing his agitation*] You look—

Rom. How do I look? [*Fearing and still undetermined.*]

Mich. I—What have you there?

Rom. Where?

Mich. Under your coat.

Rom. [*Leaving the pistol in his inside pocket, and shewing his hands*] Nothing.

Mich. Something is the matter with you.

Rom. I am tired.

Mich. Come in, then, and rest yourself.

Rom. Thank you! [*Moved*] Thank you!

Mich. Whence do you come?

Rom. From—the neighbourhood of Geneva.

Mich. Did you pass through Sallancha?

Rom. [*Alarmed*] Sallancha? Why do you ask?

Mich. You have heard of what has happened?

Rom. Where?

Mich. There! At Sallancha! One Count Romaldi—

Rom. What of him?

Mich. [*Observing*] Do you know him?

Rom. I—How should a poor—

Mich. Justice is at his heels. He has escaped: but he'll be taken. The executioner will have him. At least I hope so.

Rom. [*Shudders*] Ay?

Mich. As sure as you are here.

Rom. [*Aside*] All men hate me! Why should I spare him?

Mich. I saved the good Francisco.

Rom. [*Gazing stedfastly at him*] You? Was it you?

Mich. I.

Rom. Then—live.

Mich. Live?

Rom. To be rewarded.

Mich. I'd have done the same for you.

Rom. Live—live!

Mich. I will, my friend, as long as I can; and when I die, I'll die with an honest heart.

Rom. Miserable wretch!

Mich. Who?

Rom. That Count Romaldi.

Mich. Why ay!—Unless he is a devil, he is miserable indeed. [*Music, quick march*] He'll be taken; for, look, yonder are the archers. [*They cross the bridge.*]

Rom. [*Fearing* MICHELLI *knows him*] What then? Where is Romaldi?

Mich. How should I know?

Rom. [*Aside*] Does he dissemble? They are here! I am lost! [*Retires.*]

Music. The Archers come forward.

Mich. Good day, worthy sirs.

Exempt. Honest miller, good day. We are in search of Count Romaldi, whom we are to take, dead or alive. Do you know his person?

Mich. No.

Rom. [*Comes out aside, and out of sight of the Archers*] Thanks, merciful heaven!

Exempt. [*Reads*] "Fivefeet eight" [*The description must be that of the actor's voice, size, and person: to which add*] "with a large scar on the back of the right hand."

Rom. [*Thrusting his hand in his bosom*] 'Twill betray me!

Exempt. 'Twas a bite! The wretch Malvoglio, has deposed that good Francisco is the brother of the vile Romaldi.

Mich. How!

Exempt. And that Francisco, tho' robbed, betrayed and mutilated, has endured every misery, and lived in continual dread of steel or poison, rather than bring this monster to the scaffold.

Mich. But, he'll come there at last?

Exempt. We are told, he is among these mountains.

Mich. Oh, could I catch him by the collar!

Exempt. Should you meet him, beware: he's not unarmed.

Mich. There is no passing for him or you by this valley after the storm; the mountain torrents are falling. You must go back.

Exempt. Many thanks. We must lose no time.

Mich. Success to you.

Archers re-ascend the hill.—Music.—Quick march as when they entered.

Rom. Death! Infamy! Is there no escaping!

Mich. The day declines, and you look—

Rom. How?

Mich. Um—I wish you looked better. Come in; pass the evening here: recover your strength and spirits.

Rom. [*With great emotion, forgetting and holding out his hand.*] You are a worthy man.

Mich. I wish to be. [*Feeling* ROMALDI'S *hand after shaking.*] Zounds! What? Hey?

Rom. [*Concealing his confusion.*] A scar—

Mich. On the back of the right hand!

Rom. I have served. A hussar with his sabre gave the cut.

Mich. [*After considering.*] Humph! it may be.

Rom. It is.

Mich. At least it may be; and the innocent—

Rom. Ay! might suffer for the guilty.

Mich. [*After looking at him.*] Rather than that—I will run all risks. I am alone; my family is at the fair, and cannot be home to-night. But you are a stranger; you want protection—

Rom. [*With great emotion.*] I do indeed!

Mich. You shall have it. Come. Never shall my door be shut against the houseless wretch.

[*Exit to the house.*

[*Music.* FRANCISCO *and* SELINA *approaching the bridge, he points to the Miller's house. Cheerful music; she testifies joy, and admiration of the Miller. They descend; he carefully guiding and aiding her. The Miller, supposed to hear a noise, comes to inquire, sees* FRANCISCO, *and they run into each other's arms.*

Mich. Welcome! A thousand times welcome!

Sel. Ten thousand thanks to the saviour of my father!

Mich. Your father, sweet lady?

Sel. Oh yes! discovered to me by his mortal enemy.

Mich. The monster Romaldi?

Sel. [*Dejectedly.*] Alas!

Mich. For your father's sake, for your own sake, welcome both.

Rom. [*Half from the door.*] I heard my name!

Mich. [*Leading them to the door, just as* ROMALDI *advances a step.*] Come. I have a stranger—

Sel. [*Seeing* ROMALDI, *shrieks.*] Ah!

Fran. [*Falls back and covers his eyes, with agony.*]

Mich. How now? [ROMALDI *retires.*

Sel. 'Tis he!

Music of terror, &c.

[FRANCISCO *putting his hand towards her mouth, enjoins her silence with great eagerness.* MICHELLI, *by making the sign of biting his right hand, asks* FRANCISCO *if it be* ROMALDI. FRANCISCO *turns away without answering.* MICHELLI *denotes his conviction it is* ROMALDI, *and hastily ascends to cross the bridge in search of the archers,* FRANCISCO *entreats him back in vain.* ROMALDI, *in terror, enters from the house, presenting his pistol.* FRANCISCO *opens his breast for him to shoot if he pleases.* SELINA *falls between them. The whole scene passes in a mysterious and rapid manner. Music suddenly stops.*

Rom. No! Too much of your blood is upon my head! Be justly revenged: take mine!

[*Music continues as* ROMALDI *offers the pistol: which* FRANCISCO *throws to a distance, and entreats him to fly by the valley.*—ROMALDI *signifies the impossibility, and runs distractedly from side to side: then after* FRANCISCO *and* SELINA'S *entreaties, ascends to cross the bridge. Met at the edge of the hill by an archer: he is driven back; they struggle on the bridge. The Archer's sword taken by* ROMALDI; *who, again attempting flight, is again met by several Archers.* ROMALDI *maintains a retreating fight.* FIAMETTA, BONAMO, STEPHANO, MONTANO, *and Peasants follow the Archers.* FRANCIS-

CO *and* SELINA, *in the greatest agitation, several times throw themselves between the assailants and* ROMALDI. *When the combatants have descended the hill,* ROMALDI'S *foot slips, he falls, and* FRANCISCO *intervenes to guard his body. By this time all the principal characters are near the front. The Archers appear to be prepared to shoot, and strike with their sabres; when the entreaties and efforts of* FRANCISCO *and* SELINA *are renewed. The Archers forbear for a moment; and* FRANCISCO *shields his brother. The music ceases.*

Sel. Oh, forbear! Let my father's virtues plead for my uncle's errors!

Bon. We all will entreat for mercy; since of mercy we all have need: for his sake, and for our own, may it be freely granted!

The curtain falls to slow and solemn music.

THE END.

Printed and published by T. DOLBY, 17, Catherine-street, Strand.

Theatre Royal, English Opera House, Strand.

This Evening, SATURDAY, August 19th, 1820;

Will be presented (FIFTEENTH TIME) an entirely new OPERATICK DRAMA, *in Three Acts*, called

Woman's Will---A Riddle!

WITH ENTIRELY NEW MUSICK, SCENERY, DRESSES AND DECORATIONS.
The OVERTURE and MUSICK composed by Mr DAVY, with the exception of Two Songs by Mr. PINDAR, of Bath.
The SCENERY designed and executed by Mr. CAPON, Mr. A THISELTON, Mr. GILL, and Assistants.
The DRESSES by Mr. HEAD, Mrs. BROOKES, &c. &c.

Duke of Milan, Mr. ROWBOTHAM, Count Vitaldi, Mr. BARTLEY,
Cæsario. Mr. PEARMAN, Corvino, Mr. HARLEY,
1st Lord, Mr. WEBSTER, 2nd Lord, Mr. LODGE, Officer, Mr. MINTON.
Principal Priest, Mr Moss, Attendant Priests, Mr. FISHER, Mr. KENNETH,
Children of the Chapel, Master COOTE, Miss E. LANCASTER.
Nobles of the Court, Messrs Bowman, Collingbourn, Elsmore, Jenkins, Laws, Nichols, H. Phillips, R. Phillips, Proud, Shaw, Spratley, &c. &c.

Duchess of Mantua, Mrs. W. S. CHATTERLEY,
Princess Clementine, Miss KELLY, Isabel, Miss CAREW,
Ladies of the Court, Mesdames & Misses Hobbs, Jerrolds, Lancaster, Lodge, Mansell, Mears, Miller, Newton, Shaw, Tokely, Webster.

The EPILOGUE, in Character, by Miss KELLY.

In the course of the Opera, the following new Scenes will be exhibited.
An ANTI-CHAMBER of the DUCAL PALACE. *(Gill.)* SALOON and BANQUET HALL. *(A Thiselton.)*
An ANTIENT STREET of POINTED ARCHITECTURE, selected entirely from remains of the middle ages. (Capon.)
ANTI-CHAMBER adjoining the PALACE CHAPEL. *(A. Thiselton)*

To which will be added *(NINTH TIME)* a NEW ROMANTICK MELODRAMA, *(partly taken from a celebrated Piece which has for some Weeks past attracted all Paris,)* IN THREE PARTS, founded on THE CELEBRATED TALE, called

"THE VAMPIRE"

The OVERTURE from OSCAR & MALVINA, composed by the late Mr. REEVE.
The INCANTATION and CHARM in the INTRODUCTORY VISION, by Mr. M. MOSS.
The VOCAL MUSICK selected from the SCOTTISH MELODIES——The Melodramatick Musick composed by Mr. HART.
The SCENERY, including correct Views of The BASALTICK COLUMNS of The ISLAND of STAFFA, with The GROTTO and CAVE of FINGAL, entirely new, by Mr. A. THISELTON, Mr SMITH, and Assistants.
The ACTION of the MELODRAMA under the direction of Mr T. P. COOKE.

Characters in the Introductory Vision.

The Vampire, Mr. T. P. COOKE,
Lady Margaret, Mrs. W. S. CHATTERLEY,
Unda, *(Spirit of the Flood)* Miss LOVE, Ariel, *(Spirit of the Air)* Miss WORGMAN.

Characters in the Drama.

Ruthven, *(Earl of Marsden)* Mr. T. P. COOKE, Ronald, *(Baron of the Isles)* Mr. BARTLEY,
Robert, *(a Retainer of the Baron)* Mr. PEARMAN, Mc.Swill, *(Henchman to the Baron)* Mr. HARLEY,
Andrew, *(Steward to the Earl of Marsden)* Mr. MINTON, Father Francis, Mr. SHAW.
Lady Margaret, *(Daughter to Lord Ronald)* Mrs. W. S. CHATTERLEY,
Bridget, *(Housekeeper to Lord Ronald)* Mrs. GROVE,
Effie, *(Daughter to Andrew, and betrothed to Robert)* Miss CAREW.

THIS PIECE IS FOUNDED ON

the various Traditions concerning THE VAMPIRES, which assert that they are *Spirits*, deprived of all *Hope* of *Futurity*, by the Crimes committed in their Mortal State—but, that they are permitted to roam the Earth, in whatever Forms they please, with *Supernatural Powers of Fascination*—and, that they cannot be destroyed, so long as they sustain their dreadful Existence, by imbibing the BLOOD of FEMALE VICTIMS, whom they are first compelled to marry.

The effect produced on crowded audiences by THE VAMPIRE is perfectly electrical. The applause at the conclusion of each performance has lasted for several minutes, and its success is nightly testified by shouts of approbation.—The publick demand will be answered by a repetition, every evening.

The highly successful Opera of WOMANS WILL—A RIDDLE, will be repeated this evening, and twice next week.

THE SPACIOUS SALOON

Has been again tastefully fitted up, with a NEW DESIGN, representing

AN ILLUMINATED ORIENTAL GARDEN

and will be opened as usual at EIGHT o'Clock, for the admittance of the SECOND PRICE, which commences at NINE.
Stage Manager, Mr. BARTLEY. Leader of the Band, Mr. MOUNTAIN.

Boxes 5s Second Price 3s. Pit 3s. Second Price 1s.6d. Lower Gallery 2s. Second Price 1s. Upper Gallery 1s. Second Price 6d.
PRIVATE BOXES may be had nightly of Mr. STEVENSON, of whom Places are to be taken, at the Box Office, Strand Entrance, from Ten till Four; also at FEARMAN's Library, 170, New Bond Street.
Doors open at half-past Six, the Performance to begin at Seven.—No Money returned—[Lowndes, Printer, Marquis Court, Drury Lane

On Monday will be produced *(First Time)* a new *ex-tempore*, temporary, Sketch, to be called

"PATENT SEASONS."

The Characters by Mr. WRENCH, Mr. HARLEY, Mr. WILKINSON, Mr. PEARMAN, Miss CAREW, Miss KELLY.

After which (10th time) The VAMPIRE: to which will be added *(First Time)* an entirely NEW FARCE, in Two Acts, which has been some time in preparation, to be called

WHANG FONG:
OR
HOW REMARKABLE!

The MUSICK composed by Mr. PINDAR, of Bath.
Principal Characters by Mr. PEARMAN, Mr. HARLEY, Mr. T. P. COOKE, Mr. WILKINSON, Mr. LANCASTER, Mrs. GROVE, Miss LOVE.
Mrs. PINDAR, *(from the Theatre Scarborough, being her first appearance on a London stage.)*

Theatre Royal, English Opera House, Strand.

The whole of the Audience Part of the House has been embellished with

NEW AND SPLENDID DECORATIONS.

TWELVE ELEGANT NEW CUT GLASS CHANDELIERS
have been added, and are to be lighted with WAX; in addition to a
NEW LARGE CENTRE GAS LUSTRE.
The Seats and Cushions of the Boxes and Pit, and the whole of the Upholstery Work of the Theatre, are entirely NEW.

This Evening, MONDAY, July 28th, 1823,

Will be produced (for the FIRST TIME) an entirely new ROMANCE of a peculiar interest, entitled

PRESUMPTION!
OR, THE
FATE OF FRANKENSTEIN.

WITH NEW SCENES, DRESSES, AND DECORATIONS.
The MUSICK composed by Mr. WATSON.

"THE event on which this fiction is founded has been supposed, by Dr. DARWIN, and some of the physiological writers of Germany, as not of impossible occurrence.—I shall not be supposed as according the remotest degree of serious faith to such an imagination; yet, in assuming it as the basis of a work of fancy, I have not considered myself as merely weaving a series of supernatural terrors. The event on which the interest of the story depends is exempt from the disadvantages of a mere tale of spectres or enchantment; it was recommended by the novelty of the situations which it developes; and, however impossible as a physical fact, affords a point of view to the imagination, for the delineating of the human passions, more comprehensive and commanding than any which the ordinary relations of existing events can yield." *From the Preface to the Novel of* FRANKENSTEIN.

The striking moral exhibited in this story, is the fatal consequence of that presumption which attempts to penetrate, beyond prescribed depths, into the mysteries of nature.

Frankenstein, Mr. WALLACK,
De Lacey, *(a banished Gentleman)* Mr. ROWBOTHAM,
Felix De Lacey, *(his Son)* Mr. PEARMAN,
Fritz, Mr. KEELEY,
Clerval, Mr. J. BLAND, William, Master BODEN,
Hammerpan, Mr. SALTER, Tanskin, Mr. SHIELD, Guide, Mr. R. PHILLIPS, Gypsey, Mr H. PHILLIPS,
(------) Mr. T. P. COOKE.

Elizabeth, *(Sister of Frankenstein)* Mrs. AUSTIN,
Agatha De Lacey, Miss L. DANCE,
Safie, *(an Arabian Girl)* Miss POVEY, Madame Ninon, *(Wife of Fritz)* Mrs. J. WEIPPERT.
Chorus of Gypsies, Peasants, &c. &c.
Messrs. Bowman, Buxton, Lodge, Mears, Povey, Saunders, Shaw, Sheriff, Smith, Taylor, Tett, Walsh, Willis.
Mesdames & Misses Bennett, Bessell, Dennis, Goodwin, Lodge, Jerrold, Southwell, 2 Stiltons, Vials, Vidall.

After which *(Third Time this Season)* O'KEEFE's *Musical Entertainment*, called

THE RIVAL SOLDIERS.

Captain Cruizer, Mr. ROWBOTHAM, Serjeant Major Tactic, Mr. W. BENNETT,
Lenox, Mr. BROADHURST, Sinclair, Mr. PEARMAN, Corporal, Mr. MEARS,
Nipperkin *(third time)* Mr. W. CHAPMAN,
In which Character he will introduce the Comick Song of "*THE NIGHTINGALE CLUB.*"
Mary, Miss HOLDAWAY.

To conclude with *(Second Time this Season)* the *Operatick Farce*, called

SHARP AND FLAT.

Sir Peter Probable, Mr. W. BENNETT,
Captain Belrose, Mr. BROADHURST, in which Character he will sing "*My native land, good night!*"
Solomon Sharpwit, *(second time)* Mr. W. CHAPMAN,
Nikey, *(second time)* Mr. KEELEY, Brisk, Mr. SALTER,
Rosabel, Miss HOLDAWAY, Jenny, *(second time)* Mrs. J. WEIPPERT.

Boxes 5s. Second Price 3s Pit 3s Second Price 1s. 6d Lower Gallery 2s. Second Price 1s. Upper Gallery 1s. Second Price 6d.
Boxes, Places, Private and Family Boxes, may be had of Mr. STEVENSON, at the Box-Office, Strand Entrance, from 10 till 4.
Doors open at half-past Six, begins at Seven —VIVAT REX'—No Money returned —[Lowndes, Printer. Marquis Court, Drury Lane.

☞ THE ILLUMINATED TRELLIS ARCADES
will be opened for the reception of the Visitors of the Theatre at SECOND PRICE, which will commence at NINE o'clock.

☞ *In consequence of the encreased attraction of the revived Opera, and the numerous demands at the Box-Office, The KNIGHT OF SNOWDOUN will be repeated on Wednesday and Friday.*

Mr. WALLACK
(who can perform only for a limited period previous to his return to America) being nightly received with enthusiastick plaudits, will appear in a new Character *This Evening*; and repeat the Character of *Roderick Dhu*, on *Wednesday* and *Friday*.

Miss LOUISA DANCE will appear in a new Character *This Evening;* and on *Wednesday* and *Friday*, as *Ellen*, in the revived Opera.

Mr. W. CHAPMAN, being nightly received with the greatest applause and laughter, will perform, *This Evening, Nipperkin,* and *Solomon Sharpwit;* and on *Wednesday* and *Friday*, the Part of *Macloon*.

Mr. RAYNER having received the most enthusiastick applause throughout his whole performance of the arduous Character of *Giles*, in The MILLER'S MAID, and the whole Entertainment having been honoured with the acclamations of crowded Audiences, it will be repeated *To-morrow* and *Thursday*.

Miss KELLY
will perform, *To-morrow* and *Thursday*, *Phœbe*, in The MILLER'S MAID.

To-morrow, The MILLER'S MAID, with (first time at this Theatre) the Farcetta of WHERE SHALL I DINE? and other Entertainments.
On Wednesday, The KNIGHT OF SNOWDOUN, with other Entertainments.

Cast of the Characters,

As Performed at the English Opera-House.

IN THE INTRODUCTORY VISION.

	August 9, 1820.	Sept. 26, 1829.
Unda, Spirit of the Flood	Miss Love.	Miss Phillips.
Ariel, Spirit of the Air	Miss Worgman.	Mrs. East.
The Vampire	Mr. T. P. Cooke.	Mr. J. Vining.
Lady Margaret	Mrs. Chatterly.	Miss Gray.

IN THE DRAMA.

Ruthven, Earl of Marsden, the Vampire	Mr. T. P. Cooke.	Mr. J. Vining.
Ronald, Baron of the Isles	Mr. Bartley.	Mr. F. Matthews.
Robert, an English Attendant on the Baron	Mr. Pearman.	Mr. Thorne.
M'Swill, the Baron's Henchman	Mr. Harley.	Mr. G. Penson.
Andrew, Steward to Ruthven	Mr. Minton.	Mr. Minton.
Father Francis	Mr. Shaw.	Mr. Shaw.
Lady Margaret, Daughter of Ronald	Mrs. Chatterly.	Miss Gray.
Effie, Daughter of Andrew	Miss Carew.	Mrs. Keeley.
Bridget, Lord Ronald's Housekeeper	Mrs. Grove.	Mrs. C. Jones

Retainers, Peasants, Bargemen, &c. &c.

R. Cruikshank, Del. *G. W. Bonner, Sc.*

The Vampire.

Lady Margaret. Hold! hold! I am thine;—the moon has set.

Act II. Scene 4.

THE VAMPIRE;

OR, THE BRIDE OF THE ISLES:

A ROMANTIC MELO-DRAMA,

In Two Acts,

BY J. R. PLANCHÉ,

Author of Charles the XII. The Merchants' Wedding, A Woman Never Vext, The Mason of Buda, The Brigand, A Daughter to Marry, &c.

PRINTED FROM THE ACTING COPY, WITH REMARKS, BIOGRAPHICAL AND CRITICAL, BY D—G.

To which are added,

A DESCRIPTION OF THE COSTUME,—CAST OF THE CHARACTERS, ENTRANCES AND EXITS,—RELATIVE POSITIONS OF THE PERFORMERS ON THE STAGE,—AND THE WHOLE OF THE STAGE BUSINESS.

As performed at the

THEATRES ROYAL, LONDON.

EMBELLISHED WITH A FINE ENGRAVING,

By MR. BONNER, from a Drawing taken in the Theatre, by MR. R. CRUIKSHANK.

LONDON:

JOHN CUMBERLAND, 6, BRECKNOCK PLACE,

CAMDEN NEW TOWN.

The Curtain rises to slow Music, and discovers the Interior of the Basaltic Caverns of Staffa—at the extremity of which is a chasm opening to the air—the moonlight streams through it, and partially reveals a number of rude sepulchres.—On one of these, R. S. E., LADY MARGARET *is seen, stretched in a heavy slumber.—The Spirit of the Flood rises through the ground* C., *to the symphony of the following Incantation.*

INCANTATION.

SOLO.—UNDA.

Spirit! Spirit of the Air!
Hear and heed my spell of power;
On the night breeze swift repair
Hither from thy starry bower

Chorus. [*Without,* L.] Appear! appear!

Unda. By the sun that hath set,
In the waves I love;
By the spheres that have met
In the heavens above;
By the latest dews
That fall to earth;
On the eve that renews
The fair moon's birth.

Chorus. [*Without,* L.] Appear! appear!

QUARTETTO.

By the charm of might and the word of fear,
Which must never be breath'd to mortal ear,
Spirit! Spirit of the Air,
Hither at my call repair!

MUSIC.—THE SPIRIT OF THE AIR *descends through the chasm, on a silvery cloud, which she leaves and advances,* L.

Ariel. Why, how now, sister? wherefore am I summoned?
What in the deep and fearful caves of Staffa
Demands our presence or protection?—Speak!

Unda. Spirit of Air! thy sister Unda claims
Thy powerful aid;—not idly from thy blue
And star-illumin'd mansion art thou call'd

To Fingal's rocky sepulchre—look here.
[*Pointing to Lady Margaret,* R.

Ariel. A maiden, and asleep!

Unda. Attend thee, Ariel.
Her name is Margaret, the only daughter
Of Ronald, the brave Baron of the Isles.
A richer, lovelier, more virtuous lady
This land of flood and mountains never boasted.
To-morrow Marsden's Earl will claim her hand,
Renown'd through Europe for his large possessions,
His clerkly knowledge, and his deeds of arms.

Ariel. How came she in this den of death and horror?

Unda. Chasing the red-deer with her father, Ronald,
A storm arose; and, parted from her train,
She sought a shelter here—calmly she sleeps,
Nor dreams to-morrow's hymeneal rites
Will give her beauties to a vampire's arms.

Ariel. A vampire, say'st thou?—Is then Marsden's Earl——

Unda. Thou knowest, Ariel, that wicked souls
Are, for wise purposes, permitted oft
To enter the dead forms of other men,
Assume their speech, their habits, and their knowledge,
And thus roam o'er the earth; but subject still,
At stated periods, to a dreadful tribute.

Ariel. Ay, they must wed some fair and virtuous maiden,
Whom they do after kill, and from her veins
Drain eagerly the purple stream of life;
Which horrid draught alone hath pow'r to save them
From swift extermination.

Unda. Yes; that state
Of nothingness—total annihilation!
The most tremendous punishment of heaven.
Their torture then being without resource,
They do enjoy all power in the present.
Death binds them not—from form to form they fleet,
And though the cheek be pale, and glaz'd the eye,
Such is their wond'rous art, the hapless victim
Blindly adores, and drops into their grasp,
Like birds when gaz'd on by the basilisk.

Ariel. Say on.

Unda. Beneath this stone the relics lie
Of Cromal, called the Bloody. Staffa still
His reign of fear remembers. For his crimes,

His spirit roams, a vampire, in the form
Of Marsden's Earl;—to count his victims o'er,
Would be an endless task—suffice to say,
His race of terror will to-morrow end,
Unless he wins some virgin for his prey,
Ere sets the full-orb'd moon.

Ariel. And with this view
He weds the Lady Margaret.

Unda. Ay, Ariel;
Unless our blended art can save the maid.

Ariel. What can be done? Our power is limited.
What can be done, my sister?

Unda. We must warn
The maiden of her fate. Lend me thine aid,
To raise a vision to her sleeping sight.

Ariel. Let us about it.

[*They perform magical ceremonies to the symphony of the following charm.*

CHARM.—ARIEL *and* UNDA, L.

Phantom, from thy tomb so drear,
At our bidding swift arise;
Let thy vampire-corpse appear
To this sleeping maiden's eyes.
Come away! come away!
That the form she may know
That would work her woe
And shun thee, till the setting ray
Of the moon shall bid thy pow'r decay;
Phantom, from thy tomb so drear,
At our bidding rise!—appear! [*Thunder.*

CHORUS, *without*, L.—ARIEL *and* UNDA.

Appear! appear! appear!

[*The Vampire rises from the tomb of Cromal, and springs towards Margaret.*

Vam. Margaret!

Ariel. Foul spirit, retire!

Vam. She is mine!

Ariel. The hour is not yet come.

Unda. Down, thou foul spirit;—extermination waits thee:
Down, I say.

[*Music.—The Vampire shuddering, sinks again into the tomb, and the scene closes*

ACT I.

SCENE I.—*A Hall in the Castle of Lord Ronald.*

M'SWILL, C., *and a group of Retainers, in hunting-dresses, discovered, seated round a table, drinking—the Sun is seen just rising behind the hills through the large Gothic window at the back.*

CHORUS.

TUNE—"*Johnny Cope.*"

Come, fill—let the parting glass go round;
With a stirrup-cup, be our revelry crown'd;
See, the sun that set to our bugles' sound
Is changing the night into morning.

As darkness shrinks from his rising ray,
So sorrow and care will we keep at bay,
By the bowl at night and the "Hark away,"
That awakes us, brave boys, in the morning.

[*They all rise—M'Swill hides under the table.*

Bridget. [*Calling without.*] M'Swill!

Enter BRIDGET *and* ROBERT, L.

Bri. Very pretty doings, upon my word! Here's our poor mistress, the Lady Margaret, been lost for nearly the whole night in the forest; and no sooner is she by good fortune found again, and trying to get a little rest in her own apartments, but you make all this noise, as if on purpose to disturb her.

Rob. Nay, Mrs. Bridget, don't be angry with them. They've been celebrating my lady's return.

Bri. Return! Don't tell me.—They never want an excuse to get drunk; out of the castle directly,—don't stand ducking and scraping there; go along directly, when I tell you! [*Exeunt Retainers*, L.] Where is that rascal, M'Swill? He's at the bottom of all this! But, if I—[*M'Swill attempts to steal off*, L.] Oh, oh, there you are, sir; come here, sir! [*Seizes him by the ear, and brings him forward.*] Down on your knees directly, and ask my pardon.

M'Swill. (C.) I do, Mrs. Bridget.

Bri. (R.) How came you under the table?

M'Swill. What a question, when a man has been drinking all night.

Bri. Will you never leave off taking your drops?

M'Swill. I don't take drops, Mrs. Bridget.

Bri. Here has poor Robert been running through the forest all night, seeking my lady, and peeping into all the holes of the grotto, whilst you——

M'Swill. The grotto, Mrs. Bridget! Good guide us! Why, you didn't go into the grotto, did you? [*To Robert.*

Rob. And why not, booby?

M'Swill. Oh, dear! oh, dear! the ignorance of some people—but you are an Englishman, and that accounts for it. Why, didn't you know that the grotto was haunted?

Rob. (L.) [*Laughing.*] Ha, ha, ha!

M'Swill. Ay, ay, laugh away, do; but, I can tell you, it's full of kelpies and evil spirits of all sorts; only ask Mrs. Bridget.

Bri. It's very true, Robert; and you shouldn't laugh, for they always owe a grudge to anybody that jests about them.

M'Swill. Did you never hear the storyof Lady Blanch?

Bri. Hush! don't talk so loud.

M'Swill. You know it, Mrs. Bridget.

Bri. No; but Lord Ronald is very angry with every body who circulates stories of that description; so, speak lower, if you are going to tell it.

M'Swill. Well, then,—once upon a time——

Rob. [*Laughing.*] Ha, ha, ha! Mother Bunch's fairy tales.

M'Swill. Well, isn't that the proper way to begin a story?

Bri. Go on.

M'Swill. Once upon a time——

Rob. You've said that once twice.

M'Swill. Will you be quiet with your fun. I won't tell it at all.

Rob. Well, well, then, once upon a time—what happened?

M'Swill. Once on a time, there lived a lady named Blanch, in this very castle, and she was betrothed to a rich Scotch nobleman; all the preparations for the wedding were finished, when, on the evening before it was to take place, the lovers strolled into the forest——

Bri. Alone?

M'Swill. No: together, to be sure.

Bri. Well, sot, I mean that; and I think it was highly improper.

M'Swill. Well, they were seen to enter the grotto, and——

Rob. And what?

M'Swill. They never came out again.

Rob. Bravo! an excellent story!

M'Swill. But that isn't all. The next morning the body of the lady was found covered with blood, and the marks of human teeth on her throat, but no trace of the nobleman could be discovered, and from that time to this he has never been heard of; and they do say,—I hope nobody hears us,—they do say that the nobleman was a vampire, for a friar afterwards confessed, on his death-bed, that he had privately married them in the morning by the nobleman's request, and that he fully believed it some fiend incarnate, for he could not say the responses without stuttering.

Rob. Better and better! and how came you by this precious legend?

M'Swill. The great uncle of my grandfather had it from the great grandfather of the steward's cousin, by the mother's side, who lived with a branch of the family when the accident happened; and, moreover, I've heard my great uncle say, that these horrible spirits, called vampires, kill and suck the blood of beautiful young maidens, whom they are obliged to marry before they can destroy And they do say that such is the condition of their existence, that if, at stated periods, they should fail to obtain a virgin bride, whose life-blood may sustain them, they would instantly perish. Oh, the beautiful young maidens!—

Bri. Of beautiful young maidens?—Merciful powers! what an escape I've had. I was in the cavern myself, one day.

M'Swill. Lord, Mrs. Bridget, I'm sure there's no occasion for you to be frightened.

Bri. Why, you saucy sot, I've a great mind to—[*A bell rings,* R.] I declare there's my lady's bell!—no occasion, indeed—an impudent fellow! But men, now-a-days, have no more manners than hogs.

[*Bell rings again—exit Mrs. Bridget,* R.

M'Swill. There's a she-devil for you! I don't think there's such another vixen in all Scotland. She's little and hot, like a pepper-corn. What a lug she gave me by the ear.

Rob. Nay, nay, you mustn't mind that; all old ladies have their odd ways.

M'Swill. Curse such odd ways as that, though! I shall feel the pinch for a month. Pray, Mr. Robert, as you've been in London with Lord Ronald, do you know who this earl is that the Lady Margaret is to be married to?

Rob. I only know that he is the Earl of Marsden, and master of the castle on the coast facing this island.

M'Swill. What, where the pretty Effie, your intended, lives?

Rob. Exactly.

M'Swill. He'll arrive just in time, then, to be present at the wedding.

Rob. I hope so.

Rob. That will be glorious! Two weddings in one day—such dancing, such eating, such drinking——

Bri. [*Calling without,* R.] M'Swill!

M'Swill. Ugh, choak you, you old warlock! what's in the wind now, I wonder? [*Crosses to* R.

Bri. [*Calling without,* R.] M'Swill, I say!

M'Swill. Coming, Mrs. Bridget. [*Exit M'Swill,* R.

Rob. Yes, as soon as the earl arrives, I shall certainly take an opportunity to request him to honour the wedding with his presence; how pleas'd my dear Effie would be. Charming girl, I shall never forget the hour when first we met.

SONG.—ROBERT.

TUNE—" *The Lass of Patie's Mill.*

The hour when first we met, my dear,
The hour when first we met,
I never can forget, my dear,
I never can forget.
So sweet on me those eyes were turn'd,
That beam thy cheek above,—
They look'd like lamps that only burn'd
To light the heart to love;
To light the heart to love, my dear,
To light the heart to love,—
They look'd like lamps that only burn'd
To light the heart to love.

And while they shine on me, my dear,
And while they shine on me,
I'll ne'er be false to thee, my dear,
I'll ne'er be false to thee.
Oh, never, never slight me, then,
Nor leave me, love, to say,
Like fires that glimmer o'er the fen,
They beam but to betray,
They beam, &c. [*Exit Robert,* L.

SCENE II.—*An Apartment in the Castle.*

Enter LADY MARGARET *and* BRIDGET, R.

Bri. Oh, my lady, you must not tell me! I'm sure the fright and the fatigue you have undergone have made you ill.

Lady M. Indeed, no; I feel quite recovered, I assure you, my good Bridget.

Bri. But I know better, my lady; that smile is not like your usual ones; something ails you.

Lady M. Something certainly troubles me, but my health is not affected. I would confide the cause of my uneasiness to you, but fear you will laugh at me when I tell you. It is a dream I have had.

Bri. A dream! For heaven's sake, tell me, my lady!

Lady M. A horrible one, Bridget. Last night, as I was endeavouring to join the hunters, from whom, in the hurry of the chase, I had been separated, I wandered near the famous basaltic caverns, to which the vulgar attach so many strange traditions. The storm grew violent. By the strong flashes of lightning I discovered the opening of the grotto; I entered it for shelter, and, overcome with fatigue, fell asleep upon one of the rocky tombs. On a sudden, a sepulchre opened, and a phantom approached me; I trembled; but an invisible hand seemed to prevent my flight. I could not even turn mine eyes from the apparition. To my surprise the countenance was that of a young and handsome man, but it was pale and wo-worn. His eyes, fixed upon mine with the most touching expression, seemed to implore my pity. He uttered my name, and had nearly reached me, when a beautiful being stood between us, and checked his progress. Then, oh, horror! the features of the spectre grew frightfully distorted; its whole form assumed the most terrific appearance; and it sunk into the tomb from which it had issued, with a shriek that froze me.

Bri Mercy preserve us! I tremble all over.

Lady M. I awoke. The moon stream'd into the grotto, and I sprung into the open air. I heard the voices of those who sought me. I answered them as loudly as I was able. With shouts of joy they surrounded me, and bore me safely hither.

Bri. I shall never sleep in peace again. Oh, my dear young lady!

Ron. [*Without.*] My daughter risen, say you?

Bri. But here comes your father; shall you tell him, my lady?

Lady M. Oh, no; he is such an enemy to what he calls superstition, that I dare not expose myself to his ridicule.

Enter LORD RONALD, L.

Ron. Well, my dear daughter. What, up and dressed again, already. Come, this is a happy omen. Bridget, order my henchman to ascend the turrets of the keep, and give notice of the Earl of Marsden's approach. [*Crosses, and exit Bridget.*] This day, my dear Margaret, will be one of the happiest of my life. But, what's the matter? You appear sorrowful.

Lady M. Ah! my dear father, the description we have had of Marsden has been such certainly as should prejudice us in his favour; yet, the nearer the moment approaches of his arrival, the more I feel uneasy. Oh, sir, my fate is (next to heaven) in your hands. Do not—do not make your daughter miserable.

Lord R. Why this agitation, Margaret?—I have never wished to force your inclination. I certainly desire his alliance most ardently; nevertheless, if you dislike him——

Lady M. I do not know that I shall. But you, sir, who wish me to accept him, do not know him personally.

Lord R. 'Tis true; but if he resembles his brother, you cannot fail to love him. Alas! poor Ruthven.

Lady M. You never mention his name but with a sigh.

Lord R. Is it possible I can ever cease to lament so dear a friend?

Lady M. I have heard you say he saved your life, and for that reason I revere his memory myself. But are you sure he no longer exists?

Lord R. Would that I could harbour a doubt on the subject; but, alas! the fatal scene of his death is ever present to my imagination. When called, as you know, by the sudden illness of my now lost son to Athens, I fonud Lord Ruthven, with whom he had contracted an iutimacy, hanging over his sick couch, and bestowing on him the attentions of a brother. Such behaviour naturally endeared him to me; and after my poor boy's death, his lordship being, like myself, an enthusiastic admirer of the beauties of nature and the works of art, became the constant companion of my excursions. The more I saw of him, the more I admired his extraordinary talents. In my eyes he appeared something more than human, and seem'd destined to fill that place in my affections which had become void by my son's decease. I showed him your miniature—never shall I forget his emotion on beholding it. "By heavens!" he exclaimed, "'tis the precise image my fancy has created as the only being who could ever constitute my happiness." We were on the point of returning to Scotland to learn your sentiments on the subject, when one evening—but why should I afflict you with a repetition of so dreadful a story?

Lady M. Pray proceed, sir. I sympathize in your afflictions, and feel a melancholy gratification in contemplating the devotedness and heroism which preserved to me so dear a father.

Ron. Returning to Athens, then, one evening, after a short excursion, we were attacked by some banditti. I was disarmed. Ruthven threw himself before me, and received the ruffian's sabre in his own breast. Our attendants, however, succeeded in overcoming the villains. I threw myself into the arms of my expiring friend—he pressed my hand—"Lord Ronald," said he, "I have saved your life—I die content—my only regret is, that fate has prevented me from becoming your son." Gallant unfortunate Ruthven! what a destiny was thine, to fall in a foreign land, in the flower of thy youth, deprived of sepulchre.

Lady M. How! deprived of sepulchre!

Ron. An extraordinary circumstance prevented my fulfilling that last melancholy duty. In his dying agonies he conjured me to quit the spot, lest the assassins should return in number. The moon was rising in unclouded majesty. "Place me," said he, "on yonder mound, so that my fleeting spirit may be soothed by the soft and tranquil light of yon chaste luminary." I did so—he expired—I left the body to collect our servants, who were in pursuit of the defeated villains, and, ere we could return to the spot, it had disappeared.

Lady M. Removed for plunder, doubtless?

Ron. I ne'er could ascertain. The stains of the grass sufficiently marked the spot where I had lain him; but all search was in vain. On quitting Greece, I heard Lord Marsden was in Venice. To him I sent his brother's property, and amidst it he found your picture, which, in my desire for his alliance, I had given Ruthven. The earl proposed immediately to replace the loss we had sustained in his brother, and nothing, I am confident, remains to complete our happiness but his arrival.

Lady M. Why is not Ruthven living?—Methinks I could have loved him for his preservation of you.

[*Bugle and response*, L.

Re-enter BRIDGET, L.

Bri. The earl has arrived, my lord.

Ron. Come, Margaret, let us haste and receive him.

Lady M. My dear sir, I cannot see him yet; indeed I cannot.

Ron. Retire, then, for a while to your apartment. Bridget, attend your lady.

[*Exeunt Lady Margaret and Bridget*, R.

Enter four Servants, L., *who range across the back.*

Ron. I'll fly to meet the earl.—Ha! he is here!

Enter LORD RUTHVEN, L.

My lord, the honour you have done me!—Heavens! what do I see?

Rut. Do I recall the memory of a friend, Lord Ronald?

Ron. His voice, too!—Ruthven!

Rut. Such was my name till the death of an elder brother put me in possession of my present title.

Ron. Can I believe my senses? or does some vision mock my waking sight?

Rut. My dear friend, let this embrace banish your doubts

Ron. Ruthven, my friend! But by what miracle have you been preserved to me?

Rut. Unexpected, but powerful assistance, recalled my fleeting spirit. When sufficiently recovered to join you, you had quitted Greece. The news of my brother's death reached me. I wrote to you under my new title, and, arriving in Scotland to take possession of my paternal estate, determined to give you this pleasurable surprise.

Ron. Oh, happy hour! I once more embrace my friend. Be sure, Ruthven, that my daughter would only have become your brother's bride, to acquit me of the debt I owe to you.

Rut. My generous friend! But think you I shall be fortunate enough to gain the lovely Margaret's affections?

Ron. I cannot doubt it—she has pitied your misfortunes—she has wept over your fate. She comes. [*Exeunt Attendants*, L.] What will be her astonishment—

Re-enter LADY MARGARET, R.

My dear, behold that generous friend, whose loss we have so long deplored. 'Tis Ruthven claims your hand.

Lady M. (R.) My lord, duty to a beloved parent will——

[*She raises her eyes slowly to his countenance, starts and falls, with a shriek, into the arms of Lord Ronald.*

Ron. Margaret! O, heavens! she is ill. Help there!

Lady M. [*Shuddering, and aside.*] That countenance The phantom of last night! [*Relapses into insensibility.*

Rut. (L.) What can have occasioned this emotion?

Ron. Alas! I know not. Margaret, my sweet child!

Lady M. [*Reviving.*] Pardon, my lord, this weakness —the effect of last night's adventure.

Rut. Last night!

Ron. We hunted late yesterday. My daughter lost her way, and suffered much fatigue.

Rut. Beautiful Lady Margaret, how am I to interpret this emotion?

Lady M. The surprise of seeing one whose death we were even now deploring.

Rut. Is it possible that, without knowing me, the recital of my misfortunes alone could thus have interested you?

Lady M. I am the daughter of Lord Ronald, and my heart, touched with gratitude—[*Aside.*] I dare not look at him.

Rut. With gratitude?—And what will be my gratitude, if you but deign to approve your father's generous designs? [*Crossing to her.*] Tell me, oh, tell me, you confirm them; or never, never, will I rise from your feet. [*Kneeling, and seizing her hand.*

Lady M. [*Aside.*] Heavens! how strange a thrill runs through my frame.

Rut. [*Aside.*] Then she's mine!

Lady M. These transports, my lord—

Rut. Must not alarm you. It is in the presence of your father. It is at his desire I here vow my eternal fidelity. Oh, my friend, join your supplications to mine.

Ron. (L.) My daughter is well aware of my wishes.

Rut. Speak, dearest lady, I conjure you.

Lady M. [*Aside.*] What spell is it that moves me thus? [*Aloud.*] My lord, my father has never yet found me disobedient to his will.

Rut. You consent, then?

Lady M. [*To Lord Ronald.*] My dear sir, allow me to retire.

Rut. Laay, dear lady——

Lady M. Pardon me, my lord; a strange confusion, a wild emotion overpowers me; let me retire.

[*Exit Lady Margaret,* R.

Ron. Ruthven, the wish of my heart is gratified; you are my son.

Rut. Dearest sir, I have still a boon to ask. Let our marriage be celebrated without delay.

Ron. It is my intention; and to-morrow——

Rut. To-night, my friend; business of the utmost importance recalls me to London. To-morrow's dawn must witness our departure.

Ron. Impossible! have you not to take possession of your estate?

Rut. It is but showing myself at the castle, from which I can return ere the sun sets this evening.

Ron. Well, if my daughter makes no objection, I will go plead your suit, and hear the reasons for your haste afterwards. I know not how you have infatuated me, Ruthven, but rest assured I feel for you all that a father's heart can feel. [*Exit Ronald,* L.

Rut. [*Walking about, agitated.*] Demon as I am, that walk the earth to slaughter and devour! The little that remains of heart within this wizard frame, sustained alone by human blood, shrinks from the appalling act of planting misery in the bosom of this veteran chieftain. Still must the fearful sacrifice be made, and suddenly, for the approaching night will find my wretched frame exhausted—and darkness—worse than death—annihilation is my lot! Margaret! unhappy maid! thou art my destined prey! thy blood must feed a Vampire's life, and prove the food of his disgusting banquet.

Enter ROBERT, *timidly,* L.

Rob. My lord!

Rut. What would you?

Rob. I beg your lordship's pardon for my boldness, but I am a servant of Lord Ronald's, and would fain request your lordship's patronage.

Rut. In what respect?

Rob. I am betrothed, an please your lordship, to Effie, your steward's daughter; and as I hear it is your lordship's intention to visit your estate, I——

Rut. [*Eagerly.*] Betrothed, say you?

Rob. Yes, my lord.

Rut. And when is the marriage to take place?

Rob. This evening, my lord.

Rut. [*Half aside.*] I will be there.

Rob. Oh, my lord, I was afraid to ask you—but your lordship has made me so happy.

Rut. What distance are we from the castle?

Rob. The sea is calm, my lord—we may row there in a few minutes.

Rut. Order the barge instantly, then.

Rob. Yes, my lord. [*Exit Robert,* L.

Enter LORD RONALD, L.

Ron. All is arranged to your wishes.

Rut. [*With joy.*] Your daughter consents?

Ron. She does; and I have ordered the chapel to be prepared by our return.

Rut. You go to Marsden with me, then?

Ron. Certainly; your stay is so short, I will not leave u for a moment.

Rut. My dear friend, this kindness——

Re-enter ROBERT, L.

Rob. The barge is ready, my lord.

Rut. Away! away! [*Hurried Music—exeunt,* L.

SCENE III.—*Garden of Lord Ruthven's Castle—the sea in the distance.*

ANDREW *and* EFFIE *discovered*, R., *surrounded by village Lads and Lasses, dressed as for a fête.*

Effie. (C.) What can be the reason Robert does not arrive?

And. (R.) Something has happened to detain him; he will be here soon.

Effie. I see nothing like a boat at present.

And. [*Looking off*, L. U. E.] Why, what is that, to the right, there?

Effie. Not a boat, I'm sure, father.

And. But I say it is a boat; and making for the castle, too.

Effie. Hark! father, hark!

[*A boat is seen at sea, which gradually approaches, to the symphony of the following boat-song, sung without*, L., *and growing louder and louder as the boat nears the land.*

BOAT-SONG.

TUNE—"*Ye Banks and Braes.*"

Row on—row on—across the main,
So smoothly glides our bark to shore;
While to our boat-song's measur'd strain,
So truly dips the well-tim'd oar.

Row on—row on—in yonder isle,
Impatient beauty chides our stay;
The head-land past, her sweetest smile
Our labour richly will repay.

SOLO—EFFIE.

TUNE—"*There's nae Luck about the House.*"

'Tis he—'tis he—his form I see,
Full soon he will be here,
Then, neighbours, haste—prepare the feast,
The bonny lad to cheer.
For there's nae luck about the house,
There's nae luck at a';
There's little pleasure in the house,
When my dear lad's awa'.

Chorus. There's nae luck about the house,
There's nae luck at a';
There's little pleasure in the house,
When Robert's far awa'.

[*Shouts without*, L. U. E.

Enter ROBERT, L. U. E.

Effie. (C.) My dear Robert——

Rob. (R. C.) My sweet Effie!

Effie. What has kept you so long?

Rob. Oh, I've news for you. Lord Ronald has come with me, and who do you think beside, father-in-law?

And. Nay, I'm sure I can't guess.

Rob. Lord Ruthven.

And. Lord Ruthven! why, he has been dead these twelve months.

Rob. Has he?—I believe you're mistaken, father-in-law. [*Shouts*, L. C.] Do you hear that?

And. Pho! pho! I tell you it must be some impostor.

Enter RUTHVEN, RONALD, *and Attendants*, L. U. E.

And. (R.) Merciful Providence! it is my young master!

Rut. (C.) Yes, my good Andrew; behold me restored to you.

And. Thank heaven! thank heaven! But I could not believe that I should ever have the pleasure of seeing my dear master again.

Rut. I shall never forget your attachment to our family, and your attentions to their interest. Let me not interrupt your felicity—you are about to celebrate a marriage, I think?

And. Yes, my lord. Here's my daughter, Effie, whom your lordship remembers a little girl.

Rut. She's very pretty.

Effie. Yes, my lord—that is, thank you, my lord.

Rut. You must allow me to give the bride her dowry, and patronize the whole ceremony.

And. Oh, my lord, this is such an honour. Well, then, before the dance commences, neighbours, let us go and arrange the supper-table, where we will drink our good lord's happy return.

Rob. Away with you, then.

[*Exeunt Andrew*, L., *and Peasants*, R. U. E.

Ron. I must leave you a moment, Ruthven, to give some directions to my bargemen.

[*Exit Ronald and Attendants,* L. U. E.

Rob. (R.) [*To Effie.*] Come, Effie, let's follow our neighbours. [*Going.*

Rut. (L.) [*Detaining Effie.*] Fair Effie, I would speak with you.

Effie. [*With hesitation,* C.] If Robert has no objection, my lord——

Rob. How, you silly girl, when his lordship does you so much honour. You'll find me with Andrew.

[*Exit Robert,* R.

Rut. Come nearer, charming maid.

Effie. My lord, I—I dare not, my lord.

Rut. Fear nothing. [*Aside.*] Yet, she has cause to fear. Should I surprise her heart, as by my gifted spell I may, the tribute that prolongs existence may be paid, and Margaret may (at least awhile) be spared. [*To Effie.*] How delightful 'tis to gaze upon thee thus! An atmosphere of joy is round about thee, which whosoever breathes, becomes thy slave.

Effie. My lord, what mean you?

Rut. My heart ne'er throbb'd but for one woman, and you have just her features. This morning the flame of love was extinguished in my soul; but now, now it burns with redoubled ardour.

Effie. But the lady whom you admired, my lord——

Rut. She is dead.

Effie. Dead!

Rut. Yes, dead, Effie: but in you she lives again.

Effie. What do I hear?

Rut. Oh, Effie, can you not conceive the happiness of once more beholding the object we adore.

Effie. I shall never love any one but Robert.

Rut. Happy Robert, and unfortunate Ruthven! Why did I ever behold thee, Effie?

Effie. See me no more, my lord, if that has occasioned your uneasiness. [*Going,* R.

Rut. Stay! Effie, it is in your power to console me for all I have lost. Love me—nay, start not; mine you must and shall be!

Effie. My lord, I'll hear no more. If Robert——

Rut. Think not of him; the bridal preparations are complete; my bride thou art—no power on earth shall tear thee from me! say, Effie, that you love me.

[*Taking her hand.*

Effie. [*Starting.*] Mercy on me! My lord, I—I know not what to say. My heart beats so that—Oh, pray leave me, my lord. [*Sobbing.*

Rut. You weep: those tears are for me.

Effie. No, no: indeed, my lord——

Rut. This instant let me bear thee to the priest.

Effie. My lord, for pity's sake——

Rut. You plead in vain: Effie, thou art mine for ever!

[*Bears her off,* R.

Re-enter ROBERT, R. U. E.

Rob. How long she stays—not here! Why—[*Effie shrieks.*] Heavens! what do I see—borne off, and struggling.—Villain! loose your hold!

[*Draws a pistol, and runs after them,* R.—*stage gradually darkens.*

Enter ANDREW *and* LORD RONALD, R. U. E.

Ron. Why, Andrew, said you not the Earl was here?

And. 'Twas here I left him but just now, my lord.

[*A pistol fired without,* R.

Effie. [*Shrieks without,* R.] Oh, save me! save me!

And. My daughter's voice! [*Exit,* R.

Enter LORD RUTHVEN, *wounded,* R. U. E.

Ron. Ruthven!

Rut. [*Falling,* C.] I die!

Ron. What murderous hand—

[*The moon is seen descending.*

Rut. Exclaim not, I have but a moment to live.—Ronald, swear by the host of heaven to obey my last commands.

Ron. Young man, the word of Ronald needs no oath to bind it.

Rut. I die—delay not a moment, but swear to——

Ron. I do, I do!—I swear by all that is most dear and sacred to honour and to man, to fulfil your last desire.

Rut. Conceal my death from every human being till yonder moon, which now sails in her full splendour, shall be set this night; and, ere an hour shall elapse after I have expired, throw this ring into the waves that wash the tomb of Fingal. [*Gives a ring.*

Ron. I will, I will, Ruthven!—Dear Ruthven!

Rut. Remember your oath. The lamp of night is descending the blue heavens; when I am dead, let its sweet light shine on me. Farewell! Remember—remember your oath.

[*Dies—solemn Music—Ronald lays the body of Ruthven on a bank in the garden,* R. U. E., *and kneels mournfully beside it—the moon continues descending, till the light falls full upon the corpse—Ronald rises, crosses to* L., *and the curtain drops.*

END OF ACT I.

ACT II.

SCENE I.—*The Tomb of Fingal,* R. C., *in the Caverns of Staffa—the Sea—Moonlight.*

MUSIC—*Enter* ANDREW, ROBERT, *and* EFFIE, *in a boat,* L. U. E.—*they land.*

And. (L.) Here, Robert, you may rest concealed till Lord Ronald's anger shall have subsided; or, should he be deaf to explanation, and refuse to believe Lord Ruthven's treachery, arrangements shall be made to convey you over to the mainland. Here is sufficient provision for the short time I hope you will be forced to remain. And so now bid Effie good by for awhile; I'll look out, in the meantime, and see if the coast be clear for our return. [*Exit Andrew, in the boat,* L. U. E.

Rob. (R.) Come, cheer up, Effie,—all will be well yet. It was in defence of innocence I fired, and, therefore, that act will never be a load on my conscience.

Effie. (C.) But, if Lord Ronald should get you into his power!

Rob. I will put it to Lord Ronald's self to say, whether a man should stand tamely by, and see the wife of his bosom dragged to misery and dishonour. Come, kiss me, Effie, and farewell till better times.

DUETTO.—EFFIE *and* ROBERT.

TUNE—"*Down the Burn, Davie.*"

Rob. Though vanish'd be the visions fair,
By Fancy's pencil trac'd;
And blighted all the blossoms rare
That hope's gay chaplet grac'd;
Fear not my faith!
The pang of death
Alone can bid it flee.

Then fare thee well, my only love!
Fare thee well, my only love!
Fare thee well, my only love!
Thou'rt more than life to me.

Both. Fare thee well, &c.

Effie. Though clouded now the prospect seem,
Though grief usurp the hour,
A light may break, a ray may beam,
And joy resume its power.

Enter ANDREW, *in the boat,* L. U. E.

Effie. Fear not my faith,
The pang of death
Alone can bid it flee.
Then fare thee well, my only love!
Fare thee well, my only love!
Fare thee well, my only love!
Thou'rt more than life to me.

Both. Fare thee well, &c.

[*Andrew places Effie in the boat, and exit,* L. U. E.

Rob. And now to find some hole for a bed-chamber. Rather sorry accommodations, I fancy; but the superstitions of the peasantry will keep them from disturbing my repose; and, as to other considerations, a man with a clear conscience may rest anywhere. [*Looking.*] Here's tolerable choice of apartments, as far as number goes: let me try what shelter this will afford.

[*Exit into the cavern,* R.

MUSIC.—*A boat is seen,* L. U. E., *with Lord Ronald and two Attendants in it.—Enter* LORD RONALD, *from the boat.*

Ron. Give me the torch, and wait without the cave till you see me wave it thus. [*Exeunt Attendants in the boat,* L.] How solemn is this scene. [*Places the torch in a fissure of the rock,* L. S. E.] By heaven, my soul, that lately mock'd at superstition, is so subdued by circumstances, that I could almost bring myself to give faith to every legend I have scorn'd as idle. Here is the ring—what am I about to do—what horrible suspicion flashes across my brain! Ruthven, mysterious being! what mean these ceremonies? Before, when I supposed him dying, he bade me place his body in the light of the moon; and now again. And wherefore make me swear to conceal his death till the moon be set?—But let me not reflect or pause. Unhappy Ruthven! thy friend performs his promise.

[*Throws the ring into the water,* C.—*a peal of thunder is heard, after which the voice of Ruthven,—*

"REMEMBER YOUR OATH!"

Ron. It is his spirit speaks! Ruthven, my friend, my preserver!

Re-enter ROBERT, R.

Rob. What voice was that?—Lord Ronald!

Ron. Ha, by heaven, justice hath given the murderer to my vengeance. [*Draws.*] Ruthven, this sacrifice I make to thee.

Rob. Hear me, my lord: Lord Ruthven would have wronged me.

Ron. Wouldst thou asperse the dead?—Down, villain, down! [*Attacks him.*

Rob. Nay, in my own defence, then——

[*They fight—Robert is disarmed—Ronald plunges him into the waves,* R. U. E.—*Lord Ronald rushes to the entrance of the cavern, and waves the torch—the boat approaches.*

Ron. Ruthven, thou art revenged! Away! away!

[*Ronald leaps into the boat,* L. U. E.—*Robert reaches and clings to the rocks,* R., *and the scene closes.*

SCENE II.—*An Apartment in Lord Ronald's Castle.*

Enter LADY MARGARET, *meeting* BRIDGET, R.

Lady M. Bridget, I was looking for you; I am so happy.

Bri. Happy, my lady! and Lord Ruthven and your father not returned? I'm frightened out of my wits about them: 'tis ten o'clock, and they were to have been back again ere sunset.

Lady M. You may dispel your fears, then; Lord Ruthven has this moment announced to me my father's return.

Bri. Lord Ruthven!

Lady M. On opening the casement, just now, that looks into the garden, I saw him by the moonlight, crossing one of the walks. I call'd to him, and he will be here directly, that the ceremony may commence. We must depart for London ere daybreak.

Bri. So soon?

Lady M. Yes; he has explained the reason to me. The King of England wishes him to marry a lady of the court, and he has no other way of avoiding the match, but by presenting me immediately as his wife.

Bri. And here comes your father, I declare. Well, my lady, I'll away and see that everything is ready. [*Exit Bridget,* R.

Lady M. I can hardly account for my sudden attachment to Lord Ruthven, especially after the shock his introduction gave me.

Enter LORD RONALD, L.

Lady M. Well, sir, is Ruthven coming?

Ron. Ruthven! Alas!——

Lady M. You sigh; what troubles you, my dear father?

Ron. Nothing. [*Aside.*] What shall I say to her?

Lady M. Every thing is prepared for the ceremony. Lord Ruthven has doubtless informed you of the pressing reason he has for our immediate departure: its suddenness at first alarm'd me; but, if you will accompany us, what a charming voyage—You do not listen to me—Why, father, what's the matter?

Ron. My dear Margaret, we must think no more of this union.

Lady M. Think no more of it! Have you not been yourself the cause, and do you now——

Ron. Question me not; I cannot answer you.

Lady M. Good heavens! and Ruthven who, not a moment ago, so warmly urged——

Ron. [*Starting.*] Ruthven, not a moment ago—what mean you?

Lady M. You frighten me; but Ruthven will soon be here, and——

Enter LORD RUTHVEN, *behind,* L. U. E.

Ron. Ruthven is——

Ron. [*Starting,* L.] Can the grave give up its dead? Spirit, what wouldst thou?

Rut. [*Apart to Ronald.*] Remember your oath.

Rut. Ronald, my friend, what means this wildness?

Ron My brain turns round! I saw him fall,—I heard his dying groan.—Fiend—phantom, hence, I charge thee!

Rut. Alas, he raves!

Lady M. [*Clinging to Ruthven*, R.] My father! my poor father!

Ron. [*Crosses to her.*] Touch him not, Margaret! Fly the demon's grasp!

Rut. How dreadful is this wildness. Ho! within, there!

Ron. I am not mad. Ruthven's dead! I saw——

Rut. [*Aside*, L.] Your oath!

Enter Two Servants, L.

Rut. Your master is not well, his brain is wandering; secure him, and let aid be sent for instantly.

[*Servants take hold of Ronald*, C.

Ron. Stand off, slaves!—'Tis a fiend in human shape! I saw him perish,—twice have I seen him perish! As I have life, Heaven saw and heard——

Rut. [*Aside.*] Your oath!

Lady M. [*To the Servants.*] Oh, harm him not, but lead him gently in.

Ron. That dreadful oath! [*Servants seize him.*] Stay but a moment: Margaret, promise me you will not marry till the moon shall set; then, fearful fiend, I am no longer pledged, and may preserve my child.

Lady M. (C.) Oh, my poor father!

[*Falls into the arms of Ruthven, fainting.*

Rut. Remove him gently—suddenly, I say.

Ron. No, I will not quit my child an instant; horror overwhelms me! I know not what thou art; but terrible conviction flashes on my mind, that thou art nothing human. A mist seems clearing from my sight; and I behold thee now—oh, horror! horror!—a monster of the grave—a—a Vam——

[*Falling into his Servant's arms, who bear him off*, R.

Rut. (L.) Remember!—[*Aside.*] She's mine! my prey is in my clutch,—the choicest, crowning victim!—Ha! revive, my bride.

Lady M. (R.) Where am I? Where, where is my father?

Rut. In safety, love, be sure; retired to his chamber.

Lady M. I know not what to think!

Rut. Alas! I have seen him often thus, during our travels together; his reason received a severe shock on the death of my young friend, your brother.

Lady M. Is't possible? I never knew him thus.

Rut. Rely upon the melancholy truth; but 'twill not last; so, cheer thee, lovely Margaret.

Lady M. Alas, I need your consolation! How wild a fancy seized him, that you were dead; and his request, too, not to marry till the moon had set.—Well, I will not.

Rut. [*Aside.*] Ha! [*Aloud.*] Sweet Margaret, you will not sure repent?

Lady M. Why, my good lord, so short a delay cannot be of consequence, and 'twill appease him, probably,—and such a slight request.

Rut. I reverence your motive; but if you love me, Margaret——

Lady M. You cannot doubt it.

Rut. Upon that love, then, my repose, my happiness, my life depends; swear to me, dearest Margaret, to forget these idle terrors, and to be mine—mine only—for ever.

Lady M. I do, by Him who reads all hearts, to be thine, and thine only, for ever.

Rut. Oh, happiness! Receive this ring, and let it be a sacred pledge between us.

[*Kisses the ring, and places it on her finger.*

Lady M. Ha!

Rut. [*Aside, smiling.*] Her fate is sealed.—She cannot now retract. [*Aloud.*] You shudder—what ails my love?

Lady M. A strange sensation runs throughout my frame; tears fill my eyes, and my heart beats as though 'twould burst my bosom. Methinks my father's voice still rings in mine ears, "Wed not before the moon shall set."

Rut. [*Aside.*] The hour approaches—no time is to be lost. [*Aloud.*] Think no more, I beseech thee, of these wanderings of the imagination, but let us hasten to consecrate the ties which unite us. Every arrangement must, by this time, have been made. Retire, my love, to your chamber; compose your spirits; and Ruthven then will lead thee to the altar.

[*Music.—Exeunt Ruthven and Lady Margaret*, R.

SCENE III.—*Distant View of Lord Ronald's Castle, by Moonlight.*

Enter ANDREW *and* EFFIE, L., *supporting* ROBERT.

Rob. (L.) Nay, nay, do not trouble yourselves; I have sustained no injury. But what made you come back to me so soon?

Effie. (C.) We saw the boat pass with Lord Ronald in it, and we feared some mischief.

And. (R.) So we lay-to till he left the cavern, and returned just in time to render you assistance. Yonder is the castle; are you still determined to seek him?

Rob. Yes; he has been imposed upon; and ere now, I am sure, he regrets having drawn upon me. I will lay open Lord Ruthven's villany to him; and I know his noble nature too well, to fear a continuance of his anger. Here, therefore, we will part for awhile; and when we meet again, I trust all obstacles to our happiness will be removed. Be faithful.

SONG.—EFFIE.

TUNE—" *Of a' the Airts.*"

Though many a wood and heath clad hill
Should rise betwixt us twain;
And many an envious stream and rill
Run babbling to the main;
This fond and faithful heart believe,
Howe'er apart we be,
Though in my breast it seem to heave,
Will linger still with thee.

Thus, when the silver lamp of night
Sails through the quiet sky,
And sheds its lustre pure and bright
Upon the traveller's eye;
Though o'er him still the fond orb seems
To glide where'er he'll roam;
Its faithful light as sweetly beams
Upon his distant home.

[*M'Swill sings without,* L.

And. Soft; who comes here?

Rob. By his gait, it should be M'Swill, the baron's toping henchman. [*They retire up.*

Enter M'SWILL, L.

M'Swill. My master's gone mad--there's a pretty job. If *he* had been going to be married, instead of the earl, I shouldn't have wonder'd so much; but for an old man to go mad, who can sit and drink all day, without any one to snub him for it, is the most ridiculous thing that ever came under my observation. Old mother Bridget

never lets me drink in quiet at home, so I carry a pocket pistol about with me. [*Pulls out a flask.*] Now, this is what I call my " Young M n's Best Companion;" it's a great consolation on a night excursion, to one who has so respectful a belief in bogles and warlocks, as I have. Whiskey's the only spirit I feel a wish to be intimately acquainted with.

Rob. [*Advancing and slapping him on the shoulder.*] M'Swill!

M'Swill. [*Dropping on his knees.*] Oh, lord, what's that?

Rob. Why, how now, booby? Where have you been at this time of night?

M'Swill. Eh! What, Robert, is it only you? I was just kneeling to—this stupid latchet, you see, is——

[*Pretending to fasten it.*

Rob. Oh yes, I see; but where have you been, I ask you?

M'Swill. Been! oh, I've been for Father Francis;—my lord's gone crazy, and the Earl of Marsden sent me.

Rob. & *Effie.* } The Earl of Marsden!

M'Swill. Whew! what's in the wind now?

And. (R.) The Earl of Marsden sent you?

M'Swill. Yes, to be sure; he's in the castle there, and just going to be married to my Lady Margaret.

Rob. Fool! the Earl of Marsden is dead.

M'Swill. Nay, now you're mad. My master's been telling the same story this half-hour; but the earl says it's no such thing; that he is not dead, and never was dead; that my master's out of his wits;—and off he sends me for Father Francis, to come and talk to my master, and marry my mistress.

Rob. What mystery is this? There is some foul play towards—at any rate, the Lady Margaret must know her danger. Is the friar gone?

M'Swill. Oh yes, he's there before now. The very name of a wedding made him chuckle, and waddle off at a rate, which obliged me to stop so many times for refreshment, that he has been out of sight these some minutes.

Rob. Let us haste, father; we may toil the villain yet.

[*Exeunt Robert, Andrew, and Effie,* R.

M'Swill. It appears there is something wrong, but I

can't positively pretend to say what it is; and as my flask seems as much exhausted as my speculations, I'll make the best of my way home, and ruminate how much whiskey I shall drink at the wedding.

SONG.—M'SWILL.

Tune—"Fly, let us awa to the Bridal."

Faith, I'll awa' to the bridal,
For there will be tippling there;
For my lady's about to be married,
To whom I don't know, and don't care.
But I know we shall all be as frisky
And tipsy as pipers, good lack;
And so that there's plenty of whiskey,
She may marry the devil for Mac.
So, faith! I'll awa' to the bridal, &c.

I once left the bottle for Cupid,
And bade an adieu to my glass;
I simper'd, and sigh'd, and look'd stupid,
And courted a cherry-cheek'd lass.
She turn'd out a jilt:—'twere a lie should I
Say, that it gave me no pain;
For sorrowing made me so dry, that I
Took to my bottle again.
So, faith! I'll awa' to the bridal, &c.

They say there's five reasons for drinking,
But more, I am sure, may be got;
For I never can find out by thinking
A reason why people should not.
A sixth I'll not scruple at giving;
I'll name it while 'tis in my head;
'Tis if you don't drink while you're living,
You never will after you're dead.
So, faith! I'll awa' to the bridal, &c.
[*Exit M'Swill*, R.

SCENE IV.—*The Chapel.—A large Gothic Window, through which the Moon is seen going down.*

MUSIC.—LORD RUTHVEN, *Priests, Vassals, &c. discovered.*

Rut. All is prepared; o'er the great fiend once more
I triumph! Ere yon orb shall kiss the wave,
The tributary victim shall be paid.

Bow, ye less subtle spirits—bow abashed
Before your master.
Margaret!
'Tis Ruthven calls thee. Hasten, sweet, and crown
Thy lover's happiness.

Enter LADY MARGARET *and* BRIDGET, R.

Rut. Lady, to the altar.

Lady M. I follow you, my lord—and yet——

Rut. [*Impatiently seizing her hand.*] Come, Margaret, come!

[*Distant thunder.—A loud gust of wind shakes the casement.*

Lady M. What noise was that?

Bri. 'Tis but the wind, my lady; we shall have another storm, I think, when the moon sets.

Lady M. When the moon sets!—Ah, my poor father! See, 'twill set soon, my Ruthven; let me again beseech you to delay, till then, the ceremony!

Rut. [*More impatiently.*] Nay, this is folly, Margaret. Father, commence the rites.

Enter LORD RONALD, *preceded by* ROBERT, *and followed by* ANDREW, EFFIE, *and Attendants*, R.

Rob. Make way! make way, I say! Lord Ronald shall be heard!

Ron. (L.) My daughter! my daughter!

Rut. [*Aside.*] Confusion!—Ronald!

Ron. Where is she? Give me my daughter.

Lady M. (C.) My dearest father, be calm. What wouldst thou with me?

Ron. (R. C.) Ha! do I again embrace thee. Follow him not—he drags you to the tomb.

Rut. [*Furiously.*] Margaret, we are waited for.

Ron. Barbarian! I forbid the ceremony. You have no right over her—I am her father.

Lady M. You are—you are my loving, tender father:—I will not wed against his will.

[*Throwing herself into his arms.*

Rut I'll hear no more!—she is my bride betrothed: this madman would deprive me of her.

Lady M. [*Indignantly*, R.] No!—Why this violence? Wait till the hour is past.

Rut. Will you listen to his ravings?

Ron. I do not rave. [*Loud thunder.—Another gust of*

wind blows open the casement.] See, see! the moon already rests upon the wave! one moment! but one moment!—— [*Detaining Margaret.*

Rut. Nay, then, thus I seal thy lips, and seize my bride.

[*Ruthven draws his poniard, and rushes on Ronald—Lady Margaret shrieks; when Robert throws himself between Ruthven and Ronald, and wrenches the dagger from his grasp.*

Lady M. Hold! hold!—I am thine;—the moon has set.

Rut. And I am lost!

[*A terrific peal of thunder is heard—Unda and Ariel appear—a thunder-bolt strikes Ruthven, who immediately vanishes through the ground—general picture.*

DISPOSITION OF THE CHARACTERS AT THE FALL OF THE CURTAIN.

Altar. Priest.		*Attendants.*			*Two Attendants.*
AND.	RON.	LADY M.	{ RUTHVEN, *Descending.* }	ROB	EFFIE.
R.]					[L.

THE END.

Costume.

—

IN THE INTRODUCTORY VISION.

UNDA.—White satin dress, trimmed with shells, &c.—blue satin robe—hair in long ringlets—tiara—wand.

ARIEL.—White muslin dress, with spangles—sky-blue robe—wings—tiara—silver wand.

THE VAMPIRE (RUTHVEN).—Silver breast-plate, studded with steel buttons—plaid kelt—cloak—flesh arms and leggings—sandals—gray cloak, to form the attitude as he ascends from the tomb.

LADY MARGARET.—White satin dress, trimmed with plaid and silver—plaid silk sash—Scotch hat and feather.

IN THE DRAMA.

RUTHVEN.—Silver breast-plate, studded with steel buttons—plaid kelt—philibeg—flesh arms and leggings—sandals—Scotch hat and feathers—sword and dagger.

RONALD.—Crimson shirt, with large clasps down the front—plaid cloak—flesh arms and leggings—sandals—sword and belt—Scotch hat and feathers.

ROBERT.—Gray shirt, trimmed with yellow binding—drab pantaloons—gray hat, with black feathers—sword and belt—russet boots and collar.

M'SWILL.—Red plaid jacket, waistcoat, and kelt—philibeg—flesh leggings—plaid stockings—black shoes and buckles—Scotch cap.

ANDREW.—Old man's brown coat and breeches—plaid waistcoat and stockings—old man's shoes and buckles—Scotch cap—gray wig—black kerchief.

FATHER FRANCIS.—Sacerdotal robes and tonsure.

LADY MARGARET.—The same as in the vision.

EFFIE.—Black velvet body and tabs—plaid petticoat, trimmed with black—blue ribbon in the hair—plaid sash.

BRIDGET.—Black velvet body, with point lace—red petticoat, with point lace—point-lace apron—kerchief—cap—peaked black hat, trimmed with red.

SERVANTS.—Kelts—jackets, &c.

Royal Coburg Theatre.

ACTING-MANAGER MR HUNTLEY.

First Night of an entirely New & most Impressive Melo-Drama!

SECOND WEEK OF THE SPLENDID ROMANCE OF THALABA THE DESTROYER.

☞The Rapturous Applause from Overflowing and Elegant Audiences, which Nightly hails the New Dramatic Romance, founded on the celebrated Poem of THALABA THE DESTROYER, by *R. Southey, Esq. Poet Laureat*, has surpassed the Proprietor's most sanguine Expectation.—The Characteristic Splendor of the Costume and Scenery, and the extent and ingenuity of the Machinery, are universally allowed to do ample justice to the magnificent Creation of the Poet's Imagination.

MONDAY, Aug. 18th, 1823,—And During the Week,—At Half-past Six precisely,

Will be Presented an entirely New Melo-Dramatic Romance, founded on Southey's celebrated Poem of Thalaba, *written by E. Ball, Esq.* with New Music, Scenery, Machinery, Dresses and Decorations, Called,

THALABA
THE DESTROYER!

The Music & New Overture composed by *Mr. T. Hughes.*—The Scenery by *Messrs. Wilkins, Jones, Stanfield, Jun. and Assistants.*—The Machinery by *Mr. Burroughs.*—The Properties by *Mr. Blamire.*—The Dresses by *Mr. Smythers, Messds. Cross and Follet.*
The New Ballet & Processions arranged by Monsieur Le CLERCQ, and the Piece Produced under the immediate Direction of Mr. HUNTLEY.

Thalaba, the Destroyer,......*Brought up as an Arabian Peasant,*......Mr. STANLEY.
Moath, *an Old Arabian*, Mr. HARWOOD. Samba, *a Black Slave*, Mr. SLOMAN. Hamed, *Usurping Sultan of the Isles*, Mr. BENGOUGH.
Hafna, Zalem, and Ali, *Officers of the Sultan*, Mr. HILL, Mr. HAINES, and Mr. HOWELL.
Osman, Zorar, Hasric, Karau, Morab, Abner, *Persian Chiefs*, Messrs. HONOR, COOPER, ASBURY, HOBBS, BOULANGER, FISHER.
Abdalda, *a Demon, assuming various Characters*, Mr. BRADLEY. Okba, *a Fiend*, Mr. JONES. Mountain Hag, Mr. MORRIS.
Oneiza, - - - - - *Daughter of Moath, beloved by Thalaba*, - - - - - Miss EDMISTON.
Zeinah, *Spirit of Thalaba's Mother*, Mrs. BRADLEY. Kawla, *Enchantress of the Isles*, Mrs. STANLY. Marmina, *Peri of Faith*, Miss BURNETT.
Fairy Fiends, Upas, Mrs. TENNANT. Semi, Miss GASKILL. Mosfa, Mrs. YOUNG. Cindoubree, Mrs. WESTON.

In Act II.—A NEW GRAND ASIATIC PAS DE DEUX, by Monsieur and Madame Le CLERCQ.

Act 1.

The Sepulchre of Zeinah by Moonlight, WILKINS.
AWFUL INCANTATION.
ROMANTIC PASS, WILKINS.
Cottage of Moath in the Valley of Date Trees, WILKINS.
Thalaba's Chamber in the Cottage of Moath, WILKINS.

Act 2.

COTTAGE OF MOATH BY SUN-RISE.
Impressive Appearance and Flight of the Locusts.
Apartment in the Sultan's Palace, STANFIELD, JUN.
MOUNTAINOUS PASS & MAGIC WELL, WILKINS.
Splendid Pavilion in the Sultan's Palace,
IN WHICH WILL BE INTRODUCED
A Grand Procession and Ballet.
PRINCIPAL DANCERS,
Mons. & Mad. Le CLERCQ, Masters HUMMERSTON and WIELAND.
A VIEW NEAR THE ROCK OF BADELMANDEL.
Enchanted Cavern
***Beneath** the WATERS of Badelmandel,* WILKINS.
GRAND STORM CHORUS,
And Precipitation of Thalaba & Oneiza down the Cataract of Badelmandel,
With their Miraculous Escape.

Act 3.

A RUINED CEMETERY, JONES.
ENTRANCE TO THE SILVER CAVERN,
Guarded by a Stupendous Winged Serpent, JONES.
Interior of the Silver Cavern,
COLOSSAL STATUE AND ALTAR.
Bearing the 7 Enchanted Lights & Burning Sword, JONES.
VALLEY OF THE MOUNTAINS, JONES.
Procession of Thalaba's Army,
WITH HIS APPEARANCE ON A
WAR ELEPHANT
Towers and Fortifications of Badelmandel,
Wilkins & Jones.
Desperate Conflict,
STORMING OF THE FORTRESS,
With the Destruction of the Tyrant,
AND RESTORATION OF THALABA
To his CROWN and KINGDOM.

After which will be Revived, *(Second Time these Two Years,)* the very favorite Petite Comedy, Called,

THE SECRET.

The Characters by Messrs. HILL, HAINES, HARWOOD. Mrs. POPE and Mrs. De BOOS.

☞The Proprietor ever anxious to produce Novelty, has engaged that eminent Artist, Mr. STANFIELD, (by Permission of R. W. ELLISTON, Esq.) to paint a *New Elegant Picturesque Drop Scene*, to be exhibited at the End of the First Piece.

*** In the Construction of the New Melo-Drame, founded upon the Terrific Romance of "FRANKENSTEIN," every care has been taken to avoid any points that might be deemed objectionable in Principle and Morality; and, the Manager trusts, that instead of being offensive to the Feelings of the most Fastidious, this Drama will be found to convey an instructive Lesson, through the Medium of the most Novel and Impressive Effects.

The whole to conclude with an entirely New Dramatic Romance, of a peculiar Interest, founded on the Popular and Singular Romance of the same Name, with New Music, Scenery, Dresses and Decorations, to be Called,

FRANKENSTEIN!
Or, THE DEMON OF SWITZERLAND.

Music by *Mr. T. Hughes.*—Scenery by *Messrs. Wilkins, Jones, and Assistants.*—Dresses by *Mr. Smythers. Messds. Cross and Follet.*—Properties by *Mr. Blamire.*—Machinery by *Mr. Burroughs.*—And the Piece written by *Mr. H. M. Milner.*

Frankenstein, *a Student of Geneva*, Mr. STANLEY. Clairville, *his Friend*, Mr. HILL. Mr. Theodosius, Cornelius, Maximan Lightbody, Mr. SLOMAN.
Ludolf, Mr. JACOBSON. Ruric, Mr. COOPER. Villager, Mr. REEVES.
(——————) Mr. BENGOUGH.
Clara, *Sister of Clairville*, Mrs. POPE. Maud, *his Mother*, Mrs. WESTON. Eliza, *Sister to Lightbody*, Mrs. TENNANT.
Swiss Villagers, Messrs. Morris, Proud, Waring, Boulanger, George, Dowsing. Messds. Brock, Fairbrother, Davis, De Boos, Gough, Grisdale.

BOXES 4s & 3s. PIT 2s. GAL. 1s. Doors open at Half-past 5, begin at Half-past 6. Second Price at Half-past 8.

☞ Places to be taken of Mr. A. R. BOWES, at the New Box Office, in the Grand Marine Saloon of the Theatre, and of whom may be had Private Boxes Nightly, also *Free Admissions for the Season*, and for the Accommodation of the Nobility and Gentry at the West End of the Town, at the Western Exchange, Old Bond-street, and at No. 182, Piccadilly, opposite Burlington-House. *[T. Romney, Printer, Lambeth.]*

A Note on

Frankenstein

There were many dramatic adaptations of Mary Shelley's gothic novel *Frankenstein* (1818) and both the Coburg and the English Opera House had their own versions. There is, however, some confusion about the version reproduced here. The title-page of Duncombe's edition calls the play *Frankenstein, or the Man and the Monster* while at the head of Act 1 of the same edition the play is called *The Fate of Frankenstein.* The date of its first performance at the Coburg Theatre is given as 3 July 1826. In my possession, however, is a Coburg playbill for 18 August 1823 naming the afterpiece for that night as *Frankenstein, or the Demon of Switzerland.* H. M. Milner is given as the author of the play in Duncombe's edition which is set in Sicily, but the Coburg bill of some three years earlier acknowledges Milner's play as being the foundation of the new work.

The version put on at the English Opera House in June 1823 is called *Presumption, or the Fate of Frankenstein*, but, while the alternative title is the same as in Duncombe's edition, the dramatis personae in neither of the versions of which I have seen playbills correspond to the list of characters given in Duncombe's edition.

Whether one may conclude that the 1826 version presented here is a re-working of an earlier success, I would not like to say, but here, with all faults, is the play.

MR. O. SMITH AS THE MONSTER.
in
FRANKENSTEIN.

London Pub.d by J. Duncombe, 19 Little Queen Street, Holborn.

Duncombe's Edition.

FRANKENSTEIN;

OR,

THE MAN AND THE MONSTER!

A PECULIAR ROMANTIC, MELO-DRAMATIC PANTOMIMIC SPECTACLE,

IN TWO ACTS.

Founded principally on Mrs. Shelly's singular Work, entitled,
FRANKENSTEIN; OR, THE MODERN PROMETHEUS;
and partly on the French Piece,
"*Le Magicien et le Monstre.*"

BY H. M. MILNER.

THE ONLY EDITION CORRECTLY MARKED FROM THE PROMPTER'S BOOK; WITH THE STAGE BUSINESS, SITUATIONS, AND DIRECTIONS.

AS PERFORMED AT

The London Theatres.

LONDON:
PRINTED AND PUBLISHED BY J. DUNCOMBE,
19 LITTLE QUEEN STREET, HOLBORN; AND SOLD BY ALL BOOKSELLERS IN TOWN AND COUNTRY.

DRAMATIS PERSONÆ.

PRINCE DEL PIOMBINO -	Mr. HEMMINGS.
FRANKENSTEIN - - -	Mr. ROWBOTHAM.
RITZBERG - - - -	Mr. MEREDITH.
QUADRO - - - -	Mr. GOLDSMITH.
STRUTT - - - - -	Mr. E. L. LEWIS.
JULIO - - - - -	Miss BURNETT.
(* * * * * *) - - - -	Mr. O. SMITH.
ROSAURA - - - -	Mrs. LEWIS.
EMMELINE - - - -	Mrs. YOUNG.
LISETTA - - - - -	Mrs. ROWBOTHAM.

Nobles, Guards, and Attendants on the Prince, Peasants, &c.

SCENE—The Estate of the Prince del Piombino, near the foot of Mount Etna.

TIME—From Sunset on one day, till Midnight the next.

First performed at the Coburg Theatre, July 3, 1826

COSTUME:

PRINCE DEL PIOMBINO—Green Italian tunic, richly embroidered with silver, crimson sash, white pantaloons, yellow boots. Italian cap and feathers.

FRANKENSTEIN—Black velvet vest and trunk breeches, grey tunic open, the sleeves open in front, slashed with white, black stockings and shoes.

QUADRO—Blue doublet, vest, trunk breeches, & stockings.

RITZBERG—Dark brown doublet, mantle, trunk breeches, stockings, and cloth hat.

STRUTT—Blue doublet with long tabs, dark brown vest and tight pantaloons, boots, small three-cornered cloth hat.

JULIO—White satin embroidered tunic, white silk pantaloons, scarlet bottines, white satin Italian cap.

(* * * * * *) Close vest and leggings of a very pale yellowish brown, heightened with blue, as if to show the muscles, &c. Greek shirt of very dark brown, broad black leather belt.

ROSAURA—Embroidered dress of pink satin.

EMMELINE—Short German pelisse of a dark brown, over a slate coloured petticoat, dark brown Polish cap.

LISETTA—Italian peasant.

THE FATE OF FRANKENSTEIN.

ACT I.

SCENE 1.

The Gardens of the Prince del Piombino's *Villa.—At the back a River, beyond which, Picturesque Country. On the* P. S. *side, the Entrance to the Villa. On the* O.P. *side, a small Pavilion.)*

Enter QUADRO, STRUTT, *and* LISETTA, *from the Villa, meeting male and female Villagers.*

Lis. And you think yourself a vastly great man, Mr. Strutt, I suppose.

Strutt. Philosophers are not content with thinking, I know it. My master's a great man, and I'm like the moon to the sun, I shine with a reflected brightness.

Quad. Great man, indeed! I should like to know what there is great about either of you. A couple of adventurers, whom my poor silly dupe of a master, (Heaven help him!) has brought from that beggarly place, Germany; and I suppose you'll never leave him whilst he has got a ducat.

Strutt. Pooh! for his ducats! we want his ducats, indeed! when we could make gold out of any rubbish; your worthless head, for instance, Signor Quadro. My master is the most profound philosopher, and consequently the greatest man that ever lived; to tell you what he can do is impossible; but what he cannot do, it would be still more difficult to mention.

Quad. Yes, his way of making gold, I fancy, is by conveying it out of other people's pockets. He may make gold, but he'd much rather have it made to his hand, I've a notion.

Strutt. Signor Quadro, it is fortunate for you that my master does not hear you, and that (considering the choice bottles of Catanian wine, that you have from time to time been pleased to open for me) I'm too discreet to tell him; —for, oh! signor Quadro, his power is terrible;—he could prevent you from ever passing a quiet night again!

Quad. When I've got three quarts of good Rhenish in my skin, I'll give him leave, if he can. Your master is a water-drinker, sir, he keeps no butler; I never knew any good of a man that drank water and kept no butler.

Strutt. At all events, master Quadro, that's an offence which you cannot lay to my charge; I have the most philosophical principles upon the subject;—I drink water, Signor Quadro, only when I can't get any thing better.

Quad. And that's generally the case, I fancy, when you can't find some good-natured simpleton, like the Prince del Piombino, to keep you and your master together. Instead of board-wages, he billets you upon the kitchen of any body that's fool enough to take you into it.

Strutt. Be assured of this, Signor Quadro, I am not ungrateful; when any kind friend has the goodness to take me in, I do the best in my power to return the compliment

Quad. The devil doubt you.

Strutt. But for my master, signor Quadro, don't think that all the wine in Sicily is any object to him; he could turn that river into wine if he thought proper,—I've seen him do it, sir, and convert a quart of simple water into a bottle of prime Burgundy.

Quad. Can he? can he do that? Then he has an easy way of making me his sworn friend for life. Only let him turn——I won't be unreasonable; I won't say a word about the river——only let him turn the pump in our stable-yard into a fountain of claret, and I'll never purloin another bottle of my master's, so long as I'm a butler.

Lis. And pray, Mr. Strutt, has all this philosophy and learning quite driven the thoughts of love out of your head? I suppose you fancy yourself now quite above us poor weak women?

Strutt. Not at all, my dear creature; for the man who has the impudence to fancy himself above the fairest half of human nature has sunk immeasurably below it.

Quad. Egad! philosophy has not made quite a fool of the fellow. But pray now, my good Mr. Strutt, amongst all this transmuting of metal, and converting of water, can you inform us what it is that this wonderful master of yours is doing in that pavilion, where he remains constantly shut up, day and night, and into which no mortal but himself is ever permitted to penetrate?

Strutt. You would like to know, would you?

Quad. Yes I should, very much indeed.

Lis. Oh yes, I'd give the world to know, I should so like to find out the secret.

Strutt. (*after a pause*) And so should I.

Quad. What then, you can't tell us?

Lis. Or perhaps you won't.

Strutt. Why you see——I'm not exactly certain—but I partly guess—(*they cling to him with eager curiosity*)—that is, I suspect—that it is—something that will astonish your weak nerves, one day or another.

Quad. Pshaw!

Lis. A nasty, ill-natured fellow—see how I'll serve you, the next time you try to kiss me. (*Music without.*

Quad. But hark! his highness approaches with his lovely sister, the lady Rosaura. Back! back! all of you, show him proper respect.

(*They are ioined by other domestics, male and female, who form in order. A Gondola approaches the shore, from which the* Prince, Rosaura, *and* Attendants *land. As the* Prince *advances, all salute him.*)

Prince. Enough, enough, my friends, hasten to the villa, and busy yourselves in preparations for the festival I wish to give in honour of the illustrious genius, who honours my house with his presence.

Quad. (*aside*) A festival, too! for a man who drinks no wine. Well, there's one consolation; there'll be more for those who do—and I'll do my best to make up for his deficiencies, he may depend on't.

Strutt. (*to* Lis.) If there's dancing, may I claim the honour——?

Lis. Will you try to find out your master's secret for me?—

Strutt. It is positively against his orders, to pry into his concerns; and do you know, there is but one person in the world whose commands could induce me to disobey those of my master.

Lis. And who may that be, pray?

Strutt. My mistress, you jade. (*takes her under his arm, and exeunt with* Quadro, Domestics, &c. *into the Palace.*)

Prince. I feel most deeply that rank and opulence can never do themselves greater honour, than by protecting and assisting talent and genius.

Ros. And never, surely, did genius clothe itself in a more enviable guise, than in the person of Frankenstein. How different is the unassuming modesty of his demeanour, his winning gentleness, from the harsh pedantry and formal solemnity of schoolmen in general.

Prince. Theirs is the solemn mockery of mere pretension, which genius, such as Frankenstein's, despises.—The Universities of Germany have all bent to his prodigious talent, and acknowledged his superiority :—the prince who, conscious of his merit, rewards, assists, and forwards it, not only reaps the fruit of his sublime discoveries, but becomes the sharer of his immortality.

Ros. Oh ! may virtues and talents such as Frankenstein's, ever receive the patronage and protection of such men as the Prince del Piombino.

Prince. I rejoice that my dear Rosaura's admiration of this illustrious foreigner almost equals the enthusiasm of her brother's. Has her penetration ever hinted to her that last, that best, inestimable reward with which I meditate to crown my favours towards this Frankenstein ?—

Ros. (*Turning away*) Ah, my brother !——

Prince. That blush, that downcast look, assure me, that should my admiration of his merit induce me to confer on him a gift so precious as my sister's hand, I should not in her heart find an opposer of my generosity :—I will not tax your delicacy for a frank avowal, but in your silence read your acquiescence. This night, amidst the joyous mirth that fills our halls, will I hint to our philosopher, the dearer pleasure that I have in store for him.

Ros. My dear, dear brother !—A heart like yours will ever find the secret of making all around it happy.

[*Exeunt into Palace.*

SCENE II.

A Nearer View of the Outside of the Pavilion, appropriate, as Frankenstein's *study ; practicable door, and transparent window above.* (*dark.*)

Enter Frankenstein, *from the Pavilion.*

Fran. It comes—it comes !—'tis nigh—the moment that shall crown my patient labours, that shall gild my toilsome studies with the brightest joy that e'er was yet attained by mortal man.—What monarch's power, what general's valour, or what hero's fame, can rank with that of Frankenstein? What can their choicest efforts accomplish, but to destroy ? 'Tis mine, mine only to create, to breathe the breath of life into a mass of putrifying mortality ; 'tis mine to call into existence a form

conceived in my own notions of perfection ! How vain, how worthless is the noblest fame compared to mine !—Frankenstein shall be the first of men !—And this triumph is at hand ; but a few moments and it is accomplished Burst not, high swelling heart, with this o'erwhelmi tide of joy !

Enter JULIO. O. P.

Ju. Ah ! my dear sir, I have not seen you before, to day ; I am so glad to meet with you.

Fran. (*Abstractedly*) 'Tis well, boy.—Good even to you.

Ju. There are such doings in the palace ; such feastings, and such merry-makings, and all, as they say, for you.

Fran. Why that is better ; 'tis as it should be. Doubt not, I will be with ye. Let the full bowl high sparkle, let the joyous note swell loud ; I will be there, exulting in my triumph.

Ju. Aye, but moreover than all that, I could—but I don't think I shall, because it was told to me as a very great secret—I could tell you of something that would make you so happy.

Fran. I shall, I must be happy ; the secret is my own. Leave me, boy, leave me.

Ju. Nay, now, you do not love your poor Julio ; I'm sure I know not how I have offended you ; but you never spoke to me thus harshly before.

Fran. (*embraces him*) Nay, my pretty pupil, my affectionate Julio, I must love thee, ever. I am disturbed by intense study, and for a few moments I would be alone.

Ju. If you are sure you love me, I will leave you ; but if I had offended you, I would not leave you till you had forgiven me, I would not, indeed ; we shall see you anon. I shall know where to find you, by my pretty aunt Rosaura's side. Oh, if you did but know what I could tell you ! [*He runs off.* O. P.

Fran. The time is come, the glorious moment is arriv'd. Now, Frankenstein, atchieve the mighty work, gain that best of victories, a victory o'er the grave !

[*Exit into the Pavilion.*

Enter STRUTT, *with a Ladder, and* LISETTA.

Strutt. Well now, do you know, Lisetta, I'm going to do a great deal more for you, than I dare to do for myself. I'm dying to know what my master is about yonder, but if he should catch me peeping, what a jolly thump o' the head I shall get, to be sure; and then, Lisetta, you have it in your power to break my heart, and that's a great deal worse.

Lis. Well, now, without any more ado, you put the ladder against the window, and hold it fast, whilst I mount up and see what he is about.

Strutt. Fie, for shame, Lisetta, what are you thinking about? I'll get up the ladder, and I'll report all that I see, to you below.

Lis. Well, just as you please, only I'd rather peep myself, because, you know, seeing is believing. (Strutt *places the Ladder against the window of the Pavilion, mounts it, and peeps in; a faint glimmering of light is seen through the window.)* Well, now, what can you see?

Strutt. Why, I can see a little fire, and a great deal of smoke.

Lis. And I suppose all your boasted discoveries will end in smoke.

Strutt. Oh! now I can see better;—and would you believe it, Lisetta, from all I can see, I really do think, at least it seems so to me, that my master is making a man.

Lis. Making a man!—What is not he alone?

Strutt. Yes, quite alone. *(A strong and sudden flash of light is now seen at the window;* Strutt *slides down the Ladder.)* Oh, Lord! that's too much for me!—he's raising the devil—he's blown off the top of the pavilion! —Run, run, Lisetta, or the old gentleman will have you!

Lis. Nay, then the devil take the hindmost, I say!

[*They run off.* O. P.

SCENE III.

The Interior of the Pavilion.—Folding Doors in the Back. On a long Table is discovered an indistinct Form, covered with a black cloth. A small side Table, with Bottles, and Chemical Apparatus,—and a brazier with fire.

FRANKENSTEIN *is discovered, as if engaged in a Calculation.*

Fran. Now that the final operation is accomplished, my panting heart dares scarcely gaze upon the object of its labours—dares scarcely contemplate the grand fulfilment of its wishes. Courage, Frankenstein! glut thy big soul with exultation!—enjoy a triumph never yet attained by mortal man! *(Music.—He eagerly lays his hand*

on the bosom of the figure, as if to discover whether it breathes.) The breath of life now swells its bosom.—*(Music.)* As the cool night breeze plays upon its brow, it will awake to sense and motion. *(Music.—He rolls back the black covering, which discovers a colossal human figure, of a cadaverous livid complexion; it slowly begins to rise, gradually attaining an erect posture,* Frankenstein *observing with intense anxiety. When it has attained a perpendicular position, and glares its eyes upon him, he starts back with horror.)* Merciful Heaven! And has the fondest visions of my fancy awakened to this terrible reality; a form of horror, which I scarcely dare to look upon:—instead of the fresh colour of humanity, he wears the livid hue of the damp grave. Oh, horror! horror!—let me fly this dreadful monster of my own creation! *(He hides his face in his hands; the* Monster, *meantime, springs from the table, and gradually gains the use of his limbs; he is surprized at the appearance of* Frankenstein, *—advances towards him and touches him; the latter starts back in disgust and horror, draws his sword and rushes on the* Monster, *who with the utmost care takes the sword from him, snaps it in two, and throws it down.* Frankenstein *then attempts to seize it by the throat, but by a very slight exertion of its powers, it throws him off to a considerable distance; in shame, confusion, and despair,* Frankenstein *rushes out of the Apartment, locking the doors after him. The* Monster *gazes about it in wonder, traverses the Apartment; hearing the sound of* Frankenstein's *footsteps without, wishes to follow him; finds the opposition of the door, with one blow strikes it from its hinges, and rushes out.)*

SCENE IV.

Outside of the Pavilion, as before.

Frankenstein, *in great agitation, rushes from the Pavilion locking the door after him.*

Fran. *(After a pause of much terror.)* Have all my dreams of greatness ended here? Is this the boasted wonder of my science,—is this the offspring of long years of toilsome study and noisome labour? Is my fairest model of perfection come to this—a hideous monster, a loathsome mass of animated putrefaction, whom, but to gaze on chills with horror even me, his maker? How, how shall I secrete him, how destroy——? Heaven! to think that in the very moment of fruition, when all my toils were ended and I should glory in their noble consummation, my first, my dearest, only wish, is to annihilate what I have made! Horrible object. wretched produce of my ill-directed efforts! never must thou meet another eye than mine—never must thou gaze upon a human being, whom thy fell aspect sure would kill with terror! *(A tremendous crash is heard, the* Monster *breaks through the door of the Pavilion)* Ah! he is here! I have endued him with a giant's strength, and he will use it to pluck down ruin on his maker's head. *(Music.—The* Monster *approaches him with gestures of conciliation.)*—Hence! avoid me! do not approach me, wretch! thy horrid contact would spread a pestilence throughout my veins; touch me, and I will straightway strike thee back to nothingness!

The Monster *still approaches him with friendly gesturess*—Frankenstein *endeavours to stab him with his dagger, which the* Monster *strikes from his hand;—whilst the* Monster *is taking up the dagger, and admiring its form,* Frankenstein *steals off.—The* Monster, *perceiving him gone, rushes off, as if in pursuit, but in an opposite direction.*

SCENE V.

The heart of a gloomy and intricate Forest.—Tremendous Storm, Thunder, Lightning, Rain, &c.

Enter RITZBERG,—*and* EMMELINE, *bearing the* Child.

Em. The thunder's awful voice, and the fierce tumult of the wildly raging storm, have drowned thy plaintive wailings, my poor babe, and thou art hushed to silence. Sleep on, my babe, let thy mother's throbbing bosom shelter thee. We shall find him soon,—yes, I am sure we shall.—And when he sees thy ruddy smiling cheek, and marks his Emmeline's wan and haggard features, his heart will turn to us, he will again be all our own.

Ritz. I don't believe a word of it. Talk of his heart, indeed! he has no heart: if ever he had any, it has evaporated in the fumes of his diabolical preparations. He love and protect you!—all his affections are in the bottom of a crucible; and in the wild chimeras of his science, and the dreams of his mad ambition, all his human feelings are lost and annihilated.

Em. Oh, no! my father; the enthusiasm of knowledge, the applauses of the powerful, may for a time, have weaned him from us, but my own kind, gentle, Frankenstein, can never be inhuman.

Ritz. Can't he? Well, I don't know what you may call it; but to deceive and trepan a young, innocent confiding creature, as you were, and to leave you and your child to poverty and want, whilst he went rambling in the train of a prince, after his own devilish devices;—if that is not inhuman, I don't know what is.

Em. Ah, my father; I have heard that the Prince del Piombino has an estate in this beautiful island; that he has, attached to his household, a wonderful philosopher—I am confident 'tis he—and oh! my heart tells me, that he will shortly bless us with his returning love.

Ritz. Yes, and with this fine tale; and because I could not bear to see you pining away in hopeless sorrow, have you lured me to quit my quiet, peaceful abode in Germany, and come wandering over here to Sicily. And today you must march out on a pretty wild-goose chase, to endeavour to trace him in the household of this prince; till we have lost our way in the mazes of this forest, and can't trace a path back again to the hovel I have hired. And it's my belief, that if you found him in the Prince's palace, you would be driven away from the gate like a common beggar.

Em. Oh, say not so, my father; do not destroy my hope, for in that consists the little strength that now remains to me.

(Storm rages furiously.)

Ritz. And a pretty night this for a young, delicate creature like you, with your helpless infant, to be out in.—Curses, a thousand curses on the villain——!

Em. Oh, no, my father, no!—Do not curse him.—Curse not the husband of your Emmeline,—the father of her child!

Ritz. Well, well, I won't—the damn'd good-for-nothing vagabond!—I dare'nt stir a step in this plaguy forest, for all the storm keeps such a beautiful hubbub about us, for fear of straying further out of the way; and I am sure you have no strength to waste.—But here, I have it. You stay here, exactly where I leave you; give me the child, for you must be tired of carrying it, and I'll endeavour to find the path.—When I have traced it, I'll return for you.—There, stay here, just under this tree; it will afford a partial shelter. I warrant me, that with the assistance of the lightning, which keeps flashing so merrily, I shall soon discover the path.—I think I've got an inkling of it now. (*Takes the* Child *from* Emmeline, *and goes out as if endeavouring to trace the path.* U. E. P. S.)

Em. My spirits fail me, and my strength is exhausted. Whilst I bore the child, nature gave me powers, and I could not sink beneath the grateful burthen.—Ah, what a peal was there!—Heaven itself joins in the persecution of the hapless Emmeline.—Father, father! come to me!—I sink—I die—oh, Frankenstein! Frankenstein! (*She falls on the ground—the storm still continues to rage. The* Monster *enters in alarm and wonder, stares wildly about him; at length perceives* Emmeline *extended on the ground—is struck with wonder, approaches and raises her; is filled with admiration; expresses that the rain occasions inconvenience, and that the lightning is dreadful, his pity for* Emmeline *being exposed to it, his wish to procure her shelter; at length takes her up in his arms, and bears her off.*)

Re-enter RITZBERG, *with the* Child.

Ritz. Come, Emmeline, I think I have found it at last, and we shall be snug at home before the thunder can give another growl at us.——(*Perceives that she is gone.*) Merciful Heaven! not here! Where can she be gone? Surely no danger can have approached her.—She has wandered on, endeavouring to overtake me, and has mistaken the path, and so increased our troubles. Imprudent girl!—Emmeline, my child, my girl, my Emmeline

[*Exit with the* Child, *calling aloud.*

SCENE VI.

The Inside of Ritzberg's *Cottage.—Entrance Door in Flat; in some part of the Scene, a Fire-place.*

(*The* Monster *dashes open the door, and enters, bearing* Emmeline; *he places her in a chair, and looks round for some means of assisting her; perceives the fire, discovers by touching it, that it yields heat; removes the chair with* Emmeline, *to the fire, and remains watching her. The* Child *enters, on perceiving the* Monster *utters a shriek of terror, and runs across the stage, exclaiming,* 'Mother!—mother!' Ritzberg *then enters, is likewise alarmed at the appearance of the* Monster. *The* Monster *observes the* Child *with admiration and beckons it to approach him which the* Child *refuses to do; he then softly approaches the* Child *with gestures of conciliation, the* Child *endeavouring to escape from him.* Emmeline *utters a piercing shriek*

Ritzberg *snatches up his gun, fires at the* Monster, *wounds it in the shoulder. The* Monster *puts down the* Child, *who rushes to his mother's embrace; expresses the agony occasioned by the wound; the rage inspired by the pain! would rush on* Ritzberg, *who keeps the gun presented; it is deterred by fear of a repetition of the wound; rushes out of the hut;* Ritzberg *remaining on the defensive; whilst* Emmeline *thanks Heaven for the preservation of her child.*

SCENE VII.

A Landscape.

Enter JULIO.

Ju. I can't conceive what has happened to Mr. Frankenstein; when I spoke to him this evening, he was so cross, and so abstracted, and so mysterious; and now here my father, the Prince, has given a grand festival, expressly to do him honour, and he is no where to be found. I wish I could meet with him. I think he loves me, and I would coax him out of his gloomy humour, and lead him smiling and good-natured to my aunt Rosaura, or I'd know the reason why, I am determined. (*Music.—The* Monster *furiously rushes on.*) Ah! what dreadful gigantic creature is this? (*The* Monster *approaches and seizes him.*) Oh!—help,—mercy,—spare me,—spare me!——

(*The* Monster *expresses that his kindly feelings towards the human race have been met by scorn, abhorrence, and violence, that they are all now converted into hate and vengeance; that* Julio *shall be his first victim; he snatches him up and bears him off;* Julio *crying* 'Mercy!—help help!'

SCENE VIII.

Splendid Banqueting Hall in the Palace, open in the back upon the Garden, and giving a View of the Lake. Banqueting Tables, &c.

The PRINCE *and* ROSAURA *discovered, on a Throne under the centre Arch. Company of both sexes,* Attendants, &c. *A BALLET is performed, after which the* Prince *and* Rosaura *advance.*

Prince. I know not why it is, that he in whose honour this entertainment was expressly given, should so long absent himself from our revels. Surely, for one night he might have relaxed from his deep studies.

Ros. I think he scarce will tarry longer, for I have sent Julio in search of him.—Ah! he is here.

Enter FRANKENSTEIN, *in great agitation.*

Prince. At length you are arrived. Be assured, my friend, your absence has been both felt and regretted.

Fran. Accept my humble and sincere apology. I was engaged, most intently engaged, in the solution of a Problem, on the result of which I had much at stake. *(aside)* My every hope depended on it, and the solution has stamped me a wretch for ever!

Prince. A truce to study, now, and moody thoughts.—Let the grape's sparkling juice chace from your brain all dark chimeras; partake the joy that smiles around you:—anon, I have a proposal to make to you, that will not damp your mirth, I trust.

Fran. Aye, let me be joyous; let me seek joy even at the bottom of the maddening bowl; I cannot find it in my own heart.—Give me wine;—quick, let me drain a flowing goblet, perchance it may chace——oh! no, no, it can never drive from my remembrance that form of horror that exceeds conception.

Ros. From my hand will the cup bring less of joy?—Dear Frankenstein—I would say, learned sir, what means the dreadful wildness that gleams on your countenance?

Fran. Dear and most lovely lady, 'tis the intoxication of high swelling mirth, of gratitude, of animating hilarity. Fair lady, permit the humblest of your slaves to pledge you. (*He is raising the cup to his lips, when* Quadro *hastily rushes in.*

Quad. Oh, my lord, my lord!—such intelligence of horror!—the young prince, Julio, has been murdered!

Fran. (*Dashing the cup from him.*) Eternal Heaven!—that fiend has perpetrated it!

Ros. Julio murdered!

Prince. My boy! my pretty, innocent, affectionate boy! say where, how, by whom?

Quad. He was found in the pavilion where Mr. Frankenstein pursues his studies, the door thrown from its hinges: from the mark on his neck, he appears to have been strangled.

Fran. (aside.) Then my worst fears have proved too true!

Prince. How could that lovely child provoke his fate? Robbery was not the object. Who could have the heart to harm that unoffending, darling child!

Quad. Can your highness doubt?

Prince. Speak, what mean you? On whom do your suspicions fall?

Quad. Who should it be, but this foreign adventurer this Frankenstein?

Prince. Frankenstein!

Ros. Oh, Heavens!

Quad. Has any one else access to the pavilion, or ever presumes to enter it, or would have done now, except in eager search for the young prince?

Prince. I scarcely can believe it possible; but yet his lengthened absence from the festival at the very hour, his palpable agitation when he entered.——Frankenstein, what say you to this dreadful accusation?

Fran. I say that I am guilty, guilty a thousand times!

All. Ha!

Frank. Not of the crime of murder. I could not lay a finger in the way of violence on that lovely Child. Mine is a guilt a thousand times more black, more horrible. I am the father of a thousand murders. Oh! presumption, and is this thy punishment? has my promised triumph brought me but to this?

Prince. Frankenstein! for mercy's sake explain. What horrid mystery lurks beneath thy words?

(*Shots and noise of pursuit heard without—the* Monster *rushes in through the archway in the back, pursued by* Peasants *variously armed—all shriek with horror—he rushes up to* Frankenstein, *and casts himself at his feet, imploring protection.*)

Fran. Hated, detested fiend! now reeking with the blood of innocence—fiend of malice and destruction—here on thy hated head, I now invoke a father's and a prince's vengeance. Die, monster, die! and quit the life thou hast disgraced by blood and slaughter.—(*He seizes on the* Monster—*the guards close round—the* Monster *dashes* Frankenstein *to the earth, and by an exertion of his immense strength breaks through the opposing line—the* Prince *gives the word to fire—the* Monster, *snatching up the* Officer *holds him as a target before him—he receives the shots and falls dead—the* Monster *rushes up the steps of the throne and laughs exultingly—a general picture is formed, on which the Drop falls.)*

ACT II.

SCENE I.

A Cellar belonging to the Villa, entered only by a ladder from a small Trap-door above.

Strutt. (discovered) Well, my master has done a nice job for himself, it should seem, with all his machinery and magic; the making of a man has rendered him a made man for life, and I seem destined to share all his advantages. Because his hopeful bantling chose to amuse itself with strangling a child, much in the same way, I suppose, that our ordinary brats do kittens, out of pure kindness, they have seized hold of me and popped me into this underground apartment, to keep me out of mischief; as if they thought I shared my master's propensities, and had a *penchant* for making of men and strangling of children.—And so, after having taught me philosophy, my master has left me here to practise it. Now, if this were a wine cellar, there would be some kind of consolation; I might, by the magic of a butt of good liquor, convert this dungeon into a fairy palace, and when I could stand no longer, fancy these hard stones were silken cushions. But every thing now has the appearance of a cursed uncomfortable reality. Ha! I think I hear some one coming. I suppose it's old Quadro, who is about to set me at liberty, or at least to afford me the consolation of a flaggon of his best. *(The trap-door above opens, a ladder is put down, and* Quadro *descends, followed by* Lisetta.) Ah! how d'ye do; 'm so glad to see you. I hope you are come to bring me comfort in one shape or the other.

Quad. Oh, yes! the best of all possible comfort, the news of a speedy termination to all your miseries; you will very shortly be exalted, my fine fellow, elevated, tucked up, dance upon nothing.

Strutt. Don't mention it. I assure you such allusions are altogether unpleasant to my feelings; for though you may consider my master a bit of a mountebank, I assure

you that I have never been accustomed to dance on a tight rope; and as to hanging—*(to* Lisetta) oh! you dear little creature, I have dreamt of nothing but hanging round your neck—whilst for tucking up, I had hoped we should have been both tucked up together in the bridal bed, before this.

Lis. Oh! for shame, sir!

Quad. Oh! you did, did you? I can tell you that there is a very narrow bed in preparation for you, where you will find it most convenient to lie alone, and where you will be tucked up with the sexton's shovel.

Strutt. I am surprised at your mentioning such indelicacies before a young lady.

Quad. In the confusion occasioned by the appearance of his delectable companion, your pretty master effected his escape; but I took care to grapple you. I considered the nabbing of such a fellow as you to be in my department, and so I popped you into this cellar.

Strutt. It would have been much more handsome of you to pop me in the cellar where you keep the liquor.

Quad. And you will be hanged for having aided, abetted, and assisted your master in the formation of a monster, and as an accessary in the young Prince's murder.

Strutt. Signor Quadro, you shock me. Me accused of assisting to make a man! Let me tell you I was never before suspected of such an offence; not even by the beadle of our parish, and he was a sharp chap at nosing out such matters, I warrant ye.

Quad. But now, sir, you are in my clutches, you won't get off so easy you may depend on it.

Strutt. Oh, Mr. Frankenstein! Mr. Frankenstein! this is a pretty mess you have got me into, to stand god-father to your monster.—*(he sits down in the back.)*

Lis. Now, my dear father, how can you be so harsh to this poor young man? I don't really believe he had any hand in it; in my opinion, he would not be concerned in the making of any thing half so ugly.

Quad. Did not I say it from the beginning; did not I always insist that they were a brace of vagabonds, and that no good would come of harbouring them?

Lis. But now my own good, kind, dear father, seeing that what is done cannot be undone, and that hanging this young man would only make bad worse, could not you contrive to let him go?

Quad. Let him go, indeed! and what for?

Lis. Why just to oblige me, father; for really he is a tolerably well-behaved young man enough, and not so much amiss to look at.

Quad. Oh! you think so? And then, I suppose, the next think is that you must go with him, eh, you minx? Go and see him hanged if you like.

Lis. Now my dear, beautiful father, you don't know, though you are rather old, how well you look when you are doing a good-natured action. (*She makes signs behind his back to* Strutt, *to take advantage of the opportunity and run up the ladder.*)

Quad. You coaxing Jezebel! But don't think to wheedle me out of my duty.

Lis. Now look in my face. (*places one hand on each side of his face, as if to turn it towards her*; Strutt *watches his opportunity and silently ascends the ladder*) Look in my face, and frown a refusal if you can. Will you let him go?

Quad. No, I won't.

Lis. You are sure you won't?

Quad. No, I'll be damned if I do. (Strutt *has now gained the top of the ladder.*)

Lis. Then I'd advise him to do as I shall, to be off without asking your leave, and let you enjoy the comforts of this place by yourself. (*She runs to the ladder, and with* Strutt's *assistance hastily ascends it, after which they quickly draw up the ladder.*)

Quad. Why, you jade, you vixen, you undutiful hussey, what do you mean?

Lis. Only to let you stay there, father, till the young man is out of your reach; for I could not bear that you should have his death upon your conscience, father, I could not, indeed.

Quad. Go, both of you, and people the world with monsters, if you will; you can produce none worse than an unnatural daughter.

Strutt. Good bye, old gentleman!

Strutt *and* Lisetta *disappear with the ladder,* Quadro *rushes out in a rage on the opposite side.*)

SCENE II.

The inside of Ritzberg's *Cottage, as before.*

Frankenstein *rushes in, in great agitation.*

Fran. Where am I? Let me a moment pause collect my distracted thoughts—compose, if possible, this tumult of the brain. I have fled! and wherefore fled? Had not death been welcome? But then to perish on a scaffold—loaded with infamy—branded with a crime my very soul abhors—the murder of an innocent I would have died to save. No, no, it must not be—not yet. My life has been devoted to the fulfilment of one object, another now claims the exertion of its short remainder, to destroy the wretch that I have formed—to purge the world of that infuriated monster—to free mankind from the fell persecution of that demon. This, this is now my bounden duty, and to this awful task I solemnly devote myself.

Enter Emmeline *and* Child.

Em. A stranger here! Ah! can I believe my senses—am I indeed so blest, does he come to seek his Emmeline? My lord, my life, my Frankenstein!

Fran. What do I behold? Emmeline Ritzberg! Lost, guilty, cursed wretch! thy cup of crime and misery is full. Hell yawns for thee, and all thy victims now surround thee, calling down Heaven's vengeance on thy head.

Em. And is it thus? Is Emmeline's presence, then, a curse? Farewell, then, hope.—But we'll not persecute thee, Frankenstein, for with my child I'll wander where thou shalt never more be punished with remembrance of us, and where death will soon end our sorrow.

Fran. Emmeline! Emmeline! tear not my heart with words like those. What to a guilty wretch can be a greater curse than the presence of those he has injured? Now at thy feet behold me, Emmeline, in humble agony of heart, I plead for thy forgiveness. Oh! that I ne'er had quitted thy peaceful blest abode—ne'er let into my bosom those demons of ambition and fell pride, that now, with ceaseless gnawing, prey upon my soul

Em. Not at my feet, but in my arms, dear Frankenstein, lose all the memory of sorrows past. Oh! if thy heart still owns thy Emmeline, all shall be well, be happy.—One fond embrace of thine repays an age of sorrow; in thy smiles and those of this sweet cherub, I shall again awake to joy.

Fran. Oh, Emmeline, since we parted, all has been crime; crime of so black a dye, that even to thy gentle forgiving spirit, I dare not confess it. Crime, whose punishment will be unceasing, will be eternal.

Em. Oh, no, my Frankenstein, guilt, to be absolved needs but to be abjured. Returned to virtue and domestic peace, thy Emmeline shall soothe thy every woe, and on her bosom thou'lt forget thy griefs.

Fran. I dare not hope it. But in this land I cannot hope a moment's ease. Quick, let us fly—far, far from this accursed spot, the bane of all my peace. There, to that calm retreat, where first thy angel charms awoke my soul to love, there let us quick repair. Oh, that in former and in happier scenes, I could forget the guilt, the misery that I have since been slave to.

Enter hastily RITZBERG, *Door in Flat.*

Ritz. Ha! Frankenstein here! but 'tis no time to parley; the cottage is on fire! That fierce gigantic figure of terrific aspect, waves aloft his torch, as if in triumph at the deed. (*a coarse yelling laugh is heard.*)

Fran. Ha! 'tis that hideous voice! Quick, quick, let us fly! His hellish malice still pursues me; and but with his death or with mine, will this fierce persecution cease. Could I but place you beyond his power——! (*With* Ritzberg *he attempts to open the door, they find it barricadoed from without; the laugh is repeated---the conflagration has enveloped the whole building---*Frankenstein *rushes off as if in search of some other outlet—Part of the building breaks---the* Monster *enters at the chasm, seizes on* Emmeline *and the* Child, *and bears them through the burning ruins, followed by* Ritzberg. Frankenstein *returns, perceives that* Emmeline *and her* Child *are gone, and in despair rushes after them.*)

SCENE III.

A Landscape.

Enter STRUTT *and* LISETTA. (P.S.)

Strutt. Well, Lisetta, and now having by your assistance, escaped from the clutches of that cantankerous old father of yours. What is next to be done?

Lis. Why as I have got out of his clutches at the same time, and so lost my natural protector, what do you think you ought to do next?

Strutt. Why, I suppose you think I ought to marry you?

Lis. Whilst you, perhaps, are of a very different opinion.

Strutt. Not in the least, my angel; but then my poor master, he perhaps is in trouble, and requires my assistance; and to desert him in the hour of need, I could not do it, Lisetta, no, not to possess such a treasure as yourself.

Lis. And if you could I should despise you for it. But suppose, Mr. Strutt, we were both to go and assist him. Two heads, they say, are better than one, and so are two pair of hands: and instead of having one faithful follower he would have a couple, that's all.

Strutt. What, no, you don't mean it, do you? Will you really take me for better for worse, and go with me in search of my poor dear master? Well, I always thought you were a good creature, but now you're a perfect divinity, and I'll adore you.

Lis. Who knows, perhaps Mr. Frankenstein may get married to, and then he'll have better employment than making monsters.

Strutt. Oh, that monster! don't mention him, Lisetta. If he should be with my master now, do you think you would have the courage to face him? I'm not quite sure that I should.

Lis. Oh! never doubt me; if I take him in hand, I'll bring him to his senses, I warrant me; for if a spirited woman can't tame him, he must be a very fierce ungovernable devil indeed.—(*a scream is heard without.*)

Strutt. Ah! what means that shriek? See, yonder, where the demon comes, he bears with him both a woman and a child. She does not seem to have made much of a hand of him, at any rate. Here, back, back, conceal yourself, Lisetta, I would not have him come within arm's length of you, for the world. (*he pulls her behind a tree.*)

(*The* Monster *enters, exultingly bearing* Emmeline *and her* Child, *crosses and exit.* Frankenstein *follows him with a staggering step, almost overcome with fatigue and terror.* (P.S.) *to* (O.P.)

Strutt. (*coming from his concealment.*) What, ho! Sir! master! Mr. Frankenstein! 'Tis Strutt, your faithful servant! He hears me not, but madly still pursues the fiend he cannot hope to master.

Lis. And will you, too, Strutt, be mad enough to follow him?

Strutt. Why not singly, because I think it would be to little purpose; but I'll tell you what I'll do—I'll first bestow you in a place of safety, and then I'll summon together a few stout-hearted fellows, and we'll see if we can't settle his monstership; for sooner than he should harm that poor woman and her infant, damme, he shall kill and eat me—but I'll endeavour to give him a belly-full. [*Exeunt.* (O.P.)

SCENE IV.

A tremendous range of craggy precipices, near the summit of Mount Etna. On the P.S. *a conspicuous pillar of rock stands on a lofty elevation. The only approach is from the depths below.*

(*The* Monster, *with gigantic strides, ascends from below with* Emmeline *and the* Child—*she is so overcome with fatigue and terror as to be unable to speak---The* Monster *gains the elevation, and with a cord that is round his waist, binds* Emmeline *to the pillar of rock—He returns to the* Child—Emmeline *sinks on her knees in supplication*—Frankenstein *with great difficulty ascends from below—he perceives his* Child *in the* Monster's *power—he is about to rush on him; the monster defies him—and* Frankenstein, *recollecting his former defeats, abandons his threatening gestures and assumes one of entreaty.*)

Fran. Demon of cruelty, art thou still insatiate with the blood of innocence? how many victims does it require to content thy rage? I do implore thee, I, thy creator, who gave thee life, who endued thee with that matchless strength I cannot hope to master, I, on my knees, entreat thee but to spare that innocent. If fury and the thirst of blood be in thy hellish nature, on me, on me glut thy fell appetite—but, oh! if in thy human frame there dwells one spark of humun sympathy or feeling, spare, spare that unoffending child!

(*The* Monster *points to his wound—expresses that he would willingly have served* Frankenstein *and befriended him, but that all his overtures were repelled with scorn and abhorrence—then, with malignant exultation seizes on the* Child, *and whirls it aloft, as if about to dash it down the rock*—Emmeline *screams,* Frankenstein, *with a cry of horror, covers his eyes—at this moment a thought occurs to* Emmeline*- she pulls from under her dress a small flageolet, and begins to play an air—it's effect on the* Monster *is instantaneous—he is at once astonished and delighted—he places the* Child *on the ground—his feelings become more powerfully affected by the music, and his attention absorbed by it—the* Child *escapes to its father*—Emmeline *continues to play, and* Frankenstein *intently to watch its effect on the* Monster. *As the air proceeds his feelings become more powerfully excited—he is moved to tears: afterwards, on the music assuming a lively character, he is worked up to a paroxysm of delight—and on its again becoming mournful, is quite subdued, till he lays down exhausted at the foot of the rock to which* Emmeline *is attached.*)

(Strutt *now rushes on with* Ritzberg, *and a number of* Peasants *variously armed, and furnished with strong cords.*)

Strutt. There he is! that's him! that's my gentleman! and luckily for us, he seems in a bit of a snooze—now's our time or never. On him, my lads, and bind him fast, and then we shall be all right.

(*With* Ritzberg *and others, he immediately falls on the* Monster, *and they bind him stoutly with cords*—Frankenstein *has meantime released* Emmeline—*the* Monster *makes prodigious exertions of strength to burst his bonds, but he is overpowered by the number of his adversaries.*)

Strutt. Away, away, sir, and place the lady and child in safety. I'll take care and accommodate this gentleman with snug quarters, and return immediately to attend your commands.

Fran. Faithful creature! Eternal Providence, receive my thanks; and if it be thy pleasure to inflict on me an added punishment, oh! on this guilty head alone direct thy wrath; spare those who are most dear to me, those whose innocence may challenge thy compassion! (*With* Emmeline *and the* Child *he commences the descent, and disappears.*)

Strutt. Now I think the best thing we can do is to fasten my gentleman to this pinnacle of rock; the cool air of this exalted region may give him an appetite; but he will stand very little chance of getting it gratified, unless the lava should flow from the volcano, and that may be a kind of cordial for him. (*They are binding him to the rock, the* Monster *making a furious resistance, in the course of which he hurls one of the* Peasants *to the depths below.*)—That's right, make a tight job of it, whilst you are about it; for if he once gets loose, he'll play the devil with you all; he'd crack you like so many walnuts. There, I think he'll do now; there's not much fear of his troubling us again for one while. If he gets away from here, and finds his way down to terra firma again, I'll give him leave to drink hob-and-nob with me, in the cup I have filled to celebrate his overthrow.

(They descend the precipice by means of ropes and ladders, leaving the Monster *attached to the pinnacle of rock—when they are gone, he redoubles his efforts to escape from his bonds, and at length succeeds—he surveys the chasm, and is afraid to venture down it— he firmly attaches to the pinnacle one end of the cord by which he was bound—and by means of this lowers himself down the chasm.)*

SCENE V.

A Subterranean Passage hollowed in the Mountain.

Enter STRUTT *and* Peasants. (P.S.)

Strutt. Faith, my lads, it's cold work this, climbing so near the summit of Etna, in a chill evening breeze—yes, and fatiguing work too—catching such game as we've been after is no boy's play. Lord, what a chap my master must be, to be sure, when he was making a man—he thought he might as well have a wapper at once, I suppose. Now I say, a little and good for my money. But, however, we have quieted my gentleman, and I think we have done a much better job than my master did in making him. Aud now I can tell you a secret. This passage leads to the hermitage of father Antonio; that you all know, so that's no secret; but what you perhaps do not know is, that old Quadro, the Prince's [illegible]tler, whenever he visits the holy father to confess, alwa[illegible] brings a bottle or two of prime old wine, which is [illegible]ved by the hermit in lieu of penance; and so he makes his master pay for all his sins, and purchases absolution for one by committing another. Now do you know, I really think, that we better deserve this wine than the reverend father, and my proposal is, that we adjourn to his cave and drink to the future prosperity of the heroes who subdued the monster.

[*Shout, and exeunt,* (O.P.)

SCENE VI.

Interior of the Hermit's Cave.

STRUTT *and* Peasants *discovered seated round a table.*

Strutt. Well, upon my soul, it's a monstrous pleasant retreat. And now for the little store of choice Falernian.

Peas. (who has been hunting about the cave) Here it is, master Strutt; here's his reverence's holy water.

Strutt. Out with it, then, and in with it. If his reverence should miss it when he comes home, he knows where to get more. Old Quadro's sins will always keep his cellar well stocked. So now my lads, charge your cups—(Peasants *have meanwhile placed on the table several flaggons of wine, horns, &c.*) Now for it, fill all, and mind it's a bumper. *(all fill)* Here's confusion to any creature that would harm a defenceless woman and a helpless child; for be their shape what it may, they must be monsters indeed.

Peas. Bravo! with all my heart! *(all drink.)*

Strutt. And now I'll give you another. Here's our noble selves, and may all our future enterprizes be crowned with as complete success, as that which we have now so gloriously achieved.

(They have their cups raised to their lips, when the Monster, *still lowering himself by his rope, descends from an aperture in the roof of the cavern, and stands on the table in the midst of them—they all shrink back in terror with loud cries—the* Monster, *with one blow, dashes the table in pieces —all fly in extreme fear – the* Monster *in rage dashes about the seats—*Strutt *takes an opportunity to stab him in the back, and flies leaving the dagger in the wound—the* Monster *extracts it, and roaring with pain rushes off.)*

SCENE VII.

A narrow rocky Path-way, leading to the summit of Etna.

Enter STRUTT *and* Peasants *rapidly retreating from the* Monster—*the* Monster *follows in pursuit.*—Frankenstein *enters with* Emmeline—*they are followed by a party of* Soldiers, *whom* Frankenstein *encourages to the attack of the* Monster.

[*They all go off in pursuit, from* P.S. *to* O.P.

SCENE VIII.

The Summit of Mount Etna—the Crater occupies the middle of the stage—near it is the Path-way from below—in very distant perspective are seen the sea and towns at the foot of Etna—the Volcano during the scene throws out torrents of fire, sparks, smoke, &c. as at the commencement of an eruption.

(*The* Monster *ascends from below, faint from loss of blood and overcome by fatigue—he is followed by* Frankenstein, *whom he immediately attacks and stabs with the dagger he had taken from his wound—as* Frankenstein *falls,* Emmeline *rushes in shrieking and catches his lifeless body—the* Monster, *attempting to escape, is met at every outlet by armed* Peasantry—*in despair he rushes up to the apex of the mountain—the* Soldiery *rush in and fire on him—he immediately leaps into the Crater, now vomiting burning lava, and the Curtain falls.*)

FINIS.

Disposition of the Characters when the Curtain falls.

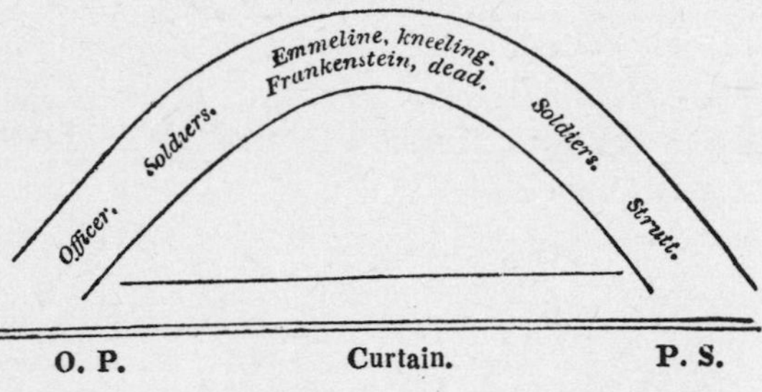

Theatre Royal, Covent-Garden.

This present MONDAY, April 20, 1829. a Play (in 3 acts) called The

POINT OF HONOUR.

The Chevalier de St. Franc, Mr. WARDE,
Durimel, Mr. C. KEMBLE,
Valcour, Mr. GREEN,
Steinberg, Mr. BLANCHARD, Zenger, Mr. ATKINS, Steibel Mr. J. Cooper
First Officer, Mr. Horrebow, Second Officer, Mr. Irwin
Keeper of the Prison, Mr. Crumpton,
Mrs. Melfort, Miss LACY Bertha, Miss JARMAN

To which will be added the Farce of

HONEST THIEVES.

Colonel Careless, Mr. DIDDEAR,
Captain Manly, Mr. HORREBOW, Mr. Storey, Mr. IRWIN,
Justice Day, Mr. EVANS,
Abel Day, Mr. KEELEY,
Obadiah, Mr. J. REEVE,
Teague, Mr. POWER,
Bailiffs, Messrs J. Cooper, Mathews, F. Sutton,
Coachman, Mr. Grant, Servant, Mr. Heath,
Ruth, Miss NELSON,
Arabella, Miss FORDE,
Mrs. Day, Mrs. DAVENPORT.

After which will be produced (*for the first time*) a New Musical Tale of Romance, called

THE DEVIL'S ELIXIR; or, the Shadowless Man.

With new Music, Scenery, Machinery, Dresses and Decorations.
The Overture and Music composed by Mr. G. H. RODWELL.
The Scenery painted by Mess. GRIEVE, T. GRIEVE, W. GRIEVE, and FINLEY.
The MACHINERY by Mr. E. SAUL. The Properties by Mr. KELLY.
The Dresses by Mr. HEAD and Miss ABBOTT.
THE ACTION ARRANGED BY Mr. FARLEY.

Francesco (*a Capuchin*) Mr. WARDE,
Count Hermogen, (*his Brother*) Mr. WOOD,
Nicholas (*the Bell Toller*) Mr. KEELEY,
Gortzburg (*Demon of the Elixir*) Mr. O. SMITH,
The Shadow King, Mr. PURDAY,
Oldburg and Stormworg (*his Agents*) Mr. HENRY and Mr. TETT,
Page, Master WATSON,
Spirits of the Elixir, Mess. Burke, Crumpton, Fuller, Goodson, May, Shegog, C. Tett, &c.
Domestics of the Count, Mess. Beale, Birt, Caulfield, Miller, Norris, S. Tett, Tinney, &c.
Mesdames Appleton, Brown, Clarke, Fenwick, Goodwin, Hudson, Nicholson, Parsloe, Perry, Phillips.
The Prior of the Silver Palm Tree Monastery, Mr. TURNOUR,
Bridesmen & Maids, Mess. Collett, J. Cooper, Grant, Heath, Matthews, F. Sutton
Mesdames Reed, Parsloe, Rountree, Ryalls, Shotter, Vials.
The Lady Aurelia, Miss HUGHES,
Ureka (*her Attendant*) Miss GOWARD.

In act II. a PAS de TROIS,
By Mesdames BEDFORD, EGAN, and THOMASIN.
BOOKS *of the Songs*, to be had in the Theatre, price 10d.

Tomorrow, Farquhar's Comedy of **THE RECRUITING OFFICER.**
Captain Plume, Mr. C. KEMBLE, Capt. Brazen, Mr. GREEN, Sergeant Kite, Mr. WRENCH,
Justice Balance, Mr. BARTLEY, Bullock, Mr. J. REEVE,
Coster Pearmain, Mr. KEELEY, Thomas Appletree, Mr. MEADOWS,
Sylvia, Mrs CHATTERLEY, Melinda, Miss CHESTER. Rose, Miss NELSON, Lucy, Mrs. GIBBS.
On Wednesday, **THE BEGGAR'S OPERA,**
Capt. Macheath, Mr. WOOD, Polly, Miss BYFELD.
With, (79th time) the Comedy of **CHARLES THE SECOND.**
King Charles, Mr. C. KEMBLE, Lord Rochester, Mr. WRENCH, Capt. Copp, Mr. FAWCETT.
Mary Copp, Miss GOWARD.
On Thursday, FARQUHAR's Comedy of **THE BEAUX STRATAGEM.**

Printed by W. REYNOLDS, 9, Denmark-court, Strand.

Theatre Royal, Covent-Garden.

THE SCENERY

Of the Devil's Elixir will be shewn in the following order:

THE MYSTIC CAVERN
OF THE SHADOW KING. GRIEVE.
Francesco's Cell. Finley
THE RELIQUARY CHAMBER
In the Silver Palm Tree Monastery. T Grieve
THE EXTERIOR OF THE MONASTERY,
AND ITS DOMAINS. T. Grieve
The Woodman's Hut and Forest. T. Grieve
The CASTLE of HARTZMERE,
And Forest in the distance. W. Grieve

Act II.

THE GRAND CHAMBER
IN THE CASTLE OF HARTZMERE. T. Grieve
The Interior of the Belfry,
IN THE MONASTERY. W. Grieve
THE SHRINE
OF SAINT ANTHONY,
Whose falling Ruins cause
THE DESTRUCTION
OF THE DEMON,
And shew the
MONASTERY on the Silver Palm Tree Lake,
The interior
Brilliantly Illuminated. Grieve

The Public is respectfully informed that
An authenticated Medical Certificate has been transmitted, announcing that
Miss SMITHSON,
is detained at *Amsterdam* by a severe indisposition—her appearance is therefore postponed till the first week in May.

Printed by W. Reynolds, 9, Denmark-Court Strand.

R. Cruikshank, Del. Bonner, Sc.

The Devil's Elixir.

The Demon Gortzburg. [*In a hollow voice.*] Brother!

Act I. Scene 3.

THE DEVIL'S ELIXIR;

OR,

THE SHADOWLESS MAN:

A MUSICAL ROMANCE,

In Two Acts,

BY EDWARD FITZ-BALL Esq.,

Author of The Pilot, The Earthquake, The Inchcape Bell, The Flying Dutchman, &c.

THE MUSIC BY G. H. RODWELL, ESQ.

PRINTED FROM THE ACTING COPY, WITH REMARKS, BIOGRAPHICAL AND CRITICAL; BY D——G.

To which are added,

A DESCRIPTION OF THE COSTUME,—CAST OF THE CHARACTERS, ENTRANCES AND EXITS,—RELATIVE POSITIONS OF THE PERFORMERS ON THE STAGE,—AND THE WHOLE OF THE STAGE BUSINESS.

As performed at the

THEATRE-ROYAL, COVENT GARDEN.

EMBELLISHED WITH A FINE ENGRAVING,

By Mr. Bonner, from a Drawing taken in the Theatre by Mr. R. Cruikshank.

LONDON:

JOHN CUMBERLAND, 6, BRECKNOCK PLACE,

CAMDEN TOWN.

Cast of the Characters,

As Performed at the Theatre Royal, Covent Garden, April 20, 1829.

Francesco, a Capuchin . . .	Mr. Warde.
Count Hermogen, his Brother .	Mr. Wood.
Nicholas, the Bell-Toller . .	Mr. Keeley.
Gortzburg, Demon of the Elixir	Mr. O. Smith.
The Shadow King { *Demons, Compounders of the Elixir,*	Mr. Isaacs.
Olburg, } *his Agents,*	Mr. Henry.
Stormburg,	Mr. Tett.
The Page	Master Watson.
Prior of the Silver Palm-Tree Monastery	Mr. Turnour.
The Lady Aurelia	Miss Hughes.
Urika, her Attendant . . .	Miss Goward.

Monks, Dancers, Servants, &c.

STAGE DIRECTIONS.

The Conductors of this work print no Plays but those which they have seen acted. The *Stage Directions* are given from personal observations, during the most recent performances.

EXITS and ENTRANCES.

R. means *Right*; L. *Left*; D. F. *Door in Flat*; R. D. *Right Door*; L. D. *Left Door*; C. D. *Centre Door*; S. E. *Second Entrance*; U. E. *Upper Entrance.*

RELATIVE POSITIONS.

R. means *Right*; L. *Left*; C. *Centre*; R. C. *Right of Centre*; L. C. *Left of Centre*; F. *the Flat, or Scene running across the back of the Stage.*

R. RC. C. LC. L.

*** *The Reader is supposed to be on the Stage, facing the Audience.*

THE DEVIL'S ELIXIR;

OR, THE SHADOWLESS MAN.

ACT I.

SCENE I.—*A Circular Cavern opening to the Sky, which appears moonlit, but stormy, with passing Clouds—a Rock of Crystal,* R., *reflecting the hues of a small flame, which burns,* L. C.—*over the fire hangs a cruise, containing the inscription "Elixir."*

MUSIC.—*The* SHADOW KING *discovered near the cruise, and two Imps blowing the fire with bellows, on which are magic characters.*

SOLO.

Blaze, blaze, thou spectre light—
Boil, compound dark and fell;
'Tis the hour, 'tis the night,
When the demon sprite
Hurries to the haunted dell.
Olburg! Stormburg! hither come.

[*Thunder—Enter* OLBURG, R., *and* STORMBURG, L.

All. Ha, ha, ha! brother!

[*They dip their cruises into the boiling elixir, and drink.*

TRIO.—SHADOW KING, OLBURG, *and* STORMBURG.

Ho, ho, ho! brothers three,
Fiends of mischief, here are we,
Quaffing the fell draught merrily.

Shadow King. The time has arrived in which to release my captive slave, who, condemned by St. Anthony's curse, hath slept a hundred years in the centre of yonder crystal rock. What! ho! Gortzburg, the time of thy penance has expired—thou most subtle of my spirits, awake! arise! the Shadow King commands thee to arise!

[CHORD.—*He strikes the rock, which splits asunder, and discovers the* DEMON GORTZBURG *in a forlorn attitude.*

All. Brother!

[MUSIC, *piano.—Gortzburg, as if roused from sleep, looks torpidly around—he stretches his limbs and wings—then leaps joyfully from the rock, and throws himself at the feet of the Shadow King.*

Shadow King. Ha, ha, ha! I, the King of Shadows, welcome thee! welcome to freedom and to vengeance. By a mortal malediction, consigned to yonder icy tomb, a mortal victim soon shall satisfy thy hate. [*Clapping his hands.*] Behold! [MUSIC.—*The back scene opens, and discovers Francesco, seated at a table, in his cell, by lamplight.*] 'Tis Francesco, the young monk of the Silver Palm-tree Monastery: of late, he hath wandered much from pious thoughts; and loves, in secret, Aurelia, his brother's betrothed bride. Hear me: Francesco is keeper of the reliquary, in which stands deposited the fatal cruise of that soul-intoxicating elixir, which, for offering to St. Anthony, thou wast doomed to a century of torpor. Weak-sighted mortals! out of their own precautions, work thou thy revenge—behold thy victim. [*Pointing up to Francesco in the cell,* L.C.] I see, by the malice flaming in thine eye, thou read'st my thoughts—no more. The moon begins to fade—we must all away.

[*Scene closes.*

CHORUS.

Away, away, through earth and sky—
On demons' wings, we fly! we fly!
With fell intent,
On mischief bent,
We fly! we fly! we fly!

[*The Shadow King ascends on a fragment of the rock—Olburg, Stormburg, and Imps, fly up—The Demon Gortzburg, with an attitude of denunciation, rushes out,* L.

SCENE II.—*Francesco's Cell.—A door in flat,* L.

MUSIC.—*Enter* GORTZBURG, L. D. F., *he advances with hurried strides, undraws the curtain, and discoveres* FRANCESCO, *sleeping on a pallet,* C. F.

Fra. [*Through music.*] Aurelia! bright vision! where art thou, Aurelia? [*Gortzburg waves his hand, and the form of Aurelia appears by the side of Francesco—she plays on the lute, and sings.*] There again, beautiful image! stay till I enfold thee to this burning heart.

AIR.—AURELIA.

Bright as sunbeams to the valley,
Like the shade of summer tree;
Pure as dewdrops to the valley,
So my love shall prove to thee.

[*He starts from his dream—the figure fades from his grasp, and the Demon exultingly vanishes.*

Fra. Gone! Alas, 'twas but a dream—a wild, deceiving dream; and Francesco, the love-stricken guilty Francesco, has only to cherish in secret his unhappy passion—till, like a canker in the bud, it consumes, destroys him. [*Loud knocking at the door,* R.

Nicholas. [*Without,* R.] Ho! good Francesco! ho!

Fra. Who, with this unusual violence, demands Francesco?

Nic. Open, pray—'tis I, Nicholas, the bell-toller.

Fra. Nicholas, at this unusual hour. [*Opens door.*] Now, Nicholas, enter freely.

Enter NICHOLAS, *tumbling in,* R. D.—*his dress in disorder, his nightcap on, and a lamp in his hand.*

Nic. (C.) Oh! a—h! Is that you, kind Francesco?

Fra. (L. C.) Truly, 'tis I—what wouldst thou?

Nic. Oh! I've been so terrified.

Fra. Terrified! at what?

Nic. I've been dreaming, all night long, about—about—oh, my heart! about the devil's elixir. Oh! [*Sighing.*

Fra. [*Laughing.*] Indeed: what do you know about devils' elixir?

Nic. Why, I know that our good patron, St. Anthony, took a bottle of it away by force, a hundred years ago, from the claws, [*Alarmed.*] the hands, I mean, of a certain gentleman, and locked it up in the reliquary chamber yonder—under I don't know how many seals, in order to prevent future mischief.

Fra. I confess I have heard something of this strange story before; and I also know there is a casket in the monastery, sealed as you describe, and covered with dust, which, it is reported, contains the famous flask of St. Anthony's wine; but neither my superstition nor my curiosity, although I am keeper of the relics, has ever led me to examine it.

Nic. Ah, Francesco, if, like me, you had ever been desperately in love—oh, bless you, I was once as tall as yourself, but love has wasted me like a taper, downwards: heigho!

Fra. Poor Nicholas! but what has your or my being in love to do with the devil's elixir?

Nic. Why, if a man drink but one drop of that diabolical compound, he becomes quite angelic, assumes the appearance of his most envied rival, and usurps his place in the affections of the mistress of his heart.

Fra. Indeed! instantly becomes like his most envied rival, and usurps his place in the affections of the maid of his heart? So the story goes [*Aside.*]—would I could possess myself of such a talisman, become like my brother Hermogen, and obtain Aurelia's love.

Nic. What did you say?

Fra. Who has put all these idle fancies into your brain, simpleton?

Nic. Simpleton! I learned the whole particulars from my grandmother, Howetz Wonwenzbrune, who knew things.—She had the honour of being burned for a witch—she was no simpleton, whatever I may be; besides, you must know, I'm the seventh son of a seventh son, and in my time have seen such noises and heard such sights as would make all your hair stand on end, like the spikes of a *shiver-de-freeze* fence. So, when I fell in love with Urika Kolgranx—the prettiest girl in all Saxony, who likes very tall lovers, and only laughs at me because I'm a trotting mushroom, as she calls me—then I began to long for a drop of the devil's elixir, and I should certainly have made a desperate effort to obtain it—I'm sure I should—had I not reflected on its conditions—oh, horrible!

Fra. Why, what are its conditions for the important service it renders you?

Nic. Frightful! during life you are to have no shadow, and when you die, instead of its being all up with you, it's all down with you. [*Points down.*

Fra. You had better retire to your pallet, my good fellow; trust me, honest prayers are much more likely to serve a lover's cause than evil spells.

Nic. Ah! that's all easy enough for them to say that hav'nt been dreadfully in love, like me: I'll warrant me, you'd soon alter your chime if you were but to fall in love with my pretty black-eyed Urika, for about five minutes, or with her mistress, the handsome Lady Aurelia, or with—

Fra. [*Starting.*] Lady Aurelia! why have you mentioned her name?—has any one dared to breathe?—

Nic. Mercy on me, what's the matter? I meant no harm, I'm sure; don't I know that Lady Aurelia is soon to be married to your good brother, Count Hermogen: I'll ring the bells merrily on that day, if I never ring them again—bless me, does any thing ail you, good Francesco—how pale you turn.

[*Holding the lamp to Francesco's face.*

Fra. Insolence! dare you attempt to peruse my features?

Nic. Oh no, I'm not learned enough to peruse any thing; I meant no offence; I was afraid you were suddenly indisposed—I—

Fra. Forgive this haste: [*Crossing to* R.] study and watching have changed my temper much, of late. Benedicite—oh, Aurelia! [*Exit abruptly,* R.

Nic. (C.) Oh, benedicite,—now I've got absolution, my heart does feel somewhat relieved. [*Going—returns.*] Only to think, I dreamt that I actually had swallowed a dose of that elixir, and that I had got no shadow; well, it would be no great loss. What if I should have walked in my sleep, and actually have done as I dreamt—I'm so nervous I don't know what I'm about. [*Setting fire to the tassel of his cap.*] Goodness preserve me, I don't see that I have any shadow—I've got no shadow, and flames of fire seem sporting all about my head—I'm bewitched, light-headed, undone—oh, help!—I've got no shadow.

[*Staggers out,* L.

SCENE III.—*The Reliquary Chamber.—A Gallery at the back, running from* R. *to* L. *with a grand Antique double Staircase,* C.—*Portraits of Saints, &c.—painted Windows in flat,* R. *and* L., *through which the moon shines.—Massy Volumes on Shelves in the lower part of the Chamber—Gothic Table and Chair, with a cloak on it —a very ancient Coffer, sealed, standing on the floor, in front of the Stairs,* C., *on which is inscribed* "DEVIL'S ELIXIR."

MUSIC.—*Enter* FRANCESCO, C. D. F., *in the gallery, with a lamp in his hand.*

Fra. What strange influence hurries me to this reliquary chamber—wild distraction guides my wandering footsteps. [*Descends.*] Alas! Francesco, was there none other to love, but only she, the fairest, the betrothed of thy brother? thy brave, happy, happy brother Hermogen. What if this cunning elixir, of which our monks, our

learned and pious monks, stand in such awe, guarding it like a pernicious treasure, really, truly, should contain the magic qualities they dread—oh, to possess Aurelia, loving as I love, would it be madness in me to seize the fatal cruise and drain it to the very dregs? what else shall quench the fire in my raging despairing breast—the casket—'tis somewhere here. [*Going up to the casket*, C. MUSIC.—*He holds the lamp to the inscription and reads it.*] Why does my heart palpitate?—what shakes me thus?—the saints appear to frown upon me—away with superstition; ought I to shrink from the inspection of a vain chimera, which it should be my pride, my duty, to expose? It shall be so; [*Rending the seals.*] the keys are here—[*Attached to his girdle.*—MUSIC.—*He unlocks the coffer, a light diffuses itself through the apartment, and a bottle of luminous red rises.*] 'Tis here! how luminous and fantastic; yet, what is there to daunt my resolution? Nothing—bid children tremble. [MUSIC.—*He snatches the cruise and advances, and, as he holds it up against the lamp, the* DEMON, GORTZBURG, *rises suddenly within the coffer, observing his actions.*] My hand seems frozen to the cruise. [*The portraits change.*] Great powers, do my eyes deceive me? the figures of the saints are changed to black infernals, threatening and denouncing. What have I done? [*Thunder.*] Back, back, ill-omened compound: be thou good or evil, Francesco fears thine influence. [CHORD.—*As he turns towards the coffer, it shuts, and, with the Demon, vanishes.*] Horror! the coffer disappeared! I dream—yet this cruise—frightful conviction—
[*Holding up the cruse and gazing at it.*

Enter HERMOGEN, R., *in the gallery.*

Her. Brother, brother Francesco!

Fra. Confusion! My brother Hermogen! Where to conceal this testimony of my weakness—there! [MUSIC—*He hastily places the cruise on table*, L., *and covers it with the cloak, as Hermogen descends the stairs*, L.] Thou here, brother Hermogen, at midnight?

Her. (L. C.) Yes, Francesco. A sudden and secret embassy in the service of my sovereign calls me for a short period from my home. On my route past your monastery, I have entered, to bid you, my brother, farewell.

Fra. Dear Hermogen!

Her. On my return, Aurelia has consented to become

my bride. Promise me, Francesco, that thou wilt join our hands, quit the monastery for a time, and witness the happiness which, shared with thee, trust me, will prove the greater.

Fra. [*Wildly.*] No, no, I cannot accept thy bidding!—must not—dare not!

Her. Dare not! You indulge too much of this strict penance, Francesco. Fasting and watching may be all good enough in their season, but a man isn't a chameleon, to exist upon air. You appear to me strangely altered in your looks of late; too much abstinence, my young hermit—depend on it, too much abstinence won't do. No, no; a little good eating now and then—ay, and a little good wine, too.

Fra. [*Alarmed.*] Wine! Are not such luxuries denied our order?

Her. [*Aside.*] Now, I suppose, I've hurt his sanctity. Yes, wine! Why, Francesco, how you tremble! This agitation—brother——

Fra. Fatigue, or, perhaps——

Her. Ah, you are destroying yourself with this watching, as you term it. I wish you'd never consented to lead a monastic life; you know I was always the first to oppose it. Look at me, how well and happy I am. What peace of mind can these gloomy cells offer you, equal to that which liberty, and the affections of my Aurelia, are capable of bestowing on me?

Fra. [*Wildly.*] Oh, Hermogen!

Her. Francesco, speak! This emotion—seat yourself. [*Hands the chair.*

Fra. [*Shuddering.*] Cold, cold as death!
[*Sinks into the chair.*

Her. Courage, courage—I'll cover you with this cloak.

Fra. [*Grasping his arm.*] No, no—forbear!

Her. [*Struggling, lets fall a miniature.*] Nay, I insist. [*Snatching off cloak, discovers the bottle.*] The devil!

Fra. Discovered!

Her. [*Laughing.*] Ha, ha, ha, ha! Wine, by Jupiter! Oh, Francesco! [*Gravely.*] Are not such luxuries strictly denied your order? Ha, ha, ha, ha!

Fra. Hear me: you know not what you utter.

Her. Perhaps I shall know what I taste.

Fra. [*Alarmed.*] Do not touch it—'tis a precious relic.

Her. Oh, well, if it's a relic—I know your scruples,

and e'en let it remain where it is; but, to my thinking, it looks very much like Syracuse wine. I do love a cup of Syracuse; however, if you promise to attend my nuptials, as I requested, keep your flask for your own private tippling; if you refuse, out goes the cork.

[*Approaching the wine.*

Fra. [*Hastily.*] Stay, stay—I comply with your demand.

Her. That's well said—now you look like yourself. So farewell to your sternly frowning cloisters and grim saints—I say no more. Now, then, beneath Aurelia's lattice, to cry once more adieu, then to my mission, and swift return to love and happiness. Farewell! Remember your promise. [*Exit up the gallery*, R.

Fra. [*After watching him out, sits dejectedly at the table*, L.] Yes; for you, love and happiness may, indeed, await; for me—— What is it he has dropped? [*Takes up the picture and crosses to* R.] Heavens! Aurelia's portrait! Those crimson lips—those blue eyes smile on me.[*Kissing the picture.*] Dear treasure, rest for ever next my heart! I'll cherish thee as the miser treasures up his gold—wear thee even in death. But have I ceased to remember who and what I am? Ah, fatal destiny! Yet, till I beheld Aurelia, I was happy—ah, how happy! The swelling anthem, and the heart-inspiring benediction, composed my every joy; now, the monastery has become a prison; my cell a dungeon—hope forsakes me. [*Crosses to table*, L., *and takes up the cruise.*] Mysterious draught! hadst thou magic in thee, I would entreat to become like Hermogen, to wear his form, and win Aurelia's love—hadst thou virtue to ease a moment's anguish, [*Hesitates.*] perhaps thou'lt give me *death.* [MUSIC—*pause.*] Yet what should I fear, already so lost in love, so wretched, and despairing:—The trial shall be made. Come, then, come, fatal potion! though for one instant, make me blessed as Hermogen, or, otherwise, I cannot be more cursed than is Francesco! [*Drinks—thunder.*

[MUSIC.—*Enter the* DEMON, GORTZBURG, *in the gallery*, R., *he appears suddenly on the top of the stairs*, C., *and exclaims, in a hollow voice*, Brother!—*The whole of the scenery sinks; the garments of Francesco fall off and disappear, discovering him dressed as Hermogen; Enter* OLBURG, R., *and* STORMBURG, L., *in the gallery, while it is falling—the Demons repeat the word*, Brother! *and vanish, leaving Francesco transfixed*, L. C., *while the scene changes.*

SCENE IV.—*Sunrise.—Rustic Bridge in the Foreground—A Cut Wood, and View of Hartzmere, in the distance.*

Fra. Wonderful powers! Where am I? Who am I? [*Seeing his dress.*] It is true, then, this elixir has changed me. Will it give me an Aurelia? If so, what have I to deplore? Liberty breathes around me like the perfume of these groves; love lights his beams in my heart, as the morning sun gladdens the hills with his golden light. Yet it must be that some demon mocks my senses. If so, juggling fiend, appear, and——

Enter NICHOLAS, *with a little bundle on his shoulder*, L.

Nic. Fooh! here I am at last.

Fra. [*Going*, R.] Nicholas here! I must avoid him, or——

Nic. Save your countship; pity a poor devil, who is without means.

Fra. Countship! For whom do you take me?

Nic. Do you think I don't remember Count Hermogen, whom I want so much to hire for my master, because he's going to be married to Lady Aurelia, my Urika's mistress? Pray do hire me, Sir Count, that I may live under the same roof with Urika Kolgranx; I shall require no wages, but bread and cheese and kisses.

Fra. [*Aside.*] 'Tis plain he doesn't recognise me—how is all this? Are not you Nicholas, the bell-toller of the monastery?

Nic. I am Nicholas, the bell-toller that was this morning, so please you; but the belle I desire most to ring is Urika Kolgranx; so I've just run away from my high church preferment, mounted my steeple-crowned hat, packed up my wardrobe in this pocket handkerchief, and set out in order to seek preferment in Urika's heart. I hope your countship won't go for to think that I've acted very improperly.

Fra. There are others in the world, who have acted exactly like yourself, Nicholas. But, if you are about to visit your mistress, you can doubtless inform me how far we are at this moment from the chateau Hartzmere, the residence of Lady Aurelia.

Nic. Scarce a quarter of a league from this woodman's hut. Don't your countship recollect that? [*Aside.*] Your great men are remarkable for short memories.

Fra. Yes, yes, I remember me now. I am proceeding to Hartzmere—you can follow me.

Nic. Bravo! I'm let! But doesn't your countship think a little better livery would be an advantage? I might find a suit big enough even in yonder cottage.—The old woodman there has smart sons, well-made fellows, like me; I dare say, for a few pieces, out of that well-filled purse which graces your countship's side——

Fra. A purse, too! [*Seeing the purse.*] So—here take money, and equip thyself; you'll overtake me on the way. [*Giving money.*

Nic. Here's advancement! A new doublet for thee, Nicholas! I'faith, thine elbows have been on the look-out for one long enough. You have only to tarry a moment, master of mine, and you shall see me as rapidly transmogrified, as if I'd swallowed a magnum of the devil's elixir, bottle and all. [*Exit,* L.

Fra. Sirrah——But I forget myself. Who comes here? Hermogen, as I live.

[*Runs behind the trees,* L. S. E.

Enter HERMOGEN, R."

Her. Farewell, my Aurelia!—farewell to the turrets of Hartzmere! Till we meet again, good angels hover round and guard thee.

BALLAD.—HERMOGEN.

I've seen and kiss'd that crimson lip,
With honied smiles o'erflowing;
Enchanted, watch'd the op'ning rose
Upon thy soft cheek glowing;
Nor ever deem'd thy beauty's spell
A purer charm could borrow;
But, oh! I had not then beheld
Thy parting look of sorrow.

Although, in nature's garland gay
A thousand hues be twining,
Can one surpass the snow-white flower,
Through dew-drops meekly shining?
Dear maid, thine eye may prove less blue,
Thy beauty fade to-morrow;
But, ah! my heart can ne'er forget
Thy parting look of sorrow.

[*Exit,* L.

SCENE V.—*A Forest.—The Woodman's Hut,* L.

Enter FRANCESCO *from the back,* R. S. E.

Fra. Strange that I, who have so often wandered through every intricacy of this dark forest, should now find my footsteps bewildered in its leafy mazes. But my mind is ill at rest—distracted. Why do I tremble to find myself alone? Guilt hath made a coward of my heart—the very rustling of the foliage scares me like a timid deer. Ah! have I wandered back to the woodman's hut? Nicholas! Nicholas, I say.

Nic. [*Within the Cottage.*] Coming, master! coming, sir count!

Fra. Hermogen again! Like an accusing spectre, he crosses my every path. Cover me, ye boughs—hide me from his just disdain! [*Rushes back behind the cottage.*

Enter HERMOGEN, L.—*he crosses to* R. *as* NICHOLAS *enters from the hut,* L.

Nic. There, count, how do I look?

Her. Fellow!

Nic. He doesn't know me—so much for fine clothes. I always said the tailor made the gentleman. Is it possible your countship so soon forgets an old acquaintance?

Her. Acquaintance! you!

Nic. To be sure: I'm not proud; I'm Nicholas—handsome Nicholas, as the girls call me: he's still in the dark: laud bless your countship's noncomprehensibleness, I'm not my own gentleman, not I—excuse my laughing—I'm only your gentleman.

Her. My gentleman!

Nic. To be sure; mine's all outside show: and, when I tell you I am the ass in the lion's skin, you must recollect me.

Her. Not I; I never beheld you till this moment.

Nic. He wants to get off taking me into his service, but it won't do: [*Aside.*] dear your excellence, didn't you just now hire me?

Her. Not to my knowlegde.

Nic. I'm Nicholas: you see I wanted nothing but a good dressing.

Her. Take it, then. [*Beats him violently.*

Nic. [*Falling.*] Oh! help! murder! I'm not your servant—I'm not Nicholas—I'm—[*Exit Hermogen,* L.]—Oh, my poor bones! gone—he may return: a precious service—indeed, I'll to my heels and run.

Enter FRANCESCO, L. S. E., *meeting him.*

Fra. Gone—I am no longer in danger.—Well, Nicholas, you cut a fine figure, indeed.

Nic. [*Staring, and in doubt.*] How's this? he comes in here, and he went out there?

Fra. Are you not satisfied!

Nic. [*Rubbing his back.*] Oh, yes, perfectly.

Fra. Do you not already retain sufficient marks of my favour.

Nic. That I do, your countship, in black and blue, I'll be sworn. [*Aside*] it's the devil I've let myself to, and I've got his coat on—flame colour, too!—oh, dear! how shall I get out of this scrape?

Fra. Follow in my train.

Nic. Follow his train—that means his tail, I suppose. Yes, master, I will. [*Stepping the contrary way.*

Fra. Is that what you call following? why, you are going the contrary way.

Nic. Bless me! so I am, I declare.

Fra. Do you forget who I am?

Nic. [*Aside.*] No, indeed, I don't. He wants an excuse to pummel me again: he, he! I don't forget that your grace's mightiness never beheld me till this moment.

Fra. [*Beats him.*] Knave! take that, and that, and remember, the next time you attempt these sort of jokes, to practise them on persons less irritable than your new master. [*Exit*, R.

Nic. O—h! o—h! between the trimming of the one, and the basting of t'other, never was livery so laced as mine: I'll be sworn, my back is as striped as that of a zebra. My new master—I strangely suspect he's the old one in disguise; but, if he should really and truly be Count Hermogen, it were folly in me to lose my place. I wonder whether he has a shadow—how stupid in me not to observe; if he has a shadow, then he's flesh and blood, like myself; if he has no shadow, he's the unmentionable one: but I'll follow, at a distance, and observe—if it should be my master, I'll brazen it out.—I've got impudence enough to outface the very devil. Ha, ha, ha! [MUSIC.—*He is about to follow* FRANCESCO, *when the* DEMON GORTZBURG *starts from behind a tree and suddenly appears before him.*] Oh! [*Staggering off*, L.] That's somebody what's got no shadow. [*Gortzburg disappears*, R.

SCENE VI.—*The Castle of Hartzmere, entered by an Archway*, L.,—*over the Archway a Verandah, on which are Orange-Trees, in Vases of Porcelain, and a practicable window, covered with a Venetian blind*, L., *in flat.—A Rose-Tree*, L.—*The Forest of Hartzmere at the back*, R.

Enter AURELIA, *from the grotto*, R.

SONG.—AURELIA.

I hear him,—yes, returning, 'tis the accent of my love:
Ah, no, 'tis but the nightingale, which sings in yonder grove.
Too silly bird! too silly bird! had I but wings as thou,
I'd fly away and seek my love beneath each greenwood bough;
And, by his side, I'd wander through the daisied meadows gay,
While hamlet bells were ringing, in the merry month of May.

I hear him—yes, I hear him—gentle throbs my bosom swell,—
Ah, no, 'tis but the murmur of the streamlet in the dell.
Too silly stream! too silly stream! if I like thee could roam,
On every bank I'd seek my love, 'neath every flower in bloom;
And, by his side, I'd wander through the daisied meadows gay,
While hamlet bells were ringing in the merry month of May.

Enter URIKA *from the Castle*, L.

Uri. Ah, my dear young lady! what can possibly render you so melancholy? so soon to be married, too; the anticipation of a wedding always puts me into delightful spirits. I prophesy the count will return much sooner than you expect; in the meantime, wouldn't it be far more agreeable to be admiring your bridal dresses, than to be pining in sad solitude, and heaving heighos to every flower in the forest?

Aur. I had an ill-omen'd dream last night, Urika:

methought the wedding-ring, which Hermogen press'd on my finger at parting, chang'd to a fiery serpent, which encompassed me in its terrific folds.

Enter FRANCESCO, *in the background, listening.*

Uri. You screamed so, in your sleep, that even I, who am no coward, was frightened almost out of my wits: it was, indeed, a strange dream; but I have no faith in dreams; I've been dreaming of a husband for these four years, and hav'nt so much as received a single offer, except from little Nicholas, the bell-toller: and see, my lady, as I foretold, here is the count already, returned in safety.

Aur. Already returned—so unlooked for—ah, my dear Hermogen! welcome! welcome!

[*Francesco advances, she rushes fondly into his arms.*

Fra. What transport! thus welcomed by Aurelia.

Aur. (C.) A thousand apprehensions had inspired me in thine absence: the torrent which, at this season of the year, is apt to overflow its banks—the banditti, said to haunt the borders of the forest——

Fra. All these dangers have I avoided, by sending on my embassy a trusty messenger in my stead, that I might fly back to love and Aurelia.

Aur. Dear Hermogen!

Fra. To-morrow, Aurelia consents to become my bride?

Aur. Can my heart deny thee? But, enter now the castle: welcome, welcome, my loved Hermogen!

Fra. Oh, joy! oh, ecstasy.

[*Exeunt Francesco and Aurelia into the Castle,* L.

Uri. So, now we are coming to the end of the chapter: the count has but to return, a bachelor, to his own chateau once more; to-morrow night, he will be lord and master here, and my lady a happy bride. I'm to be bride's-maid. By the bye, I've no time to lose—I must be thinking of the bridal wreath. I may as well gather the roses now,—they say, they should always be plucked before the moon rises or the evening dew falls. A bouquet for myself, too. [*She plucks the roses,* L.—*Evening.*

MUSIC.—*Enter* NICHOLAS, R., *his dress soiled and torn.*

Nic. 'Tis my darling, Urika, gathering a rose: I dare say, she's thinking of me.

Uri. [*Singing.*] Fal, lal, la, la, lal, la! A rose, jasmine, a lily [*Stooping.*] of the valley. [*Screams.*] Oh, that horrid ugly toad!

Nic. Ugly toad! oh, then, she can't be thinking of me.

Uri. The saints defend me! what queer little man are you?

Nic. Your queer little man, Urika; don't you know me?

Uri. That insignificant wretch, Nicholas, I declare. Why, what, in the name of patience, do you want here?

Nic. I'm coming to be your fellow-sarvant: I've hired myself as the count's head man. Instead of my ringing the bell, in future, the bell is to ring for me.

Uri. You! such a booby!

Nic. Ah! but, booby as I am, I saved the count's life, within this half hour.

Uri. You! impossible.

Nic. But I say it's all possible. The count was crossing the ford, when the force of the torrent swept him off his horse; his other servant couldn't swim, but I could, like a frog—so in I plunges, and drags out his countship by the skirts.

Uri. Indeed; and pray where may the count be at this moment?

Nic. At the woodcutter's cottage, changing his wet clothes; while I came forward, to prevent alarm.

Uri. I tell you what, Mr. Nicholas: when I knew you first, at Konizburg, you were always accounted the biggest pilferer in the village; it's my belief, you've joined the robbers in the forest, and have come hither, with this pretty story, to rob this mansion; but know, to your confusion, you pitiful sirrah, that the domestics are well armed; and, what adds more to your shame, is, that the count is at this moment in the castle.

Nic. (L. C.) Nay, but, Urika, it can't be; I—

Uri. Go along about your business—don't touch me—I despise you more than ever I did. In pity, I shan't send out the butler, with his long fusee, to shoot you; but, if you remain more than five minutes, you are a dead man. [*Exit,* L., *closing the door.*

Nic. I'm a dead man! she despises me more than ever—the count already arrived—what does it all mean? Oh, it's only done to intimidate me—she and her butler with his fusee. But here comes the count, and now she'll soon tell a different story.

Enter HERMOGEN, *in the dress of a fisherman*, R.

Her. Have you announced my return and safety?

Nic. It was unnecessary, because, I can assure you, from the first authority, that your countship is already in the castle.

Her. This is some blunder of yours.

[*A bell ringing at the castle door*, L.

Nic. [*Aside.*] It's all right—he's got a shadow; if I hadn't seen his reflection in the water, he might have gone to the bottom for what I had cared. There's the fusee!

Enter Servants and URIKA, *on the verandah, presenting a fusee—Nicholas runs out frightened*, R.

Her. 'Tis I, Count Hermogen—open the door.

Uri. [*On verandah.*] Impostors! you are detected. As you would avoid the anger of the count, fly and save yourselves. [*Exit*, L.

Her. Insolent! stay!

FINALE.—CONCERTED MUSIC.

Her. (C.) Repelled! and from Aurelia's door;
Distraction, sure, my mind consumes!

[*The Venetian blind is drawn up, and discovers Francesco and Aurelia at a banquet, in flat*, L.

A stranger in that banquet bower—
And, horror! he my form assumes.

Aur. Silent night and listening grove,—
Mark—oh, mark, the song of love!

[*Shuts the blind.*

Her. To him, that strain-afflicting sound!

Nic. [*Running in* R. *with a ladder.*] Master, see what I have found.

Her. This way—this way.

Both. Without delay.

[*Nicholas places the ladder against the verandah*, L.

Her. Soon on yon head be vengeance poured—
Now, hated rival, dread my sword!

[*Ascends and enters castle.—Nicholas beats his breast and follows—as he reaches the summit of the ladder, the Servants, armed, enter the balcony—while Nicholas, terrified at the sight of a fusee, falls down the ladder, dragging with him the orange-trees with a crash.*

Ser. Ruffians, ruffians, disappear!

Nic. [*Falling.*] O—h! oh dear!

Nic. [*Getting up and limping.*] Oh, my back! my head!
Murder! I'm dead! I'm dead!
Oh!

[*They fire a fusee—Nicholas runs off*, R.—*Servants retire*, L.

Enter Domestics hastily, from the Castle, with lights, and armed.

Cho. This dreadful tumult! consternation!
Oh, sight of fear! oh, desolation!

Enter HERMOGEN *and* FRANCESCO, *fighting*, L., *Aurelia parting them.*

Aur. Mercy, help—forbear, forbear—
Hear, oh hear, Aurelia's pray'r!

[*Hermogen is held.*

Enter Attendants.

Her. [*Struggling*, R.] Coward! think not woman's tears
Shall aid thy life, or shield thy fears.
Coward!

[*Breaking away, and striking Francesco—they re-encounter, and fight off*, R.

GRAND CHORUS.

Oh, hour of woe! oh, consternation!
Thunder crashing,
Lightning flashing,
Oh, misery! oh, desolation!

[*The storm rages—Aurelia faints—Servants pass to and fro with torches, and the* DEMON GORTZBURG *appears with a torch of flaming fire in his hand, forming a picture of consternation.*

END OF ACT I.

ACT II.

SCENE I.—*A magnificent Apartment in the Castle of Hartzmere, with a large window, discovering the tops of forest-trees,* R.—*A couch, flowers, &c.,* L.

AURELIA *and* URIKA *discovered, watching the flashes of lightning, which are visible through the window,* C. F.

TRIO—AURELIA, URIKA, *and* PAGE.

Aur. Night still thickens! fiends of thunder
Battle through the cloudy air;
Forest-boughs are cleft asunder;
Nature mocks my wild despair.

Enter Page, through the window, C. F.

Aur. Ah, what tidings?
Page. [*Turning aside.*] Still, he comes not.
Aur. Kill me, lightnings from the sky;
Uri. & *Page.* Calm thee! calm thee!
Aur. [*Weeping.*] He is absent: kill me, &c.
Uri. & *Page.* Do not weep so.
Aur. Let me die.

DUET—URIKA *and* PAGE.

Dearest lady, calm this sorrow,—
Let not grief thy bosom tear;
Peace shall sweetly smile to-morrow:
Calm, oh calm, this wild despair.

[*The* DEMON GORTZBURG *flies past the window from* R. *to* L.—*A storm.*

TRIO.—AURELIA, URIKA, AND PAGE.

Nature rages; fiends of thunder
Battle through the cloudy air;
Forest-boughs are cleft asunder—
Heaven save us from despair.

[*Pause—music dies away, then becomes more animated—A cry without,* "The count! the count!"

Aur. [*Seeing Francesco,* L.] Ah, tis he! my lord! my love! my life! [*Rushing towards him.*

MUSIC.—*Enter* FRANCESCO, *hastily, with his sword drawn,* L.

Fra. (L. C.) The furious sword of my opponent had well nigh stricken me down, when our attendants rushed forward: their numbers compelled him to fly.

Aur. (C.) Thank heaven!

Fra. How my heart throbs, and my temples burn: demons seem to haunt me; the vivid lightning scorches me; save me, angel, save me! thou—— [*Falling wildly at her feet.*

Aur. [*Supporting him.*] What ails thee, love? Speak, Hermogen,—'tis thy Aurelia.

Fra. To hear thy voice, and not reply, Aurelia, were to be dead to heaven's own melody: say on, fair creature,—let the hallowed accents of those lips, expanding like the rich perfume of consecrating censors, disperse the unhallowed forms that chased me, even to the sanctuary of these arms. [*Crosses to* R.

Aur. Ah, that deadly paleness: wine there, Urika: quick! he swoons! he dies!

[MUSIC.—*The Page, having brought in wine, Urika kneels,* L. C., *and holds the goblet—at that instant The* DEMON, GORTZBURG, *rises behind her,* L., *and fills the goblet from the devil's cruise.*

Fra. (R.) Horror! there, there again!

Aur. (C.) What alarms thee?

Fra. Seest thou nothing, Aurelia? Thrice it crossed me in the forest; the demon! does it not startle thee? See, see there, Aurelia! [*Pointing to* L.

Aur. I see but Urika and the Page.

Fra. Thou art innocent, but I—does not this goblet overflow with liquid fire? Do these treacherous eyes still, still deceive me?

[MUSIC.—*Aurelia takes the goblet from Urika, out of which ascends a blue flame.*

Aur. But in thy wild imagining, the horror that thou speak'st of lives: neither fiend nor flame is here. Drink, Hermogen, and heaven will bless the draught.

[*The Demon vanishes—distant thunder heard.*

Fra. [*Taking the goblet, which is still flaming.*] It must be—this is frensy, all; yes, I will drink—Aurelia's hand can minister naught unholy. To thee I drink, Aurelia.

[MUSIC.—*He drinks—the Page crosses to* R., *receives the cup from him, goes off with it,* L., *and returns—the sky appears blue, and moonlit.*] It refreshes me: my heart palpitates with new rapture.

Aur. Blessed sounds! Open the casement—admit the pure reviving air. [*Urika opens the window,* C. F.] Lo! what a beamy sky. Love's mariner, the moon, hath launched her silvery vessel on the blue sea of night: be thou calm as she, Hermogen.

Fra. Beautiful Aurelia! come, seat thee by my side, —here, in this gay alcove, the sweet flowers twining around us, like love around our hearts, and I'll breathe to my Aurelia vows so tender, that spirits, as they pass, shall pause to listen, and wish such orisons were raised to them.

Aur. Meanwhile, that every heart may share Aurelia's joy, spread the rich banquet—weave the festive dance.

Enter Attendants, bringing in tables, with banquet, &c.—Francesco leads Aurelia to a seat at the table, L. U. E.

MUSIC.—*Enter* DANCERS, R., *who perform a waltz.*

Enter HERMOGEN, R., *at the conclusion of the dance, in his original dress—the Dancers start, and point him out to Francesco, who advances,* L. C.

Fra. What stranger art thou that stealest thus unbidden to our feast—thy name?

Her. Shall I utter it aloud, that all may hear? What if I say,—Francesco!

Fra. In these bright halls, oh, utter not that name: Francesco lives no longer; he's dead.

Her. (R.) And Hermogen?—

Fra. (L.) Who says I am not he?

Her. I'll prove thee what thou art. [*Going.*] Let him not escape.

Fra. [*To the Attendant.*] A betrayer!

Aur. [*Coming wildly between them.*] Frenzy fires my brain: here are two, yet one so like the other, that both seem Hermogen.

Her. Dearest Aurelia, I am he, thy love; look on me, Aurelia.

Aur. Ah, well thought! he that is my Hermogen, let him show the miniature, the semblance of myself, which I at our last parting gave.

Her. [*Aside.*] Oh, fatal loss!

Fra. 'Tis here, here, in my bosom cherish'd. [*Shows it.*

Aur. [*Rushing into his arms.*] My Hermogen, my husband, shield me, save me.

Fra. Drag hence yon miscreant! [*Attendants seize Hermogen.*

Her. Misery! misery! speak for me, Aurelia; know'st me not thou? for, oh, I think, were there an hundred Aurelias present in others' eyes, in my eyes there could be but one Aurelia, and thou thyself that she.

Fra. Away! away!

Enter NICHOLAS, *running,* L.

Nic. Stay, stay, I'll soon set this all to rights, I promise you.

Uri. You, indeed! ha, ha, ha!

Nic. Yes, I indeed, madame pert: [*Aside to Urika.*] you bring forward that silver lamp—there, now hold it, just so, and I'll soon show you which is my master.

Fra. Begone!

Aur. Nay, pardon my curiosity—my fears, my anxiety: Urika, do as he desires. [*Urika holds up the lamp.*

Nic. Now observe! [MUSIC.—*Nicholas walks before the lamp, and his shadow passes on the wall.*] Well, what did you see?

All. Nothing.

Uri. Nothing, but your silly self.

Nic. (R.) Look again; [*Walks as before.*] there, don't you see my silly self's shadow.

Fra. [*Aside.*] A—h!

Uri. What of all this?

Nic. What of it? this of it: he that's my master has got a good substantial shadow to his heels; and he that is not my master, yet so exactly like him, must have drunk "devil's elixir," as grandmother used to say, and lost his shadow.

Her. Instant to the proof.

[MUSIC—*Passing the light, his shadow appears,* R.

Nic. Huzza! huzza! this is the real count! this is my dear flesh-and-blood master: only look at the other, [*Pointing at Francesco.*] how he shrinks back—he's afraid—he's a coward: ha, ha, ha! [*Laughs.*]

Fra. [*Drawing his sword,* L.] Dog! this temerity! die!

MUSIC.—*Francesco rushing across to Nicholas,* R., *they all look for his shadow, but seeing none they recoil from him, while he appears rivetted to the spot.*

Nic. Bravo! where's the shadow! oh dear, I begin to be alarmed.

[*Staggers out with Urika, terribly alarmed*, R. U. E.

Fra. Confusion! have I rushed madly into the snare? let me not meet Aurelia's looks: lost wretch that I am, hide me, for ever—to a dungeon lead me!

[*Exeunt Francesco*, L., *Hermogen and Aurelia*, R. *followed by Attendants.*

SCENE II.—*Interior of Ancient Belfry, with a suspended Lamp.*

FRANCESCO *discovered on a bed of straw, in flat*, L.

Fra. [*Rising.*] How awful has solitude become to me: Francesco a prisoner! [*Advancing.*] Too soon will my gaolers return, armed with monastic power, to extort confession from these guilty lips: ruin and shame await me: oh, Aurelia, Aurelia! and all this I endure for thee, while thy heart can never sympathize in my tortures. What's this struggling at my breast: Aurelia's picture: I'll not gaze on thee again; away, sweet sorceress! I'll dash thee from me, and for ever.—Yet wherefore should I? is beauty Aurelia's crime? one fond parting look—but this place—so dark, so dismal—dim as the night of death to lovers' eyes—would it were light as day. [*Looks at the picture.*—MUSIC.] Ah, Aurelia's name has magic in its tone: morning's light, as 'twere, obeys its potent spell; what marvel Francesco is Aurelia's slave! Who would not consign life's best enjoyments to hang one instant on the ripe delicious crimson of these honied lips?

[*Kissing the picture—the Demon Gortzburg appears suddenly*, R., *and, pointing mysteriously to the lamp, it beams with radiant light.*

Gor. [*In a hollow voice.*] Brother!

Fra. Ah! how horrible, to turn from the contemplation of this to thee! Fearful being, why callest thou me brother?

Gor. [*Taking from under his dress the Devil's cruise.*] All who drink of this become brothers in iniquity, why not in name?

Fra. Avaunt, and leave me; penance and tears shall absolve me. [*The Demon laughs, and points to Aurelia's portrait.*] This thy spell: I'll trample on it: I'll—[*Gazing at the picture.*] Aurelia, I have not the courage to resign thee: I cannot even struggle.

Gor. Why not possess the original?

Fra. How?

Gor. Confirm our contract by an oath.

Fra. Do demons require oaths?

Gor. Ay!

Fra. Then I am not wholly lost: I can still return to—

Gor. To despair. Behold! witness thy brother's dreams.

MUSIC.—*The Demon waves his hand, advances to the back scene*, R., *it opens, and discovers Aurelia dressed as a bride, playing on a lute, Hermogen lying on a couch, and Nicholas reposing at his feet—a soft peal of bells heard.*

Fra. (L. C.) Horror! Aurelia already attired as the bride of Hermogen: the bridal peal rings in mine ears—fly, demon; snatch her from his arms,—make her mine.

Gor. On one condition.

Fra. Name it.

Gor. Ere the convent clock strike eight, at twilight, I promise thee Aurelia as a bride—if thou refuse her hand ere that hour, swear to become, with the last stroke of the clock, my slave for ever.

Fra. As Francesco never can refuse the hand of Aurelia, he fears not to swear: I swear!

Gor. Enough; we meet at eight!

Fra. Bear me to Aurelia's feet.

Gor. Ha, ha, ha! [*Laughs.*

MUSIC.—*The Demon touches Francesco's breast—he falls on a straw pallet in flat*, L.—*A cloud passes, and as it disappears, Francesco is discovered on the couch*, R. *in flat, in Hermogen's place, while Hermogen and Nicholas appear on the straw bed of Francesco*, L. *in flat—the scene* R. *in flat closes, and the Demon vanishes*, L., *during a peal of thunder.*

Nic. [*Lying on the straw bed*, L. *in flat.*] Yaw! what the deuce ails me? if this comes of sleeping on a page's cushion, I'd much rather lie on my straw in the old belfry again: [*Getting up, and rubbing his eyes.*] I'm certainly troubled with the night-mare: tossing and tumbling—tum—toss—eh! why, where am I? Oh dear! Mas—master!

Her. How now, Nicholas, whence that cry—heavens! what place is this? do I dream? yet this is straw on which my limbs repose: this wretched hovel for my gilded chamber! [*Rising, and coming forward,* L.] What base treachery has conveyed me hither?

Nic. (C.) In my opinion, the devil whisked us hither in a whirlwind. Sure, I should know these rafters—yes, this is my own bell-rope; we are locked up in the old belfry—the very place where the prior ordered your countship's double to be confined. Oh dear! They said he'd be burned for a sorcerer. If they should be after burning your countship in his stead, they'll be after singeing me as your familiar.

Her. (L.) Frightful reality! Can it be permitted that bad spirits triumph over pure and virtuous hearts? Our innocence——

Nic. Innocence! Let's think of our escape, dear master, and leave innocence to those that want it.—Would you believe it, when the prior's garden was robbed, I discovered the way the thief went. [*Aside.*] I was the thief myself, though I never confessed it. The grapes were dreadfully sour—it was punishment enough to have eaten them. [*Aloud.*] The secret door lies hidden beneath this tapestry; we can't discover it without a light. I know where to procure one—I'll feel for my tinder-box. Keep up your courage, master—I'll return in an instant. [*Exit,* L.

Her. (C.) Despair suddenly occupies my mind; my destiny seems vainly to contend with anguish. I feel that this solitary abode is not merely intended to be my prison, but, perhaps, my grave. Farewell to every joy!

SONG.—HERMOGEN.

No more amongst the mountains
  Shall the hunter's horn invite me;
No more amongst my comrades
  Shall the feat of arms delight me.

The lattice wreath'd with roses sweet,
  The vesper twilight bell,
Love's signal sound, and lady's smile,
  And every joy, farewell!

Farewell, my neighing charger,
  That to battle often bore me;
Farewell, my glitt'ring banner,
  That in conquest flutter'd o'er me.

The courtly hall—the festive board,
  With music's tuneful spell,—
The spurs of gold, and lady's smile,
  And every joy, farewell!

Re-enter NICHOLAS, *hastily, with a lamp,* L.

Nic. [*With fear.*] Oh, oh dear! They are coming! I see them through the chinks of the door—the monks from the monastery!

Her. Whom want they? What seek they?

Nic. It's you they want—me they want. They say that, when you practise your sorceries, I blow the fire—that, when you drink devil's elixir, I drain the bottles. Help me, master, help me to open the door. [*Opens the door,* R. S. E.] See, see, master, the secret passage!

Her. Which leads to——

Nic. To St. Anthony's shrine, through the prior's garden.

Her. [*Going.*] Let us begone. [*Nicholas cautiously holds the lamp against him.*] Why do you survey me with the lamp?

Nic. A suspicion entered my mind that you might be ——Nothing like light and shade. In future, I'm resolved always to examine the dark side of a man's character before I trust him. Now I'm satisfied—I've not the shadow of a doubt remaining.

[*Exeunt through the secret passage,* R. S. E.

SCENE III.—*St. Anthony's Cell and Fountain—a rude flight of natural steps in the background, leading to a small Gothic door,* C. F., *and over it an ancient clock, at 7.*

Enter URIKA, *Bridesmen, and Maidens, wearing white favours,* L.

URIKA *and* CHORUS.

Eve of Allhallows, we hail, we hail!
    At St. Anthony's well,
    And St. Anthony's cell,
No demon can ever prevail.
    Then sound, sound the bell,
    At St. Anthony's well;
    Here, scorning each spell,
'Mid mirth and 'mid glee,
Our fair lady's wedding shall be, &c.

Enter NICHOLAS, *hastily*, L.

Nic. (L.) What is all this, good people? What does it all mean, Urika?

Uri. (C.) A pretty bridesman, indeed, to ask such a question! Where have you been, sir—you, a page, not to know that your poor terrified lady has resolved, by my advice, to be married at St. Anthony's shrine, where, on Allhallows' Eve, just as the vesper clock has stricken eight, no evil spirit can take advantage of mortal innocence?

Nic. So, so, an excellent way of cheating the devil—let a woman alone: ha, ha! I must run and apprise my master, or the bride will be getting impatient: I know ladies don't like delay on these occasions. [*Runs out*, L.

Uri. Where's the fellow gone, now, I wonder? Did ever anybody see the like? no attention, no respect, indeed!

MUSIC.—*Enter* FRANCESCO, R., *leading in* AURELIA, *as bride, followed by the Prior, Monks, Servants, &c.*

Fra. This hallow'd earth trembles beneath my guilty feet! The confiding, unsuspecting Aurelia,—those looks which once so charmed me, already speak unconscious daggers.—Ah! the clock—'tis time. Now, Aurelia, shall we to the altar?

Aur. Yes, my Hermogen, here thy truth is proved: no demon may, unscourged, approach, on this night, yonder cell. Take my hand, lead me to the shrine.

Fra. [*Leading her towards the cell.*] My Aurelia! my bride!

MUSIC.—*Enter* HERMOGEN, *who rushes wildly in, from* L. U. E.

Her. Hold! these impious rights suspend! this place, even now, is polluted by a fiend: the poison of his breath is on thee, holy prior: he seeks here, even, to possess a victim, guileless, innocent—that victim is Aurelia.

Pri. (L. C.) Seize him, let him not pass the count, lest we again mistake the innocent for the guilty: drag him to his doom! [*They seize Hermogen*, L.

Her. Well, to my doom; the cruel stake and the red exterminating fire cannot exceed the torture of living to behold Aurelia yon monster's bride; I go, yet one word is struggling at my heart—a name I fain would utter—my brother, my poor Francesco!

Fra. [*Wildly.*] What! what of him?

Her. Where is he at a moment like this?—his tears—his prayers—Is there no good, pitying angel, to bear to him my dying benediction? to whisper in his ear that the lost, lost Hermogen, perished innocently and untimely, —bless thee, Francesco, wherever thou art! haply we shall meet no more on earth; but, when we meet in heaven, I'll tell thee—tell thee all! To death! to death! [*Going*, L.

Fra. Stay! to death—must it be to death?

Prior and Monks. To death!

Fra. No, no, no! [*Aside.*] Sunk as I am in shame, I will not, cannot become the assassin of a brother who has blessed me. I dare to die the self-consigned victim of a punishment, horrible, but deserved, but I dare not live beneath the sting of remorse which no tortures can surpass.—Hermogen, I resign Aurelia!

All. How!

Fra. Do not ask of me why, or how, or wherefore; know that my distracting love for Aurelia has been, shall be, my only crime. I am not what I seem—who I am, what I am, man shall never know; my secret and my sufferings are my own. Farewell, Aurelia: only this remains,—take back the fatal semblance of thyself, my joy and ruin; one kiss, one tear, and then farewell for ever!

[*Kissing the miniature and giving it to Aurelia, who crosses to Hermogen*, L.

Gor. [*Without.*] Brother!

Fra. Oh! [*Shuddering.*] the demon's voice; the clock is well nigh eight, and I have refused Aurelia's hand. [*Approaching Aurelia and recoiling.*] So best! [*Wildly.*] Doom, doom, I await thee! [*Clock strikes eight.*

Gor. [*Furiously.*] Brother!

Fra. The clock strikes!—Where shall I fly for refuge? Ah, yon holy sanctuary—this night—All Hallows' Eve! Hope sustains me—ah! come, demon, come, and snatch thy victim from the altar, which a penitent is not denied to approach.

[MUSIC.—*He hurries up the broken stairs—the Demon enters from foreground and pursues him—the steps crumble beneath the Demon's feet*—FRANCESCO *enters the cell of St. Anthony.—The Demon is striken with a thunderbolt—the shrine falls and overwhelms him in flames and ruins.—The whole of the back scene descends and presents——*

SCENE IV.—*A Rustic Bridge and Waterfall by moonlight, with the Monastery of the Silver Palm-Tree Lake, brilliantly illuminated.*

FRANCESCO *discovered on the bridge, with a crozier in his hand, and attired in his monk's habit.*

Her. [*Seeing Francesco.*] Francesco, arrived at last? Ah, Francesco, why this long delay?

Fra. [*Descending.*] A sad pilgrimage called me from the monastery; the soul of a victim was to be saved—penitence, an act of forbearance, and good angels, have accomplished the task; and Francesco, never unmindful of thy bidding, is here to bless your nuptials. [*They kneel.*] Brother! [*With force.*] Sister! bless you! bless you! bless you! [*Picture.*

DISPOSITION OF THE CHARACTERS AT THE FALL OF THE CURTAIN.

Monks.				*Peasants.*
	NICHOLAS.		URIKA.	
PRIOR	HERMOGEN.		FRANCESCO	AURELIA.
R.]				[L.

THE END.

Costume.

HERMOGEN.—*First dress:* A green velvet jerkin, open at the vest, richly trimmed with gold—sleeves puffed with white satin—broad-topped cap of same—white feathers—scarlet pantaloons, trimmed on the outside with gold binding, edged with black—boots. *Second dress:* A fisherman's blue jerkin and trunks, with slashes in the sleeves, showing a check shirt, trimmed with red binding—blue stockings—black shoes—dark brown cap—black leather belt, and sword.

FRANCESCO.—*First dress:* Monk's gown of dark brown, with cowl—white cord round waist, with black and red rosary, and cross, suspended—russet boots. *Second dress:* The same as Hermogen's first dress. *Third dress:* Same as first.

NICHOLAS.—*First dress:* Black jerkin and trunks, trimmed with red—a large bell of red cloth formed on the back of jerkin—another in front of his steeple-crowned hat—blue stockings—goat-skin shoes. *Second dress:* Yellow jerkin and trunks, trimmed with dark brown.

PAGE.—White tunic, trimmed with blue and silver—white stockings, shoes, hat, and feathers—blue scarf.

PRIOR.—Black gown, with cape and hood, bound with white—small round black cap—white ruffles and gloves—blue ribbon and order—shoes and buckles.

MONKS.—White gowns, with red capes and cowls.

SERVANTS.—Brown tunics, trimmed with red and white—scarlet breeches—russet boots.

SHADOW KING.—Blue body and pantaloons—gray gauze drapery, trimmed with purple foil—a black net shirt, trimmed with dark foil—dark gauze wings—sandals.

GORTZBURG.—Red body, arms, and legs—half tunic of brown and silver tissue—red sandals, and wings (to work.)

FIENDS.—Dark red and blue gauze dresses—red gauze wings—red and blue sandals.

DANCERS.—White breeches, trimmed with blue and red—black flies, trimmed with ditto—blue stockings, and black shoes.

AURELIA.—Long sleeved white satin dress, richly trimmed with gold, &c.

URIKA.—Blue velvet body, trimmed with silver—yellow silk skirt, trimmed with blue.

DANCERS.—White gauze dresses, trimmed with white satin ribbon.

Adelphi Theatre,

BY AUTHORITY OF THE] *STRAND.* [LORD CHAMBERLAIN

UNDER THE MANAGEMENT OF MESSRS. TERRY & YATES.

THE PUBLIC ARE RESPECTFULLY INFORMED THAT BY

☞ THE GRACIOUS PERMISSION

OF

HIS MAJESTY,

An Order has been issued from the Lord Chamberlain's Office, empowering this Theatre

TO REMAIN OPEN TILL FURTHER NOTICE.

HARLEQUIN & the EAGLE, or, the MAN in the MOON & his WIFE!
Having been received with the most unbounded Shouts of Laughter and Applause, will be repeated every Evening.

Monday, Jan. 8, 1827, & every Evening till further Notice,

Will be performed, with entirely NEW MUSIC, SCENES, DRESSES, &c. a NEW NAUTICAL BURLETTA, called

THE FLYING
Dutchman!

Or, THE PHANTOM SHIP.

"THE FLYING DUTCHMAN" is said to be an Amsterdam Vessel, which about a Century ago sailed from that Port;—the Master's Name was [illegible], whose constant Boast it was, that "he always would have his own Way, in spite of the Devil."
[illegible] doubling the Cape, they were a whole Day trying to weather *Table Bay*, the Wind encreasing a-head of them, and *Vanderdecken* walking the Deck, and [illegible] swearing fearfully—just after Sun-set, he was spoke by a Vessel, who asked him if he did not mean to go into the Bay that Night, to which *Vanderdecken*, with a tremendous Oath, replied, "he would not, though he should Beat about till the Day of Judgement." *Vanderdecken* never did go into *Table Bay*, and is believed to undergo the Doom he so desperately dared. His Vessel is still seen in the *Cape Seas* in foul Weather, sailing against the fiercest Storm, with every Inch of Canvas set, striving in vain to reach her Home, or to send Despatches to Relatives by other Vessels.
The Hints upon which the Drama is founded, were taken from a short and interesting Article in *Blackwood's Magazine*, from whence also the above Account is extracted.

The New Overture and the Whole of the Music composed by Mr. G. HERBERT RODWEL

The Dresses, by Mr. GODBEE and Mrs. STILLMAN. Properties, by Mr. WOODYER. New and extensive Machinery, by Mr. EVANS.
The Whole of the SCENERY by Messrs. TOMKINS and PITT.

The Melo-Dramatic Business under the Superintendence of Mr. T. P. COOKE.

Captain Peppercoal, *formerly Captain of a Trade Ship*, Mr. TERRY.
Lieut. Mowdrey, Mr. ELLIOTT. Tom Willis, *Mate of the Enterprize*, Mr. SALTER.
Mynheer Von Swigs, *Purser*, Mr. SANDERS. Smutta, *a Slave*, Signor PAULO. Sentinel, Mr. BUXTON.
Peter Von Bummell, *a Cockney Dutchman, a Dabbler in the Law*, Mr. JOHN REEVE.
Toby Varnish, *his Friend, a Physical Marine Painter and a Bear*, Mr. WRENCH.
Vanderdecken, *Captain of the Flying Dutchman*, Mr. T. P. COOKE.
Sailors, Soldiers, Slaves, Sprites of the Deep, &c. &c.
Rockalda, *an Evil Spirit of the Deep*, Mr. MORRIS. Lestelle Vanhelm, Miss BODEN. Lucy, Mrs. H. HUGHES.

SUCCESSION OF THE SCENERY, &c.

Rockalder's Cavern-Mysterious Appearance of Vanderdecken

OAK CHAMBER IN FORTRESS, formerly belonging to Vanderdecken. Pitt.

Deck of the Enterprise—Sun Set at Sea—Approach of *Tomkins*

THE PHANTOM SHIP

SEA VIEW Off the CAPE. *Tomkins* HAUNTED CHAMBER in the FORTRESS. *Pitt*

ROCKY PASS on the SEA SHORE. *Tomkins.*

ROMANTIC VIEW, NEAR CAPE TOWN. *Tomkins.*

EXTERIOR OF FORTRESS BY MOONLIGHT. *Tomkins*

Vanishing of VANDERDECKEN and LESTELLE.

Rising of the Sea Mist—The Scene enveloped in Darkness—The

Phantom Ship in Full Sail

ON THE OPEN SEA. **GIGANTIC CLIFF.** *Tomkins.*

INUNDATION of the DEVILS's CAVE. *Pitt*

After which will be played, a favorite Burletta, in One Act, called

Curiosity Cured

Mr. Curious, Mr. SANDERS. Charles, Mr. ELLIOTT. Mikey, Mr. SALTER.
Miss Grace, Mrs. TAYLEURE. Sally, Miss DALY.
Kitty Curious, Mrs. FITZWILLIAM!
Billy Pitt - Mrs. FITZWILLIAM!!
Mrs. Erudite, Mrs. FITZWILLIAM!!!
Janet Sqareitz, Mrs. FITZWILLIAM!!!!
Mary Jones, Mrs. FITZWILLIAM!!!!!

R. Cruikshank, Del. G. W. Bonner, Sc.

The Flying Dutchman.

The Crew. Ah! Vanderdecken! Vanderdecken!

Act II. Scene 3.

THE FLYING DUTCHMAN;

OR, THE PHANTOM SHIP:

A NAUTICAL DRAMA,

In Three Acts.

BY EDWARD FITZ-BALL, ESQ.

Author of The Pilot, Inchcape Bell, Floating Beacon, Father and Son, Innkeeper of Abbeville, Earthquake, Devil's Elixir, &c.

PRINTED FROM THE ACTING COPY, WITH REMARKS, BIOGRAPHICAL AND CRITICAL, BY D.— G.

To which are added,

A DESCRIPTION OF THE COSTUME,—CAST OF THE CHARACTERS, ENTRANCES AND EXITS,—RELATIVE POSITIONS OF THE PERFORMERS ON THE STAGE,—AND THE WHOLE OF THE STAGE BUSINESS.

As now performed at the

ADELPHI THEATRE.

EMBELLISHED WITH A FINE ENGRAVING.

By Mr. BONNER, from a Drawing taken in the Theatre by Mr. R. CRUIKSHANK,

---

LONDON:

JOHN CUMBERLAND, 6, BRECKNOCK PLACE,
CAMDEN NEW TOWN.

Costume.

CAPTAIN PEPPERCOAL.—A naval captain's coat of the old school—Cassimire waistcoat and breeches—striped silk stockings—round-toed shoes—paste buckles.

LIEUTENANT MOWDREY.—Lieutenant's blue coat—Cassimire waistcoat—blue trousers—boots—black stock.

PETER VON BUMMELL.—*First dress:* A Dutchman's outrè brown suit, with white sugar-loaf buttons—red stockings, with clocks—square-toed shoes, with red roses—old English high crowned hat, with red band and rosette—long neckcloth. *Second dress:* As a shepherdess, pink and white gown, with a stomacher—large straw hat.

TOBY VARNISH.—*First dress:* Striped shirt—nankeen jacket—white waistcoat—nankeen trousers—straw hat.—*Second dress:* a bear's skin.

TOM WILLIS.—Check shirt—sailor's jacket and trousers.

MYNHEER VON SWIGGS.—Dutch sailor—blue jacket, with white sugar-loaf buttons—belt—large blue trousers.

SAILORS.—Check shirts—blue jacket and trousers.

SMUTTA.—White calico jacket, trimmed with red binding—white vest—white trousers, tied with broad red binding below the knees—dark brown flesh-coloured stockings—red slippers—white hat, with red binding.

SLAVES.—Similar to Smutta, but without hats.

SENTINEL.—Soldier's blue jacket, with red skirts, buttoned breast high—cross belt—white serge breeches—black gaiters—soldier's cap, with dark green upright feather in front.

VANDERDECKEN.—Green old-fashioned dress, with white sugar loaf buttons—belt—high boots—old English hat—red feather.

LESTELLE VANHELM.—*First dress:* Open pink gown—white sarsnet and pink trimming—an old English stomacher, as a shepherdess. *Second dress:* White muslin—flowing hair.

LUCY.—Blue muslin dress.

ROCKALDA.—Sorceress's sea-green dress, trimmed with sea-weed and shells—tiara on her head, with long black veil fastened from the back of the head.

EIGHT WATER IMPS.—Green sea-weed dresses, with grotesque nondescript masks.

Cast of the Characters,

As Performed at the Adelphi Theatre.

Captain Peppercoal, formerly Captain of a Trade Ship	Mr. Butler.
Lieutenant Mowdrey, a young Sea Officer	Mr. Hemmings.
Peter Von Bummel, a Cockney Dutchman, a Dabbler in Law, alias a benighted Shepherdess	Mr. J. Reeve.
Toby Varnish, his Friend, a physical Marine Painter, and a Bear	Mr. Yates.
Tom Willis, Mate of the Enterprise	Mr. Smith.
Mynheer Von Swiggs, Purser of the same Vessel	Mr. Saunders.
Smutta, a Slave	Signor Paulo.
Vanderdecken, Captain of the Phantom Ship, the Flying Dutchman	Mr. O. Smith.
Rockalda, an Evil Spirit of the Deep	Mr. Morris.
Lestelle Vanhelm, Niece to Captain Peppercoal	Mrs. Fitzwilliam.
Lucy, her Attendant	Miss Apjohn.

Sailors, Slaves, Water-Imps, &c. &c.

STAGE DIRECTIONS.

The Conductors of this work print no Plays but those which they have seen acted. The *Stage Directions* are given from personal observations, during the most recent performances.

EXITS and ENTRANCES.

R. means *Right ;* L. *Left ;* F. *the Flat, or Scene running across the back of the Stage ;* D. F. *Door in Flat ;* R. D. *Right Door ;* L. D. *Left Door ;* C. D. *Centre Door* · S. E. *Second Entrance ;* U. E. *Upper Entrance.*

RELATIVE POSITIONS.

R. means *Right ;* L. *Left ;* C. *Centre ;* R. C. *Right of Centre;* L. C. *Left of Centre.*

R. RC. C. LC. L.

*** *The Reader is supposed to be on the Stage, facing the Audience.*

THE FLYING DUTCHMAN;

OR, THE PHANTOM SHIP.

ACT I.

SCENE I.—*Rockalda's Cavern, opening to the Sea—a flame burning on a projecting piece of Rock,* R. S. E.—*the stage half dark.*

MUSIC.—ROCKALDA *discovered seated on a Grotto Throne,* R., *with a trident wand—she rises and walks round the stage during the symphony.*

AIR.—ROCKALDA.

Sweetly sleep, thou silv'ry moon,
  Thy light is on the sea ;—
The fragrant samphire opes her lip,
  And breathes a kiss to thee.

Then here, in many an antic form,
  In goblin mirth and glee,
I'll weave to-night the mystic dance,
  And breathe a kiss to thee. [*Waving her wand*

Chorus heard without, L.

Cho. We'll weave to-night the mystic dance,
  And breathe a kiss to thee.
Roc. We'll weave to-night
  The mystic, mystic dance,
Cho. [*Without,* L.] And breathe a kiss to thee.
  We come, we come, we come!

Enter eight little grotesque Water Imps, two and two, alternately from R. *and* L., *with coral and small conch shells in their hands.*—MUSIC.—*The Water Imps dance around Rockalda—they blow their conch shells—and at the conclusion of the dance Rockalda waives her wand, when the eight Water Imps exeunt* R. *and* L.—*Thunder—Stage dark.*

SOLO AND CHORUS.

Roc. The billows roll, the planets fly,
  Clouds and darkness wrap the sky,—
  This sudden discord—speak! unfold!

Cho. [*Without,* L.] 'Tis Vanderdecken comes!

[*Clouds roll over the sea.*

Roc. Oh, so near!—
Let him appear!

[*Waves her wand, and seats herself on her grotto throne,* R.—*Thunder.*—SOFT MUSIC.—*The dark clouds disperse—the gong vibrates, and Vanderdecken, amid blue fire, appears from the waves, his features pale and haggard, and holding in his hand a black flag, emblazoned with a white Death's head and cross bones—he descends, advances to Rockalda, and, placing the flag at her feet, bends his head in token of deep submission—the stage becomes lighter.*

Van. [*Kneeling,* C.] Mighty genius of the deep, behold me at thy feet. My century having expired, I come to claim its renewal, according to thy promise—give me, once more, to revisit my native earth invulnerable, and, if I please, invisible, to increase the number of thy victims; and name thy own conditions.

Roc. [*Rising.*] Son of the wave, I understand, and, in observance of thy wish, receive this mystic garment.

Enter WATER IMP, R. S. E., *with a mantle, which he presents to Vanderdecken, and exit,* R. S. E.

And henceforth, in the mortal combat, be thou by this touch invulnerable. [*She touches him with her wand.*] And now go seek a bride to share thy stormy fate. Rockalda's fatal death-book make her sign, and become my slave. She's thine, and thou shalt renew thy present respite when another century has expired; but, remember, on earth, as the shadow of man is silent, so must thou be. Voice is denied thee 'till thy return; lest, in thy treachery, thou disclose to human ear the secrets of the deep.

[MUSIC.—*Vanderdecken rises and expostulates by action.*

Roc. Thou urgest in vain—speak, and the charm is broken; and, at the third appearance of thy phantom ship, thy fate lies buried in the dark depths of the ocean for ever.

AIR.—ROCKALDA.

My summons twice thy phantom-ship shall be,
Which, thrice appearing, calls thee back to me.
To speak on earth beware!
That instant, ocean's flood
Consigns thee to despair.

Invisible Chorus.

That instant ocean's flood
Consigns thee to despair.

[*Thunder—Vanderdecken takes up his death-flag and retraces his steps amid the waves—he ascends in blue fire as the scene closes.*

SCENE II.—*A Chamber in the Fortress—in the centre pannel in the flat the picture of a Ship under sail, bearing a date,* 1729

Enter LESTELLE *and* LUCY, R.

Lucy. It must be near the time, ma'am, when your lover generally steals from his concealment, and crosses the river at the back of the fortress, to discourse with you at the lattice unbeknown to your uncle. All's quiet —I don't hear the boat—no. Ah, ma'am, Lieutenant Mowdrey's a charming gentleman, and Mr. Varnish, his man, is a charming gentleman's gentleman. Heigho! I feel quite troubled with the ongwee, as Mr. Varnish calls it.

Les. Ah, you've been poring over another of those horrible German tales, I suppose, Lucy, and are now come hither to indulge me with your company, because you fear to sit alone.

Lucy. No, no, ma'am; instead of perusing a story, I've been composing a story, and one that would read charmingly in print—your own, for instance.

Les. Mine, Lucy!

Lucy. Yes, truly, ma'am, and I'm sure it would appear vastly interesting; we only want a spectre to render it a perfect romance. Listen, ma'am: you are destined by your cruel guardian to marry a man whom you never saw, one Mister or Mynheer Von Bummel, who is hourly expected from the other side of the ocean; now, you love a gallant officer whom you have seen, and who, under the disguise of a portrait-painter, contrives to obtain an interview, and to steal your heart—

Les. Now, Lucy, did I ever confess that?

Luc. No, ma'am, but your eyes and your sighs are sad blabbers of secrets—and who, because the lieutenant admired the portrait of the handsome shepherdess in the next room, and said it was an angelic resemblance of yourself, contrived this dress to appear even more like the picture which he so much admired. [*Alluding to the dress worn by Lestelle, which is almost a fac-simile of the portrait painted in the second scene of Act II.*] Ha! madam—but to my story: your guardian finds out your little attachment, locks you up, and forbids your lover the house; but he, like a true knight, only tarries in ambush till he can fairly carry off his mistress from the Cape of Good Hope, and sail away with her to England, the land of liberty and joy. [*Courtesies to Lestelle.*] Now, ma'am, how do you like my long story?

Les. The denouement, exceedingly; but you have omitted a little sort of an underplot between yourself and a certain Mr. Varnish. Ah, Lucy! now, pray don't blush.

Capt. Peppercoal. [*Without,* L., *in a passion.*] Come along, Smutta.

Enter CAPTAIN PEPPERCOAL, L. D., *followed by* SMUTTA.

Capt. P. [*Patting Smutta on the head.*] Good Smutta. [*Turning to Lestelle.*] O Letty, Letty, what's this I hear? So, you want to desert, eh? want to quit the ship—to decamp from your old fond fool of an uncle and guardian, under whose care you've been reared and educated like a gentlewoman? Fire and fury! what wind will blow next, I wonder? I am ready to expire with vexation.

Les. My dear uncle, what has happened to occasion this agitation?

Capt. P. Who says I'm agitated? Feel my pulse—count it.

Les. [*Feeling his pulse, and counting rapidly.*] One, two, three, four, five—

Capt. P. Who the devil says I'm agitated? I'm as calm as the Dead Sea; and, if I was not the mildest of tempers, as meek as a dove, and as gentle as a lamb, I'd take—— but I won't say another word; look at this—look at this, I say.

Takes a key out of his coat-pocket, and holds it up to Lestelle.

Lucy. (R.) Lauk, sir, you'll frighten my young lady into *high sterricks.* D'ye think she doesn't know a key when it's shown to her?

Capt. P. [*Crossing,* C.] O yes, or any thing else. And pray, madam [*To Lucy.*], what's that to you? I'll lock you up with her; you shall neither of you have the privilege of an old caterpillar, to crawl over the extent of a withered gooseberry-leaf, till Lestelle has become Mistress Von Bummel.

Lucy. Von Bummel! what a name!

Capt. P. What's that to you? 'tisn't yours. [*Crosses back to* L.] Mrs. Von Bummel—that's your name that is to be. I gave my word to the lad's father, my old messmate, that you should marry him; and when an old seaman, like me, gives his word, damme, he sticks to it through fire and water! Mistress Von Bummel.

Les. I'll die a million times first!

Capt. P. You'll do what first?

Les. I'll die first.

Capt. P. You'll die! well, then, die—die and be——

[*Placing his hand to his mouth.*

Les. No, sir; though in all things else I am willing to obey your inclinations—in this one instance, which concerns the whole happiness of my life, I am resolved to follow the dictates of my own reason.

Capt. P. Follow the dictates of your own reason! follow the dictates of your own fiddle-de-dee. Who ever heard of a woman having any reason of her own? No, no,—you shall follow the dictates of my reason; and whom I say marry, you shall marry, though the fellow were as ugly as a sea-horse, and as clumsy as a porpoise! What, you wanted to cheat your old uncle, did you? by pretending to be twanging your harp at your window every night, when you thought I had turned into my berth, as naturally as an old blind peacock to its perch: but it won't do, Letty. Here was the old faithful Smutta —you should have given this dingy mastiff a bone, to have prevented him from barking. Ha, ha, ha!

Les. & *Lucy.* } Smutta! He!

Capt. P. Speak, Smutta, and don't grin.

[*Pushes him to Lestelle.*

Smutta. Iss, massa: him creep vere him bid him into large hogshead—vatch him all night—him see two men climb him up window dere—him tink dem to be two big tieves—see dem go him back in wood—hide him boat in long grass—Smutta so honest, tell massa.

[*Turns to the Captain, who strikes Smutta on the head.*

Capt. P. Damn your honesty! tell your story.

Smu. [*Rubbing his head.*] Massa, him set Smutta swim across water—cutty him cord—and let him boat row himself down to him devil, missy—dere now.

Les. Ah, Smutta, you little thought that you were rendering me most unhappy.

Smu. O dear—him tought him save you troat from be cut—if him vex you, him cry him eyes out—oh, cursee him boat—and cursee him cord—and cursee him—— O—h? [*Thumping his hat.*

Capt. P. [*Kicking him.*] Get out of the house, you howling baboon!

Smu. O, tank you, massa, much obliged.

[*Exit Smutta,* L. D.

Les. This inhumanity is insupportable—not content, since my poor mother's death, with keeping me a prisoner in this gloomy fortress——

Lucy Which every body says is haunted by the Flying Dutchman, who comes here once in a century to visit his old habitation, and to carry off poor young maidens by stealth to his den under the sea.

Capt. P. I wish he'd come and carry you off, and then I should be rid of one plague, at all events. Flying Dutchman, flying devil—I don't believe a word of it; though they do tell me, that the old lady that's painted in the turret chamber, with a long marlinspike in her fist, with a crook at the end of it, was the dead Dutchman's dead wife; and that the old sea-trunk that stands under the window contains the clothes in which he last beheld her.

Lucy. Dear me, how I should like to see them.

Les. And I.

Capt. P. No doubt: woman's curiosity would peep into any thing—but I promised to the person of whom I bought the fortress to give the old trumpery sea-room, or they'd have been flung overboard long ago: your mother was so superstitious an old noodle, she would have thought it an ill omen to have disturbed them; and there they might remain till doomsday for any curiosity of mine. As for the pictures, they take up no room—they hang close to the wall, and are pretty furniture enough; and, for the box, I don't believe a soul knows how it came into the fortress.

Lucy. [*Aside to Lestelle.*] I thought that box was full of papers;—if I don't peep into it one of these days, I'm no true woman. [*Stage a little dark—thunder heard.*

Capt. P. It's coming on a rough night; therefore, turn in and go to bed: you had better do that than try to

cheat your old uncle; see, here's the key of this door, [*Pointing to* L.] and if you escape now, curse me but it shall be through the keyhole—so, go to bed.

Lucy. [*Aside to Lestelle.*] Tell him, you're not sleepy, ma'am.

Les. I'm not sleepy, uncle.

Capt. P. Well, then, go to bed and lie awake—I heard you, ma'am. [*To Lucy.*

Les. My dear uncle, you won't lock me in.

Capt. P. I'm damned if I don't, though. [*Going,* L.

Les. [*Coaxing him.*] You are too good-tempered.

Capt. P. No; I'm cursed ill-tempered.

Les. [*Following him to* L. D.] Now, my dear uncle.

Capt. P. I'm not to be wheedled; I am sixty and seven, and I was never wheedled by a woman since I was the height of a marlinspike. Egad! you are pretty, too. [*Kisses her.*] Upon my soul, I don't wonder that men are wheedled sometimes—there, good night.

[*Exit Captain Peppercoal,* L. D., *banging it after him and locking it.*]

Capt. P. [*Without.*] There, I've locked the door; go to bed, both of you.

Lucy. There's conduct, ma'am, to leave us by ourselves this stormy night. [*Thunder heard—stage darker.*

Les. How the thunder rolls; I wonder where Mawdrey is now?

Lucy. And Varnish, poor fellow. [*Thunder again heard, and the stage becoming darker and darker.*] There again, there goes another whiz. Just look at the date on that picture, ma'am.

Les [*Turns up stage, close on* L. *side, looking at the ship in the scene.*] Well, what of it?

Lucy. (R.) That's one hundred years ago—you remember the story, ma'am—once in a hundred years. [*Lucy pointing to the picture of the ship.*] That, you know, is called Vanderdecken's ship: [*Thunder.*] if the old Dutchman be not taking his rounds to-night, I'm much mistaken. Don't stand so far off, if you please, ma'am; [*Lestelle crosses to Lucy.*] I think I see the ghost of that Flying Dutchman in every ray of the moonlight.

[*Stage quite dark.*

DUET—Lestelle and Lucy.

Les. 'Tis the hour when spirits wander,
Wander lonely through the night;

Lucy. The moon has risen pale in beauty,
Dark clouds veil her silv'ry light.
Les. } *Lucy.* } 'Tis the hour, &c.
Both. 'Tis the owl in sullen humour,
Flaps the casement with her wing.
Bird forsaken, seek the forest,
And never here thy omens bring.
Lucy. Her accents still I hear;
Les. They die upon the ear. [*Thunder.*
Both. { Such chilling sounds burst from the deep
When Vanderdecken comes—ah!

[*The ship in the scene becomes illumined with crimson fire—Lestelle crosses hastily to* R.

Both. { To bed—to sleep—
With a prayer our lips we'll close.
Softly, softly, seek repose—
With a prayer our lips we'll close.

[*The air, expressive of fear, dies away, and they exeunt* R., *trembling with alarm.*

SCENE III.—Music.—*The Ship's Deck, with set waters and setting sun—dark clouds progressively rising—kegs, trunks, and coil of rope on stage—Crew discovered.*

Tom. [*Looking through a hand telescope,* L. U. E.] Huzza, lads—I see land! land!

The Crew. Huzza—land! land!

Enter PETER VON BUMMEL, R. S. E., *with a red leather foraging-cap on, and his head tied up.*

Pet. Land! land! where, mister sailorman! Show it me—where is it?

Tom. [*Still looking through the telescope.*] Why, there—no—now I can't diskiver it, shiver me if I can; nothing but water and the clouds rising o' the sudden! 'Gad, my masters, if it continues to blow thus, we are likely to get a blusterous night on it; so near port, too—that there's awkward!

Pet. You shouldn't call out land, when there's no land; bag my books, but you are coming the old Bailey. I'll let ye see, I'm a lawyer: you shouldn't do so when you know I have been sea-sick the whole voyage. [*Puts his hand to his mouth.*

Tom. By the glass I could have swored I seed the top of Table Mountain; but now the weather's got so hazy and so dark, one can scarcely see a cáble's length from the bows. [*Thunder.*] Hawl taught there, we shall have a storm—Yo! ho!

Pet. A storm, oh dear! here have I come all this way as snug as a nut in its own shell, and now, on the very crack of landing, we are to have a storm: oh that I were at my desk in Chancery Lane again. Why, the sky looks as black as the seams of a hackney clerk's Sunday coat, just rubb'd over with its Saturday night's ink. [*Thunder.*] O—h! oh dear!

Tom. It must be—there, there, it goes again: see there she goes, top-gallants and all. [*Looking across* L. U. E. *to* R.] Ay, ay, we shall have a visit. [*To Peter.*] Did your honour never hear of the Flying Dutchman?

Pet. [*Sitting down on the deck,* R., *and leaning his head against the side.*] No; but I've heard of the lying Dutchman, who sold tulips and bulberous roots in Fleet Market.

Tom. This is no land-lubber I'm speaking of, but the right real arnest Flying Dutchman, Vanderdecken, whose cutter drives constantly against the wind.

Pet. Well, that's nothing to brag of: hav'nt I done the very same thing, when I came from Margate in the steamer.

Tom. Belay! belay! This is no steamer, but a happerition, your honour; and a gang of devils what brings letters aboard of honest men's ships: but no good comes to them that has communications with sich dispatches—the weight on 'em is enough to sink the stoutest bit of oak that ever studded the salt sea.

Von S. [*Comes forward with a flask.*] Yaw, mynheer—dat ish all true.

Pet. [*Rising up, and mimicking.*] Dat ish all true, you superstitious old wig-block—what do you know of—O—h, I'm very ill, oh!

Von S. You had vetter go below.

Pet. I'm very ill below already.—[*Von Swiggs offers Peter the flask, from which he drinks, and returns it.*]—Oh dear, my stomach is like a skittle-ground,—nothing but heaving and pitching going forward from morning to night. Heigho!

[Music.—*Thunder and lightning—the setting sun and warm sky descend, and black clouds rise in its place—stage dark.*

Tom. Lights there—lights in the binnacle—what do I see?—a drowning man within hail—a rope, a rope!

[Music.—*Sailors throw out a rope at the side of the vessel,* L. U. E., *when Vanderdecken appears on the ship's side like a drowning Seaman—the Crew assist him on board—he seems exhausted—Von Swiggs gives him his flask.*

Tom. There, drink, poor fellow—Heaven help him.

[MUSIC.—*Vanderdecken trembles and drops the flask at the word "Heaven"—the Crew start, and exclaim,* "Vanderdecken! Vanderdecken!"—*Vanderdecken recovers himself suddenly, and, taking out letters, offers them to Tom Willis and the rest, who all reject them in apparent alarm—by this time, Peter has got seated on a keg,* R.

Tom. No, no, your letters are sealed with dead lead. Letters to your friends, indeed: if reports speak true, your friends have been stowed in the last hold long before now.

[MUSIC.—*Vanderdecken implies,* "*No, no*"—*he takes a letter from his bosom, tied with blue riband—Kisses it—weeps—points to the superscription—opens it—presses it to his breast—shows it to the crew—then wildly tenders its answer, sealed with green wax, to Tom Willis.*

Tom. [*Reads without touching it:* "*To Miss Lestelle Vanhelm, who lives in the second street, Stancen Yatcht Quay, Amsterdam.*"] Why, to my certain knowledge, no such person lives there; the street was pulled down sixty years since, and a large church now stands in its place.

Pet. [*Rises, and advances next to Vanderdecken.*] Bag my books, what's that I hear—Miss Lestelle Vanhelm—why, that's my wife as is to be. I'm now going to the Cape on purpose to marry her. Sailors, when I arrive, I invite you all to the wedding—plenty of grog, and all that—ah! you may stare! [*To Vanderdecken.*] Look here, here's the licence, and here's dad's letter of introduction—look here [*To Willis.*] "L-i-c-e" [*Spelling each letter.*]—there, you read.

[MUSIC.—*Vanderdecken, with a malicious smile, takes the letter—reads it with a start—conceals it, and offers his own in exchange, which Peter is going to take, when Tom Willis pulls him back.*

Tom. (R.) What the devil are you about?

Pet. (R.C.) What the devil are you about, lugging one so.

Tom. Touch one of them bits of paper, and we sink into Davy Jones's locker like a shot.

Pet. Oh, give me my letter!

[*The Sailors seize Peter, who faints in their arms,* R.

Tom. Slew him taught there—and you [*To Vanderdecken.*] quit the ship, can't ye.

[*Vanderdecken offers his letter more wildly, which they still refuse—he threatens, and places the letter on the deck.*

Pet. I will have my letter.

MUSIC.—*Peter attempts to snatch the letter, when it explodes—a sailor is about to seize Vanderdecken, who eludes his grasp, and vanishes through the deck—Tom Willis fires on* R., *Von Swiggs on* L.—*a Sailor falls dead on the deck—Vanderdecken, with a demoniac laugh, rises from the sea in blue fire, amidst violent thunder—at that instant the Phantom Ship appears in the sky behind—Vanderdecken and the Crew in consternation exclaim* "Ah! Vanderdecken! Vanderdecken!" *as the drop hastily falls.*

END OF ACT I.

ACT II

SCENE I.—*The Seacoast.*

Enter MOWDREY, L. S. E.

Mow. How unfortunate! the boat gone; cut from her moorings, and not yet recovered. This very night Lestelle had consented to elope and fly with me to happy England: now, how am I to cross the river which runs near the balcony of her chamber?—She must expect me still in vain. What new stratagem can I possibly devise? Varnish! where is that rascal? always loitering behind. His wit shall again assist me. Varnish, I say!

Enter VARNISH, L. S. E.

Var. Here, sir!

Mow. Dog! where have you been?

Var. Dog am I, sir? I'm a faithful follower of my master, at all events; or, if I am a dog, perhaps it is with living on the bark of the trees, for the deuce a bit of animal food has passed my lips since yesterday, and that's enough for any body to snarl at. Dog, indeed!

Mow. Ah, if you loved as I love; but you, you've no heart.

Var. No; I wish I had a heart, if it was only a sheep's heart;—but no, Lucy has my heart. Ah, sir, if you did but know—what is your single suffering compared to my double one? you suffer only with love—I, with love and hunger at the same time. I have two appetites, one for love and another for eating. Oh, my poor bowels!

Mow: [*Looking out,* R.] There she is again!

Var. Anything to eat, sir?

Mow. I'm sure 'tis Lestelle at the lattice, yonder.

Var. Do you see anything of my Lucy, sir?

Mow. Hold your tongue, sir. She waves her handkerchief.

Var. I'll wave mine.

Mow. That was to have been the signal, and—[*Still looking out,* R.] Now—the boat gone—what steps am I to take?

Var. Those which lead back to the cutter, sir. [*Rain and distant thunder.*] The storm beginning again. Come, sir, won't you go? ar'nt you hungry?

Mow. What! return, and without Lestelle? What have you seen in my conduct, sirrah, to presume that a little fatigue or a drop of rain should divert me from an enterprise in which my heart—my life—is involved?

Var. Yes, and my life, also. I don't know how it is; but with you, sir, difficulty only seems to increase your ardour; while, with me, it brings on a sort of don't-carishness—a kind of a want to go—to sleepishness, which are wonderful sickners to a man of my constitution. Eh! ah! what do I see? [*Looking towards* L. S. E.] Can I believe my eyes?

Mow. What new folly now? has the fellow taken leave of his senses?

Var. O, sir! I spy nothing less than Chancery Lane, Lincoln's Inn, and the Court of Equity, running a race through the back woods of Africa.

Mow. And which gets out first?

Var. Not Chancery, you may be assured.

Pet. [*Without,* L. U. E.] Hillio h—o! hillio! ho!

Var. Hillio! h—o! o—h! Eh? no—yes it is—it is either Peter or his fetch, and I should as soon expect to see the one as the other. Now I see him, he's coming down the cliff—he's there! he's here—he approaches—he is in my arms, my own arms—my own Peter Von Bummel.

Enter PETER, *harassed,* L. U. E., *a large green bag in his hand.*

Pet. No, it can't be! my old acquaintance in *statty quo.* Toby Varnish, the 'potticary's boy from Fleet-Market. Oh, my Toby! come to my arms. [*Embrace.*

Mow. (R.) Varnish, you know the stranger?

Var. [C.—*To Peter.*] My master. [*Peter bows,* L.

Var. When I first cleaned physic-bottles for Dr. Dosemdead, Peter here came over from Holland to find out the justice, and study the practice and cunning of the law—the practice and cunning came naturally. I taught him that in a single lesson.

Pet. [*Pompously.*] I studied very hard; I studied like—like a donkey, I did; my ears were constantly on the stretch; when a haccident occurred that quite upset all my great points.

Var. A haccident! what haccident?

Pet. A letter from dad to return to Holland, and equip myself like one of the house of Bummel. [*Turning round.*] I hav'nt worn these clothes for years.

Var. What a fit!

Pet. I then set sail immediately for Africa, in order to get married to the niece of an old friend of his, Miss Lestelle.

Mow. [*Aloud.*] Lestelle!

Pet. Bless me! what ails the gentleman? He bawls out like the court crier, who drowns other people's noises by calling silence himself. What is it?

Var. What is it? surprise, to be sure—ha, ha! surprise.

Mow. [*Furiously.*] There never was, there never shall or can be——

Var. So fortunate an affair as this: only to think that my pupil, Peter Von Bummel, Esq., Lord High Chancellor of England as is to be——

Pet. As is to be.

Var. Only to think, now, that he, I say, should prove the anxiously expected bridegroom of Miss Vanhelm, and that he should have the good luck to meet with us, on his way to the fortress.

Pet. Bag my books! good luck, sure it is; for somehow, while I was studying my maiden speech to my wife that is to be, I lost sight of the runners who set me ashore, and, but for meeting you, might have roared out for a haberus corporus till next term.

Var. That's not the worst, my dear Peter: without the assistance of counsellor me, and my master here, Miss Vanhelm will never get married to the young stranger, who has already won her affections.

Pet. Young stranger! that's me; affection—loves me already—heard of my fame—how things flies abroad. Not have her? Who's to serve the writ of ejectment? Mr. Toby, eh?

Var. Mr. Peppercoal.

Pet. The devil he is!

Var. Yes: he wants you to sign away your property

under the idea of marrying his ward; and then he intends to marry her to—to whom did we understand, sir?

Mow. To one—one Vanderdecken, the—

Pet. I know the fellow well enough—a blue-looking chap, with hair all about here. [*Pointing to his chin, nose, eyebrows, &c.*] He stole my letter of introduction. A ghost, I think, they called him; but, if I don't pop him into the spiritual court, say I'm a fool.

Var. [*Aside.*] Now, what does he mean, sir?

Mow. I cannot even guess.

Pet. But how did you come by your information respecting—

Var. Respecting yourself? Oh, from Miss Lestelle; my master here is—is—

Mow. A friend to her brother: we sailed together in the Quiver.

Pet. Quiver! no, it won't do—it don't dart into my recollection that she ever had a brother, or a father, or a mother either. But she might—she might—the law allows it; so, if you can and will serve the intended bridegroom of Miss Vanhelm, sign, seal, and deliver, eh?

[*Crosses to* C.

Mow. From the bottom of my heart, will I advocate the cause of Miss Vanhelm's lover.

Var. So will I.

Pet. That's brave—give me your scribblers. [*Taking both their hands.*] Now, then, lead into court. [*Turns to Varnish.*

Var. Thus attired, we cannot: Captain Peppercoal, who has heard of my knowledge of you, apprehensive lest I should put you on your guard against his wicked plot—

[*Peter turns to Mowdrey.*

Mow. And fearing, from my esteem for his brother, whom he has disinherited for—

[*Peter turns to each, as they speak.*

Var. For honesty—

Mow. And knowing, likewise, my regard for the sister——

Var. Forbids us the house till after her marriage with Vanderdecken——

Mow. Till after Vanderdecken has married the young lady.

Pet. Till after her marriage with Vanderdecken. [*Then looking at Mowdrey, and again at Varnish.*] Well, now, it's your turn, I believe. [*To Varnish.*

Var. [*To Peter.*] I say, what have you got in that bag?

Pet. What a lawyer always likes to carry.

Var. What's that?

Pet. A good suit! but you shall see. [*Feeling within the bag.*] Hollo! hollo!

Var. Anything wrong?

Pet. Yes, something is wrong. [*Smelling his fingers.*] The nasty beasts—hang me, if those confounded sailors hav'nt purloined my Wellingtons and pea-green Dashaway, and left in its place an old tarry jacket and trousers—[*Pulling out of the bag an old patched jacket and trousers.*]; here's a flaw in the indictment for ye.

[*Folding up the trousers with his thumb and finger, and pointing to a large patch.*

Mow. A very good disguise, and will do for me.

Var. That may do for you, bnt what will do for me—What am I to do? I can't stay behind, if I go upon all fours—Varnish in the rear—I can't bear that.

Pet. You must go upon all fours, and bear it into the bargain; see, here's part of a bear's skin, which I bought of our purser, to get stuffed and set in a glass-case in Lestelle's bedchamber, when we are married.

[*Takes a bear's head out of his bag, and holds it to Varnish.*

Var. Do you suppose I'll make a beast of myself—I won't do it to please anybody.

Mow. Let's return to the cave, pop on our disguises, and hey to carry the fortress.

Pet. Carry the fortress! that's too much, my shoulders wouldn't support it: if I carry off the lady, the fortress may carry off itself.

Mow. Come along, follow me! [*Exit Mowdrey,* R.

Var. [*Crosses to* C.] I won't make a beast of myself to please any body; I won't bear it.

Mow. Silence, sir, and follow me.

Pet. If you don't, I won't go with you. I'll give you the bag. [*Throws the bag over his shoulders—Exeunt,* R.

SCENE II.—*A Turret Chamber in the Fortress, with a large practicable window,* C. F.—*on one side in flat* R. *the Portrait of a Shepherdess with the sea-trunk beneath it, near* R. S. E.—*on the other side of flat,* L., *a Portrait of Vanderdecken—under the window,* C., *a table covered with baize—pens, ink, writing-paper, lute, books and work-basket—a screen near* L. U. E.—*stool and Gothic chair.*

MUSIC.—LESTELLE *tuning her lute*—LUCY *on her knees, with a bunch of keys in her hand, examining the trunk.*

Lucy. I've tried every key in the bunch, and all to no

purpose: if I thought it would not be discovered, this lock is in so crazy a state that—

Les. Not for the world, Lucy; I forbid such an action.

Lucy. But the dress of the Shepherdess, ma'am, one hundred years old—how the fashion of it would amuse us.

Les. No, no: I require no other amusement than the melancholy of my own thoughts.

Lucy. [*Brings forward the lute.*] How provoking! [*Throwing down the keys.*

Les. Never mind; come and sit by me, [*Sits near* L.] I'll sing you a ballad; I was taught it by my mother when a child—it relates to the Flying Dutchman. It seems as though the sad looks of that picture [*Pointing to the Shepherdess* R. *in flat.*] quite frightened it out of my memory.

[*Lucy takes her work-basket, and brings forward a stool and sits down to work* R., *at a distance from Lestelle.*

Lucy. There, ma'am, do you sing and I'll work.

Les. You must know, Lucy, the song I'm going to sing;—'tis said 'twas her song, the wife of Vanderdecken.

SONG—LESTELLE

Return, O my love, and we'll never, never part,
While the moon her soft light shall shed:
I'll hold thee fast to my virgin heart,
And my bosom shall pillow thy head.

Vanderdecken appears behind the large window in the flat, which he opens and closes during the first part of the song.

Les. I think it proceeded thus.

SONG—(*Continued*).

The breath of the woodbine is on my lip,
Impearl'd in the dews of May;
And none but thou of its sweetness shall sip,
Or steal its honey away.
No, no, never no,
Shall steal its honey away.
Return, O my love, &c.

Cho. Yes, yes, and my bosom shall pillow thy head.

[*During the second verse and termination of the air, Vanderdecken rises through the sea-chest and leaves the lid open—he goes near the screen and listens, lays his hand on his heart, and turns to the picture of the Shepherdess, which he contemplates and weeps—then falls into an attitude of abstraction and admiration of Lestelle, during the remaining part of the song. He stands behind her chair, and on the last note of her song, the lid of the chest falls with a loud crash—he starts, and hurries behind a large cloak, which hangs on the* R. *of flat—the women scream and run to* L. D.—*Vanderdecken vanishes unperceived through a secret pannel, and the cloak falls down.*

Lucy. [*Kneeling.*] Murder! Sure, ma'am, it seemed to me as though the lid of that very trunk had opened and shut with a violent crash: oh, my poor little heart, how it does beat. I'm sure this place is haunted by Satan and all his imps; that cloak, too, was frightened.

Les. Why, Lucy, what will you be alarmed at next?

Lucy. I'm sure I don't know, ma'am.

Les. I declare you render me almost as ridiculous as yourself: when any of the furniture creaks, or the wind blows down a cloak, or even a door opens, I tremble so that—

Lucy. [*Rising from off her knees.*] Ah, ma'am, it's a great pity we are not both married: we are not fit to live alone, I'm sure, ma'am; and you'd be more nervous did you know what Smutta told me last night.

Les. Why, what was it?

Lucy. [*Mysteriously.*] He says, ma'am, that in the neighbourhood of this very place is a cave called the Devil's Cave, and in that cave lies a Magic Book—oh! I don't know how many hundred years old, and do you know, ma'am, they do say Vanderdecken's ghost sometimes spirits away young women to set their names in that book, when they immediately become victims to himself and Rockalda, the hag of the waters.

Les. What a horrible story. [*Captain Peppercoal bangs* L. D.—*Lestelle and Lucy scream and hasten to* R. D.—*Lucy throws her apron over her head.*] Oh, 'tis my uncle,—don't be frightened, Lucy.

Lucy. [*Replacing her apron.*] Lord, ma'am, how can you be such a coward.

Enter CAPTAIN PEPPERCOAL, L. D., *with a letter in his hand.*

Capt. P. Why, Letty, what's the matter with you: you shrieked out as if you had been—may my ship's anchors come home if your cheeks are not as white as the mainsail after a six months' bleach.

Les. Oh, my dear sir, I've been so terrified.

Capt. P. What, another hobgoblin story, eh? It's like your thinking the ship's picture in the next room hoisted sail because the moon happened to shine on it, ha, ha! Nonsense—but away with all these moonshine fancies—he's come—ha, ha, ha! the dear boy—he's here.

Les. He, who?

Luc. Not the Flying Dutchman, I hope?

Capt. P. No, no, the Walking Dutchman—here he is—here's Von Bummel's hand, sure enough; and here comes young Von Bummel, as like his father as water is to water. Hollo! Smutta! bear to leeward there! clear the gangway! [MUSIC.

Enter VANDERDECKEN, *shown in by* SMUTTA, L. D.

Welcome, my dear boy, how are you? how like old Von, to be sure. Well, what sort of a voyage have you had?—I'm afraid rough; you look as if you had been a little sickish, but it's all over now—here's Letty—here's your wife that is to be; look at her—isn't she a trim-built vessel, from keel to topmast, eh? [*Lestelle gets to* L.—MUSIC.—*Vanderdecken starts at sight of Lestelle—he takes off his hat and bows to her—his eye wanders from her to the picture of the Shepherdess.*] I see what you mean, why couldn't you speak; you fancy there's a bit of a likeness between that old picture and my Letty; I have heard that said before, though I don't know why it should be, but if you are fond of old pictures, I have plenty of them in this house.

Lucy. Sir, sir, if you talk of likenesses, the one there of the Flying Dutchman is exactly like—

[MUSIC.—*Vanderdecken, unperceived, stretches out his hand, and the portrait of himself changes to a resemblance of Peter Von Bummel.*

Capt. P. Ha, ha, ha! nonsense.

Lucy. But it was like him if Old Nick hadn't changed him this instant.

Capt. P. Why, Letty, what are you doing there, twiddling up in a corner? Why don't you give the young man a little encouragement? And you [*To Vanderdecken*], why don't you speak to her—bring her to an anchor—speak to her.

[MUSIC.—*Vanderdecken is somewhat disconcerted—a thought strikes him, and he declares himself dumb.*

Les. } Dumb!
Lucy. }

Capt. P. What does he say?

Lucy. He says he's dumb, sir!

Capt. P. Oh, then that's what he meant by—[*Mimicks the action of Vanderdecken.*] Dumb! I didn't bargain for

that; but, I say, the despatches are as dumb as yourself on that subject.

[MUSIC.—*Vanderdecken runs to the table and writes, and gives it to Peppercoal.*

Capt. P. Don't look so frightful—very awful correspondence. [*Reads.*] "*I was struck dumb by lightning on my passage hither*"—Poor fellow! "*I am assured that I shall recover my speech in a short time.*" Well, come, that's not so bad; and as the women generally like all the talk to themselves, why, perhaps, it may be all the better in the end, and to-morrow shall be the wedding of yourself and Lestelle.

Les. To-morrow, uncle! Uncle—

Capt. P. Ay, to-morrow: a dumb husband will be all the better for you, and the sooner you're married, the longer you'll have all the talk to yourself; therefore, give me your hand, and give me yours. [*To Vanderdecken.*] You shall be spliced to-morrow morning.

[*A loud knocking is heard at* L. D. *as he is about to join their hands.*

Enter SMUTTA, *hastily*, L. D.

Smu. Oh, massa, there's anoder Mynheer Von Bummer man vid blind old sailor man, and dam large a bear, massa.

Capt. P. Another Von Bummel? why, there is but one Von Bummel, and here he stands.

Smu. Him so big all round.

Capt. P. And you said something about a bear, too.

Smu. O ees, massa, such him wapper!

Capt. P. O ho—I smoke the plot—Lucy, come here. [*Lucy comes down,* R.] I do believe the bear is your lover. [*To Smutta.*] Hearkye, show up this other Von Bummel, and keep the bear below. [*Exit Smutta,* L. D.] My friend, do you step behind the screen—I'll soon settle this business. [*Vanderdecken goes behind the screen.—To Lestelle and Lucy.*] Oh, fie upon you both, you ought to be ashamed of yourselves—where is he?

[MUSIC.—*The bear growls without,* L.

Enter MOWDREY, *with a long rough staff, and dressed as an old Seaman, followed by* SMUTTA, L. D.

Mow. Sarvice, your honour. I hopes you'll excuse a poor distrest seaman vots got no better means of a livelihood than by showing off poor bruin what's below there to the land swobs!

[*Bear growls without—Smutta starts, as if frightened.*

Mow. There's a woice, your honour—how he runs over the gammon.

Capt. P. Egad! but you shan't gammon me!

Mow. If you'll allow him to come up, he'll sing the young ladies a song; but, first and foremost, I does my duty by piloting into port Mynheer Von Bummel, whom your wonderfulness has been on the look out for, I reckon.

Capt. P. [*Aside.*] I have, and I'll let you know it presently.

Enter PETER VON BUMMEL, L. D.

Pet. I'm arrived, old Coaly. [*Exit Smutta,* L. D.

Capt. P. Well, and who are you, now you are arrived?

Pet. My name's Peter Von Bummel—I'm the son of your old friend.

Capt. P. You're not a bit like the son of my old friend.

Pet. You needn't blow me up for that, that's my father's fault.

Capt. P. Well, if you are the son of my old friend, prove it—show me your testimonials—where's your documents?

Pet. [*Aside to Mowdrey,* L.] As I've lost my letter, I'd better authenticate myself by a little of my native Dutch. [*Going up to Peppercoal.*] Ich, ich, mynheer! Yaw! yaw! Kaller de Holland kesta spreken.

Capt. P. Yaw! yaw! the fellow brays like a jackass. You my old friend's son—[*Noticing the portrait.*]—Damn me if it isn't the Flying Dutchman!

Pet. (C.) Dutchman—Dutch, me no Dutch—but I'll have you up, old hatchet-nose!

Capt. P. Old hatchet-nose; but I'll be calm! [*Aside.*] I see through it all, and I'll have a scheme in my turn—sit down a little.

Pet. I'll sit down, but I can't sit down a little. [*Turns round.*

Capt. P. And, hearkye, perhaps you'll entertain the ladies in the meantime with some of Bruin's antics, while I order in something to refresh your weary limbs.

Mow. (L.) Thank your wonderfulness—if I makes too free, I hopes you will excuse my nonsensicalness.

Capt. P. (R.) [*Aside.*] I will—I'll have you all in the bilboes in two minutes. [*Exit Captain Peppercoal,* L. D.

Les. My dear uncle, for heaven's sake don't leave us: we—

Mow. [*Throwing off his hat.*] Lestelle, is it possible you do not know me—let us fly—

Les. Hush! hush! my suitor, Von Bummell, is hid behind the screen!

Pet. [*Taking the lute off the table.*] What, another Von Bummell behind the screen!—we'll have him out.

[*Mowdrey throws down the screen,* L.—*Vanderdecken has vanished.*

Mow. Your apprehensions are in vain—[*Placing his arm round Lestelle.*]—hear me.

Pet. [*Coming down,* R.] Hollo, my friend, what are you at? [*Hits him with the lute.*

Mow. Keeping my word with you: didn't I promise to advocate your case?

Pet. But remember, I'll do all the rest. [*They retire up.*

Enter VARNISH, *as a Bear,* L. D., *dancing*

Var. I can bear it no longer [*Running up to Lucy,* R.U.E.]—charming Lucy [*Kneels.*], behold at your feet one who is dying for—

Lucy. Help! Murder! O—h!—[*She screams—almost faints—they support her to the chest in consternation.*

Var. [*Taking off the bear's head.*] How deucedly unlucky. [*Placing his head on the table under the window.*] If I had but taken off my infernal head first.

[*Returns to Lucy—Peppercoal, with a sword, climbs up a ladder outside the window in the flat, which he opens, and snatches the bear's head off the table.*

Capt. P. [*Disappearing.*] The rogues! [*All start up.*

Mow. Rogues! did you hear that?

Var. Somebody knows us!

Lucy. Varnish! dear Varnish!

Var. Where's my head—I've lost my head! [*Hides behind the screen,* L.

Enter CAPTAIN PEPPERCOAL, L. D., *with a sword in one hand and the bear's head in the other;* SMUTTA *and Slaves following him.*

Capt. P. Come along—I'll find 'em out, I warrant. Out with that fellow directly.

[*Pointing to Mowdrey—Scuffle—Lestelle and Lucy hurry off,* R. S. E., *while Mowdrey and Peter fight off,* L. D.—*The scene is upset, and Smutta leads forward Varnish by the ear—Captain Peppercoal holds up the head, and then throws it to Varnish.*

Var. Give me my head—how my poor head has been knocked about.

Capt. P. Now, sirrah! what have you to say to this? Confess the whole plot, or—

Var. Well, then, there is a plot.

Capt. P. And you are come to help him.

Var. Yes, sir, I'll try it on a little; my master intends to carry off your niece this very night, in the disguise of the Flying Dutchman, sir; and so we come here just to—

Capt. P. Just to let me into the secret; but you shall remain as security for their good behaviour. What shall we do with him?

Smu. Put him in wine-cellar, massa.

Var. In the wine-cellar—oh ho! Cape Madeira in abundance—that's not so bad.

Capt. P. If you dare to crack a single bottle, or to draw a cork, I'll have you stifled in sawdust—damme, I'll stop up your mouth with sealing-wax.

Var. I must try to make an impression;—sweet Mister Pepperpole, do but hear me.

Capt. P. Don't sweet me—I'm a compound of crab-apples and vinegar! away with the rascal.

[*Smutta and Slaves seize Varnish.*

Var. I won't go—no, by no manner of means—I'll see you all black, blue, red, green; and there [*Strikes Slaves, &c.*]—oh, help!

[*Slaves force Varnish out,* L., *Captain Peppercoal following.*

Smu. Oh, him poke out poor Smutta's little right eye.

SCENE III.—*A lonely Pass—Stage half dark.*

Enter MOWDREY *and* PETER, L.

Mow. I can endure this suspense no longer—I'll return and rescue Varnish and Lestelle, my adorable Lestelle.

Pet. (L. C.) Your adorable Lestelle! my adorable Lestelle!

Mow. Bah!

Pet. Bah! There's contempt of court for ye! I've a great mind to ask him for his card, only I'm afraid he'd give it me.

Mow. I'm so mortified, I'd shoot myself for half-a-crown!

Pet. I wish I had half-a crown!

Mow. What did you say?

Pet. I say I wish I had half-a-crown.

Mow. Why, sir?

Pet. Because then I should have half-a-crown.

Mow. You're a contemptible fool!

Pet. [*Looking him in the face, and stamping with his foot.*] What, sir!

Mow. You're a contemptible fool; and I'd call any man a contemptible fool that acted as you do!

Pet. Oh! if you'd call anybody a contemptible fool—I don't take it personal—I think I had better adjourn, sir. I hope I don't offend, but if you would only recommend me to the nearest vessel bound for England, I should be so—

Mow. [*Crossing to* L.] You can rest awhile here. In a few hours expect me; you shall then have the advantage of my cutter—impertinent fool!— [*Exit,* L.

Pet. His cutter! O dear! that's an insinuation I don't like; he robs me of my wife as was to be, and then I'm to have the advantage of his cutter [*Draws his finger across his throat.*]; but I'll be too sharp for him!

Smu. [*Without,* L.] Massa! massa!

Pet. Here comes one of his cutters!

[*Goes off hastily,* R., *and returns as Smutta runs in,* L., *with a letter.*

Smu. It's only Smutta.

Pet. Keep off, keep off—if you touch me, I'll bring my action for assault and battery.

Smu. Me bring no salt, nor no buttery, massa; me bring only pretty kind letter from Miss Lucy, Miss Lestelle's maid.

Pet. A letter for me, from Lestelle's maid—I'm awake, I smell a rat.

Smu. Dam him rat, massa—him no smell him rat.

Pet. Yes, you do smell like a rat. [*Reads.*] "*People set to watch at night—the only way to pass is to assume the disguise of the Flying Dutchman, which Smutta has provided.*' [*To Smutta.*] You've got the disguise all ready? "*Write a line, to put us on our guard. Fail to come, and another will carry off your mistress.*—LUCY." [*Kisses the letter.*] I don't know which to love most, the mistress or the maid; but I've been sworn at Highgate, and shall take the mistress. [*Crosses to* L.—*Smutta holds out his hand, and Peter shakes hands with him—Smutta still holds out his hand.*] I hav'nt the least idea what you mean. [*At last, as recollecting.*]

Oh, ah, certainly; I shall do everything that's correct. I am the most liberal fellow on the face of the earth, when I have any money; but—[*He fumbles in his pocket, and then exclaims, putting his finger to his nose.*] I shall see you by and by. [*Exit*, L.

Smu. Now, what de devil him mean by—[*Mimicks the action of putting his hand to his nose.*] Oh, him so dam plase, him forget to give present to poor Smutta. [*Exit*, L.

SCENE IV.—*The Turret-Chamber, as before—Peter Von Bummel's Picture continues in the frame in the flat*, L.—*Stage dark.*

TOBY VARNISH *discovered, seated on the oak chest, with the bear's head.*

Var. (R.) So, old Peppercoal was afraid of his wine, and, after keeping me a quarter of an hour in the cellar, locks me up here, in the dark, too—makes me a sort of state prisoner—in one of the best rooms, too. Ah! footsteps; should it be Lucy—it's the old sea-monster!

Enter CAPTAIN PEPPERCOAL, *with a candle in his hand*, L.—LUCY *following.*

Capt. P. Let me see: there are two or three points I must question this fellow about. Harkye— [*Lucy comes cautiously in*, R., *and blows out the candle—then runs to Varnish.*] The candle gone out—I thought I heard somebody give a puff. [*Hurries and secures the door.*] Are you there, fellow?

Var. [*With Lucy*, R.] No, sir, I'm here; I'm a fixture.

Capt. P. Ugh! I should be sorry to take you at a valuation. Enjoy yourself in the dark till my return. [*Exit*, L.

Var. I'll amuse myself as well as I can. [*Kisses Lucy.*

Lucy. If you do that again, I'll scream out.

Var. Pray don't; he's coming already.

Lucy. No, no, not so soon: I never do things by halves, though you do.

Var. Eh?

Lucy. He can't readily procure a light—I've poked out the kitchen fire, and upset the tinder-box at the same time. My mistress is locked up, and I have coaxed Smutta to carry a letter to your master, who is to come here disguised as the Flying Dutchman.

Var. Come here! what, to-night? Then he'll get murdered—I shall get murdered—you'll get murdered—we shall all get murdered.

Lucy. Is the man mad? When he knocks, you have only to open the blind [*Shows a rope-ladder.*], throw out this rope-ladder, and you'll soon see the consternation every one except ourselves will be in.

Var. Not they, indeed: why, don't you know, in order to gain time, and save my own bones, I've told old Firecoal—Charcoal—Peppercoal—what's his name? that my master is actually coming here, as the Dutchman's ghost, this blessed night.

Lucy. Was ever anything so unlucky?

Var. What shall we do? Perhaps he won't come.

Lucy. O yes! here's his reply to my note. [*Drops paper.*] No, it isn't—I've dropped it.

Var. There's a pretty piece of business! The only way is, neither to answer his signal nor to throw out the ladder. Perhaps you could quit the fortress, and give him notice.

Lucy. Impossible! Hark!

Enter CAPTAIN PEPPERCOAL, L. D., *with a loaded pistol, screening the candle with the lappet of his coat—Lucy takes advantage, and steals to the door*, L.—*Stage light.*

Capt. P. I had great difficulty to light it—somebody had poured water into the tinder-box; but it sha'nt go out this time, I'm resolved. [*Lucy shuts the door*, L.] Who's that? Lucy! where the devil did you drop from?

Lucy. Through the door, sir—thought you called for a light. [*Points for Varnish to pick up the letter.*

Capt. P. So I did, half an hour since. Why, what's all that winking and nudging about? [*Varnish hums a tune while picking up the letter.*] Come, sir, hand over those despatches, or I'll drive a bullet through your topmast.

Var. Want the head, sir? [*Tendering the bear's head.*

Capt. P. You shall want a head presently. [*Strikes the bear's head with his pistol.*

Var. Don't do that, sir—you'll make my head ache.

Capt. P. Come, give it— [*Snatches letter from Varnish.*] Now, march aft.

Var. (R.) March what, sir?

Capt. P. (C.) March up the room; and you [*To Lucy.*] keep out of the bows—none of your telegraphing. Now, keep quiet, while I read the letter. [*Reads.*] "*Recollect to be at the window in the large room, and wait till I give three knocks.*" [*Varnish creeps behind Captain Peppercoal, and *places the bear's head over Captain Peppercoal's shoulder—Lucy laughs—and Varnish retreats to the sea-chest, sits on it, and places his hat on the bear's head.*] If you have any regard for the head on your shoulders, take care of that in your hand. [*Continues reading.*] "*Be sure to be punctual at the time. Your's,* THE FLYING DUTCHMAN." So, so, this is the room, is it? I shall sup here.

[*Mumbling over the letter—advances towards* R.—*Varnish gets across to Lucy,* L.

Var. [*Aside to Lucy.*] Why, that's not my master's writing.

Lucy. What? how?

Capt. P. Come, march over the side of the ship, march!

Lucy. Well, I'm going, and happy am I to give you notice that I wouldn't live another day in your service if—

Capt. P. Get out, or—

Lucy. Sea-bear! and is this the return for a poor servant's merits.

Capt. P. Get out! and take your little merits with you. [*Exit Lucy, grumbling,* L. D.] Now, sirrah, we shall soon come to action! Hollo, there! bring up some grog and biscuit.

Enter Two Slaves bringing in a tray and wine, L., *a small supper-table with cloth laid, an extra cloth folded, two lighted candles, wine, horn cups, knife, plates, &c.*

Var. Going to get drunk, and I shall get murdered, I suppose; what can it mean—not my master's writing! if the real ghost should come—

Capt. P. [*To Slaves, who have placed the table,* L.] Sheer off! [*Exeunt Slaves,* L.—*Captain Peppercoal runs after them to kick them.*] Sit you there; [*Varnish sits at table.*] now, fill a bumper to the health of the Flying Dutchman.

Var. [*Trembling.*] I can't, sir.

Capt. P. Drink, sirrah! Drink, sirrah!

[*Captain Peppercoal gives wine to Varnish; and, just as he is about to drink it, Peter knocks violently at the window—Varnish lets the cup fall, and sinks on his knees,* R.

Capt. P. [*Laughing.*] Ha, ha, ha! Well, sir, why don't you hoist your sail, and open the window to his ghostship.

Var. [*Imploringly.*] N—o! no, sir!

[*Captain Peppercoal snatches up a pistol.*

Capt. P. But I say yes; yes, blubber, open the window, sir, or I'll pop a bullet through your topmast, I will.

Var. Ye—ye—yes, sir! O—h! o—h! I see his cloven foot through the—I smell brimstone—I! o—h! [*Captain Peppercoal presents the pistol.*] Yes, sir.

[*Varnish opens the window and falls, as Peter, with an enormous mask, hat, and feathers, presents himself at the window in flat—a dark lantern in his hand.*

Pet. [*In a gruff voice.*] B—oo!

Capt. P. [*Throws the candle and candlestick and fires a pistol at Peter.*] Miss'd him, by Jupiter.

[*Runs out,* L. D.—*Varnish gets behind the screen.*

Capt. P. [*Calling without,* L.] Smutta, get a blunderbuss; give him a raking fire at his stern, and blow away the gingerbread work!

Pet. [*Through the window.*] What am I to do? They smoke the plot below—twenty of 'em at my heels—here's a reception for a lover: I—[*Pistol fires without,* L. U. E.—*he tumbles in at the window and overturns the table, &c.*] I'm shot! o—h! [*His mask falls off.*

Var. [*Throwing down the screen.*] Spare all I have, and take my life.

Pet. [*Getting up and putting on his mask the hind part before.*] Toby! my Toby. Oh!

Var. Peter, my Peter, oh! [*Noise.*] They return; what's to be done—they've taken away the ladder! [*Looking out of the window.*] Ah! the rope ladder—here it is; follow me; but first lock that door.

[*He flings the rope ladder out of window and escapes, while Peter locks the door,* L.

Pet. Don't go without me.

Var. [*Behind the flat.*] Hollo! the rope ladder has given way.

Pet. The ladder given way! what am I to do? [*Noise at* L. D.] No closet, no outlet; a chest—fast! confusion! [*Snatches a knife from the table and forces the lock open.*] Devil take the knife, I've cut my finger; I'll tie it up with old Peppercoal's table-cloth.

Capt. P. [*Without*] Bear a hand.

Pet. They're coming; box open, in I go! I fancy myself in England,—I've got a private box all to myself.

[*Gets into the box,* R.—*A crash without.*

Enter CAPTAIN PEPPERCOAL, L. D., *with* SMUTTA *and Four Slaves with sticks, having forced the door.*

Capt. P. [*With a pistol.*] How the devil came you to miss; and such a mark, too!

Smu. [*With a gun.*] Him sure him hit him somewhere.

Capt. P. Well, I won't have the house turned topsy-turvy, nor my niece terrified in this manner; away with those infernal pictures, I'll give them no longer quarter; take them out of the house; and, as for that cursed old chest, toss it into the sea; let it swim after its master, the Flying Dutchman. Go down, and fetch up a soldier or two from the garrison. Ill—ill—ugh!

Exit, L. D., *in a violent passion—they are removing the pictures and conveying the box out as the scene changes.*

SCENE V.—*A Lonely Pass.—Stage half dark.*

Sailors. [*Without*, R.] Yo ho! yo ho!

Enter TOM WILLIS, VON SWIGGS, *and Sailors*, R.

Tom. [*Entering.*] Ah, ha, ha! I tell ye, Von, it's too late,—we must aboard the Enterprise again. Captain's leave was only for two hours, just to hail the fortress and gain signals of his honour, Mister Von Bummel; and here you, who have took upon you to be our pilot, have brought us by a round-about circumbendibus sort of a way like a rope's coil, to just where we set sail.

Von S. Ugh! Ich sall tell you vot it ish, mynheer: it ish dat deffil Vanderdecken, vot haf bewilder mein senses; it ish he who haf leaf met his dance all about, like der cork and de screw, tweest a tweester.

Tom. Belay, belay: you were out of your latitude on these shores, and we out of ours to trust to your gogriphy; howsomdever, we'll pipe all hands at daybreak, and be off to the wedding, and salute the bride with one of old Nepton's consarts, too,—three hearty cheers and a boatswain's whistle. Afraid of the Dutchman, eh, Von? Now, if I were to see him on dry land, I'd snap my finger at him myself, and call him an impostor sailing under false colours.

All. And I—and I.

Von S. Dat's a tefflish goot a joke: I'll tell you a story.—Onch on a time, Vanderdecken—[*Thunder.*] what was that?

Tom. A storm rising; come, come, let's aboard before it gets dark: shiver me, I do see something coming. [*Looking off* R.] How it glides along, what's it like?

Von S. It's like der dibel!

[*Thunder—exeunt, terrified*, L.

Enter MOWDREY, R.—*Stage becomes darker.*

Mow. Strange, I can gain no tidings of my servant. Poor Varnish, surely old Peppercoal has not dared to restrain him: yet, were he alive, at liberty, ere now, I am but too well persuaded, he would have returned to his duty; how rejoiced will he be to learn that I have again discovered our lost boat floating in yonder creek, and that we can again cross the river, and carry off Lestelle and Lucy. Ah! sure I heard a footstep; no, 'tis merely the agitation of the waves: night thickens, and the dim clouds portend a storm; still, still he comes not. I'll delay no longer: in my solitary boat alone I'll venture, and fear no danger where Lestelle invites. [*Exit*, L.

SCENE VI.—*Stage dark.—Exterior of the Fortress, with a Verandah*, L. S. E.—*in the background, over a descent of Picturesque Rocks, the Ocean—a distant Lighthouse—the Sea slightly agitated.—Moonlight.*

MUSIC.—*Enter* VANDERDECKEN, R. U. E., *wearing a large blue mantle—he crosses the stage and looks up at the Verandah*, L. S. E., *where the notes of a harp are heard—as Lestelle sings, the words of the song affect him.*

AIR.—LESTELLE, *without*, L. U. E.

Return, O my love! and we'll never part
 While the moon her soft light shall shed:
I'll hold thee fast to my virgin heart,
 And my bosom shall pillow thy head.

During the air, MOWDREY *descends the rock*, R. S. E., *with caution—he crosses and goes beneath the verandah, near Vanderderdecken, without perceiving him—Vanderdecken threatens scornfully, and implies that he himself will bear away Lestelle, and then retires, mysteriously*, R. U. E.

Mow. 'Tis her heavenly form! all quiet—if I could but attract her attention. [*Calling.*] Lestelle! Lestelle!

Enter LESTELLE *into the Verandah*, L. S. E.

Les. That voice! I could not be deceived.

Mow. Ah, Lestelle! will you not descend and fly with me, through the dim twilight, this spot, which, but for thy presence, would be too hateful.

Les. Alas, William! I am a captive, and to-morrow I am to be hurried to the altar, and my hand forcibly bestowed on another.

Mow. While I have life it shall never be accomplished. Can you by no means descend from the verandah? these arms shall screen thee from danger and the storm.

Les. I have a scarf within; I—ah! I hear footsteps—away, if you love me, and conceal yourself. Armed men, from the garrison, are in the fortress. Fly, fly! or you are lost. [*Retires from the Verandah.*

Mow. But, Lestelle! only one word, and I—Ah!
[*Exit,* R.

Enter CAPTAIN PEPPERCOAL *and Sentinel, with a gun,* L.

Capt. P. I'm certain I heard somebody's jawing tackle at work; I shan't rest if I don't shoot somebody to-night. The wood and the rocks are full of pirates, all wanting to smuggle my Letty. You, Mr. Sentinel, keep watch outside the door, and if any one come within hail, why, dam'me, fire a broadside; let 'em hear our bull-dogs bark. I'll just look out a-head to see if there are any lurkers this way. [*Exit Captain Peppercoal,* R.

[MUSIC.—*Re-enter* VANDERDECKEN, R. S. E.—*he crosses the Sentinel to* L., *unperceived*—LESTELLE *appears in the Verandah, with a scarf—she starts at the sight of the Sentinel, and hesitates—Vanderdecken waves his hand, and a small rose-coloured flame descends on the Sentinel's gun—he retreats, in terror,* R. S. E.—*the flame follows him.*

Re-enter MOWDREY, R.

Mow. Lestelle! Dearest Lestelle!

Les. Now assist me.

[MUSIC.—*She descends into Mowdrey's arms—Vanderdecken, who is invisible to Mowdrey, comes behind, and, crossing to* L., *touches Lestelle.*

Les. (C.) How is this? A sudden chillness rushes through my veins—I faint—I die! Ah, Mowdrey, see, that horrid spectre!—support me.
[*Swoons in Mowdrey's arms.*

Mow. (R. C.) Lestelle, Lestelle! All here I behold—the trees, the fortress—nothing more. Ah, this cold hand—her bosom, too, no longer palpitates. I dare not call for aid—the water—in the hollow of my hand——

[MUSIC.—*He supports Lestelle in his arms to a bank,* R. S. E., *and hurries towards the water,* L. U. E.—*in the meantime, Vanderdecken covers her with his mantle, and Lestelle vanishes.—Exit Vanderdecken,* R. S. E.

Mow. [*Returning.*] Lestelle! my love, my life! my—horror!—lost, lost! Help, help! [*Falls.*

[*Storm.—A mist begins to arise, through which Vanderdecken is seen crossing the sea in an open boat with Lestelle, from* L. U. E.—*the storm rages violently—the boat is dashed about upon the waves—it sinks suddenly with Vanderdecken and Lestelle—the* PHANTOM SHIP *appears (a la phantasmagorie) in a peal of thunder.—The stage and audience part of the Theatre in total darkness.*

INVISIBLE CHORUS, L.

Vanderdecken, come.
The bridal-bark, the spectre band,
Over sea and over land,
Wait to guide this captain's lady home.
Then, Vanderdecken, Vanderdecken, come.

END OF ACT II.

ACT III.

SCENE I.—*The Sea-beach.*

SMUTTA *sitting on the sea-chest, in* C., *and Four other Slaves discovered, with sticks, listening.*

Smu. [*Rising.*] Nobody follow! Debbil himself never come here. Now we look into old box; me hear Lucy say nice fine ting in that box, me get him out, carry fine clothes to Lucy, so she make Smutta him chum chum.

[MUSIC.—*They all approach the box, and force it open with their sticks—when the lid flies up, Peter pops out his head, with the mask and a large hat on—they all run off,* L.

Pet. Bag my books, all off! Don't like the Flying Dutchman—eh, my masters? [*Laughing.*] Ha, ha, ha! [*Noise without,* L.] O dear, they're returning—found me out. What shall I do? I'll pop on the clothes in the box there, and pretend to be a female, lovely, virtuous, and in distress. [*Noise repeated.*] Eh! coming—then I'm going.

[*Takes the dress out of the trunk, and exit hastily,* L. S. E.

MUSIC.—*Enter* VARNISH, *with the bear's head under his arm,* L. S. E.

Var. Confound that rope-ladder, I have nearly dislocated every bone in my body; what to do, I cannot imagine, though they say two heads are better than one. I have often heard of running away with a flea in my ear, but I have run away with my head under my arm. Was ever poor devil of a painter so harassed and so hungry as I am. I could eat—dam'me, I could eat my head; I could digest—[*Seeing the box.*] an old sea-chest! Oh, ho! then I did hear voices here abouts—smugglers —robbers! and this is their hidden treasure. [*Opens the lid and looks into the chest.*] Why it's full of emptiness—there, they are going to rob somebody, and this is to bring off the spoils in; if they find me there, I shall be shot for a spy; or, [*Meditating.*] if they hav'nt opened the box, they can't do it without a hammer. Perhaps they'll carry the box to the hammer; so, if I get inside, and hold down the lid—egad, I will; it's the only way of escaping unnoticed from this place to a place where eatables and drinkables are to be had. [*Gets into the chest.*] Licensed to carry one inside. Eh! Oh, my poor bowels. What a tight fit. [*Closes the box.*

MUSIC.—*Enter* SMUTTA *and Slaves, with cudgels,* L.

Smu. All still; all quiet. Tortoise in him shell again —dam cunning, but we break him about him ears. [*Laughs.*] Ha, ha, ha! [*Slaves hit the lid of chest with their sticks.*] How you like dat, Massa?

[*Varnish, with the bear's head on, shows himself in the chest.*

Var. Fire! Murder!

Smu. Vat dat? O la! him look like large kangaroo, he, he! Smutta nebber hear kangaroo cry out murder, tho', for all dat.

Var. [*Sitting on the edge of the chest.*] Spare me! Don't you know me? I'm an Englishman—my name's Varnish.

Smu. [*Aside.*] Lucy's chum chum! Me break him all into little bones. [*With sarcasm.*] Your name's Varnish, me tink you say?

Var. Yes; Toby Varnish, Esq., footman extraordinary to Lieutenant Mowdrey, potticary's boy to his Britannic Majesty, and ordinary painter in carmine to the Empress of Nova Scotia. [*Aside—rises and crosses to* R.] There, I think I've instilled into their vulgar minds a little sense of personal respect.

Smu. Um! You great man! Smutta take you to him massa—Captain Peppercoal—eh!

Var. Take me to the devil! to old Peppercoal—my back throbs at the bare idea; I'd sooner swallow a porcupine dressed in its quills, than meet that snarling sea-griffin again. Let me go—I'll come again to-morrow.

Smu. You so rich—what you give him, massa?

Var. Give! O dear! here's a rascal in office, by instinct, wants a bribe.—Alas! I've lost my place, and now I must lose my last month's wages, or lose what is dearer to an Englishman than life, place, or money—liberty! Well, well—what shall I do? egad! I will—Now, my lads, look out—there, there's a scramble, and I brush!

[*Scatters money—They squabble, and pick it up—Exit Varnish, running* L.

Smu. Dat's mine—and dat's mine—and dat's mine—and dat's mine, mind [*Smutta turns.*] Mind dat—Eh! gone! runa! No dere—no dere; me see—me see—[*Points to* R S.E.]—he! he! he! him change himself again!

Enter PETER VON BUMMELL, *dressed as a Shepherdess, with a crook, hurried in by the slaves,* R. S. E.

Pet. Oh! Gentlemen of the jury, pity and protect a lovely young creter, who has been set on by ruffians, and compelled to screen her innocence in that cave—I think I had better be off.

[*Escapes,* R. S. E.—*The Slaves run and bring him back.*

Pet. Conduct me to the nearest vessel, if you please; I'm England bound. [*Aside.*] I wish they were bound neck and heels together. Pity me, sweet gentlemen, good-looking, fair-complexioned gentlemen. I'm only a poor trembling, palpitating little damsel.

Smu. Is, missy, me pity you ver much—you got dam a large leg, missy; fine calf undem petticoats—eh! [*Catching at the petticoat a little, and laughing.*] Ha, ha! how funny!

Pet. O fie! where's your manners? talk of a lady's calves—you might as well talk of—bag my books, if this isn't worser than—I'm in such a flutter—don't you see I'm going to faint—I—oh!

Smu. You go with us, massa—you big rogue—Smutta him know all about. Come, massa—come!

Pet. If I do—I'll—I tell ye I'm a gentlewoman, lonely, virtuous, and in want! Don't believe, eh? Well, then, I'll show ye a gentlewoman's trick for once [*Snatches a cudgel from one of the Slaves.*] There! there! there!

[MUSIC.—*Smutta and Slaves attack him—he beats them off,* L.—*He returns, and, holding up his dress, runs with violence across the stage, pursued by them,* R.—*two Slaves carry off the sea-chest,* R.

SCENE II.—*A gigantic Cliff, down which the Sea is rolling with terrific violence—a descent of rocks and sea-weed—a cave sinking still deeper into the earth,* L. U. E.—*a bank,* L. S. E.—*Stage partially dark.*

[MUSIC.—*Enter* VANDERDECKEN, *with* LESTELLE *in his arms, down rock,* R. U. E.—*he places her on the bank,* L.S.E.—*goes to the entrance of cave, and listens—takes up a shell of water, and sprinkles Lestelle's face—she revives—he exults, and implies that she must now enter and sign the fatal book—music ceases.*

Les. [*Shrieks,* R.] Enter yon dreadful abyss; sign the fatal book which consigns me to live for ever beneath the waters.—Do not terrify me—you are not, cannot be what you appear—Spare me! spare me! [*Sinking at his feet.*] Yes! ah! you weep! you relent—Mercy! mercy!

[*He gazes tenderly on her, then places her hand against his heart, as he points towards the cave.*—MUSIC.—*The symphony of "Return, O my Love," played on the flute without.*

Les. Ah! that strain—the forbidden song! It bewilders me; I am lost—an irresistible impulse urges me on. [*First verse of the song,* "Return, O my love!" *sung without, accompanied by the harp.*] That sweet enchanting strain again!

[*Vanderdecken watches her features, and leads her gently down the abyss,* L. U. E., *under the influence of the music.*

Enter MOWDREY, *on the rock,* R. U. E., *pale and almost exhausted—he descends slowly.*

Mow. Thus far, directed by the screams of my dear Lestelle, I have followed—what demon is it that still tears her from my arms? [*Lestelle screams in the cave beneath the earth,* L. U. E.] Ah! 'tis her voice—again I hear it! Yes, Lestelle, I'll follow thee—into the depths of the earth I'll follow thee—we'll live and die together!

[MUSIC.—*Exit into the cave beneath the earth,* L. U. E.—*he drops his handkerchief.*

PETER, *as a Shepherdess, with a cudgel, pops his head from amongst the rocks,* L. U. E.

Pet. [*Coming forward.*] What a horrid situation for one of the soft sex! If any of the real sex should ever be placed in a similar situation, I hope they'll get out of it as neatly as I have done. [*Noise without,* L.] More violators! down, then, maiden modesty, and up cudgel.

Enter VARNISH, *hastily,* L. U. E.

Var. [*Calling.*] Sir, master—my dear master! [*Peter holds up the cudgel at him.*] Why, what the devil are you? What! Peter in petticoats? what a wapper! What masquerading is all this? where do you come from? where have you been?

Pet. [*Singing.*] "I've been roaming, I've been roaming," &c.

Var. Oh dear! I am half mad; my master must be quite mad, or he'd never have scrambled, neck or nothing, into this infernal place. I'm sure I caught a glance of him but an instant since.

Pet. He—he's just gone on a random shot into Davy Jones's Locker there. [*Pointing to the cave.*] Don't you attempt to follow him. No, no—let's decamp.

Var. Go, and desert my master! Why, look ye, Peter: my master took me from bottle-shaking, and I'll never desert him so long as I can shake a limb in his service. He's been a good master to me, and—— [*Picks up the handkerchief dropped by Mowdrey.*] Here's his handkerchief—that's a signal of distress. [*Wipes his eyes with it.*] I'll follow; so shall you.

Pet. [*Pointing to the cave.*] What, there? No, I thank you!

Var. Coward! go, then, up yonder rock, jump into the boat, and desire old Peppercoal to send aid, lights, and ropes, to the entrance of the Devil's Cave. Mind what I say, or I'll come back again, if it be only for the satisfaction of pounching you to death in my own mortar!

[*Exit into the cavern,* L. U. E.

Pet. There's a fool for ye! Going to the devil, and calculating upon coming back again. How am I to climb up these rocks again? rather an awkward situation for a lady

[*He arranges his dress to ascend the rock,* R. U. E., *and the scene closes.*

SCENE III.—*A Room in the Fortress.—Stage light.*

Enter CAPTAIN PEPPERCOAL, R.

Capt. P. (C.) They tell me Lestelle is carried off, notwithstanding my vigilance. Now, then, I'm as completely miserable as any respectable old fellow of my character would wish to be! And what's brought me to all this? My extreme good nature—the urbanity of my disposition—my lenity towards the faults of my enemies. My tenderness for Lestelle has ruined the poor girl: I suffered her to act just as she pleased, and so she's sheered off from her weak-hearted fool of a guardian with nobody knows who: the Flying Dutchman, forsooth! Psha! the flying devil! It's all a trick—a device—false colours! Oh, here comes that jade, Lucy! Now I shall have an opportunity to worm the whole scheme out of her, and detect the fugitives before it be yet too late.

Enter LUCY, *with a band-box*, R.

Lucy. (R.C.) I'm going, sir.

Capt. P. Going! where?

Lucy. [*Pertly.*] To quit my place, sir. We gave each other notice last night.

Capt. P. Ay, ay,—I believe there was a mutual exchange of signals between us, not exactly congenial though, I think.

Lucy [*Aside.*] Congenial! why that's what Varnish says—what can he mean by congenial?

Capt. P. To be sure, at times, when I'm hard up, I'm a little rough, but I'm smooth again in an instant, nobody can deny me that.

Lucy. No, but then you are no sooner smooth than you are rough again in an instant, nobody can deny that either.

Capt. P. Why, grape and canister, if—

Lucy. Character—yes, you must give me a character.

Capt. P. I don't know that I shall: every person's character ought to be able to pass muster and take care of itself;—look at mine by land and by sea.

Lucy. Take care you don't lose it.

Capt. P. Impossible, after fifty years' standing.

Lucy. Don't be too certain: as Newton says, spots do sometimes appear in the sun's dish; you may know what

it is to want a character yourself shortly, so your servant. [*Going.*

Capt. P. [*Seizing her hand.*] If you go, I'll be——

Lucy. Not go!

Capt. P. Now there's not a soul in the house but our two selves. [*Looks round.*

Lucy. What, sir?

Capt. P. I want you to let me into a little bit of a secret.

Lucy. A little bit of a secret.

Capt. P. Tell me all about it: where is Lestelle; help me to find them out, and I'll make your fortune. If you deceive me, I'll put you in the coal-cellar, and feed you upon bread and water. Come, come, Lucy, I know you'll be a good girl; [*Gives her a purse.*] there's a key to unlock the floodgates of mystery—you understand me; now we are alone, I wish to take advantage of——

Lucy. Not of me, you wicked man. O yes, you look like a seducer!

Capt. P. I look like a seducer! did you ever see a seducer in gray hairs and a three-cornered hat? will you understand me?

Lucy. I understand too well. Don't come near me—I'll scream.

Capt. P. Well, scream,—I'm too old a seaman to be frightened at that.

Lucy. What am I to do for a reputation?

Capt. P. Get another, it will be quite as good as your last.

Lucy, Ah! help! help! what am I to do? [*Aside.*] I owe him a grudge for his unkindness to my mistress. I'll frighten him a bit. I'm lost! O—h! I'm going to faint! [*Faints.*

Capt. P. Well, faint! [*Lucy falls into his arms.*

Enter VON SWIGGS, TOM WILLIS, *and Two Sailors, with a knife and table-cloth.*

Capt. P. [*Pushing Lucy from him.*] Discovered, too!

Lucy. Defend me! save me! [*Running to Tom Willis.*

Von S. [*Smoking.*] Yaw! yaw! vot is dish Mynheer Von Peppercole, ugh!

Tom. Ay, ay, my pretty lass; tuck yourself under my arm, and if that old chap dare to clap his grappling-irons athwart your mizen again, down goes his topmast.

Capt. P. And pray, gentlemen-looking smugglers,

which I take ye to be, who desired you to wind your whistle aboard this fortress.

Tom. Nobody: we com'd of ourselves—we be no smugglers, we wants to speak with our passenger, Peter Von Bummel: he invited us all here to his wedding, ye see. On our way we fell in with Peter's bag, an old chest dashed to pieces, this knife, and this bloody table-cloth, marked with your name, by which we suspect our messmate has come by an ill end, which you must answer.

Capt. P. That baggage knows well enough that Peter——

Lucy. I know nothing, except, in my opinion, that the man who came here wasn't real flesh and blood.

Tom. That's well said, my girl! Now understand me, Master Pepperpole.

Capt. P. How dare you address me in that manner? Do you know who I am? I——Did you ever hear my character?

Lucy. [*Laughing.*] Of fifty years' standing. Ha! ha! ha! [*Exit*, L. D

Capt. P. You lubbers! Now you march after her, or I'll treat you all three to a rope's end. You know what a rope's end is, all of ye, I dare say.

Enter PETER, L.

Pet. Old Coaly, I have news for you.

Capt. P. Then take your companions away, and bring them after me. [*Exit*, L.

As Captain Peppercoal rushes out, L. D., *enter* PETER, *in his original dress.*

Tom. 'Tis he! 'tis he! huzza!

All. Huzza!

Pet. Ah, Tom Willis! I didn't see you. I'm not married yet—a married life is like——Did you ever hear of such a place as the Devil's Cave?

Tom. To be sure: our cutter lies at the mouth of it, and deuced wild anchorage it is.

Pet. Never you mind that, but come along with me. I'll cut you out a job; and, if you finish it to my satisfaction, you shall swim in grog for a month. You are not afraid of spirits, are ye?

Tom. No, your honour; so being they are not stronger as brandy.

Pet. That's your sort! Now do I feel as great—as great as Alexander at the battle of the Nile, when, like a river god, he rode on the back of his *Obstrapulos*, and rushed into the briny—briny—bri—you know what I mean; he rushed into the briny.

All. Huzza! [*Exeunt*, L. D.

SCENE IV.—*Interior of the Devil's Cave—an overhanging Rock*, L. S. E., *leading into the Cave—a grotesque Rock in the centre, resembling an antique table, and massy book, closed.*

[MUSIC.—LESTELLE *discovered, supporting herself against the rock*, L. S. E., *in an attitude of distress.*—VANDERDECKEN, R., *comes down, with a torch in his hand—he gazes at Lestelle, puts down the torch, and points to the magic book.*

Les. Thine, earthly or unearthly! never! Terrible being, thou mayst indeed trample on my mortal frame, but the soul of Lestelle is far above thy malice.

[MUSIC.—*He is angry—he takes her hand, and, approaching the book, it flies open and displays hieroglyphics—Lestelle screams, and sinks at the base of the rock—footsteps heard without—Vanderdecken listens.*

Enter MOWDREY, *from the rock*, L. S. E.

Mow. [*Calling.*] Lestelle! I am here—you are safe! Lestelle! [*He descends, and sees Vanderdecken.*] Ah, wretch, is it you? Tremble!

[MUSIC.—*Vanderdecken laughs, then draws a sword—a terrific fight—Mowdrey, after repeatedly stabbing his opponent in vain, is taken up by Vanderdecken, and furiously thrown down.*

Van. Mortal, die! [*Thunder.*] Ah, what have I done! [*He displays bodily agony.*] I have spoken! [MUSIC.] The spell which admits my stay on earth is destroyed with my silence. I must begone to my phantom ship again, to the deep and howling waters; but ye, the victims of my love and fury, yours is a dreadful fate—a hundred years here, in torpid life, to lie entombed till my return. Behold! [*Points to the book*—A CHORD.

Enter VARNISH, L. S E.—*he runs across, and hides behind the magic book.*

Mow. Is there no hope?

Van. None! Seest thou this magic book: its mystic pages, consumed by the hand of a sailor's son, on ocean born, would set ye free; but never can that be accomplished, for in Vanderdecken's absence 'tis denied that human footstep e'er seek this cavern, or pierce those flinty walls.

[*Varnish comes cautiously forward and snatches up the torch, which Vanderdecken has inserted in the ground—he sets fire to the mystic book, and, advancing triumphantly to* L., *with the torch in his hand, exclaims*, 'Tis done! 'Tis done!

Var. [*To Vanderdecken.*] What d'ye think of that? I've burnt the writings, old one. I'm a sailor's son! I was born at sea, too; my father was a stout-hearted British tar, and so was my mother!

[*Varnish joins the hands of Mowdrey and Lestelle.*

Van. [*After covering his face with his hands.*] Malediction! malediction! you triumph. But I go to my revenge. Tremble, tremble! the rushing waves which rise to welcome the return of Vanderdecken, shall bury ye deep, deep in their unfathomed darkness. Burst, stormy clouds, and overwhelm them; rise, ye many waters of ocean, cover them up for ever. [*Thunder.*] Rockalda! I come.

[MUSIC.—*Vanderdecken goes behind the rock-table, whereon the magic-book was placed, and sinks with the altar, amidst thunder and flames of red fire.—Exit Varnish, with the torch*, R. S. E.

Var. [*With a torch, on a projecting rock*, R. U. E.] Master, dear master, the rock, the rock—follow me; this way—I hear voices.

Mow. 'Tis the voice of Varnish; he has found an outlet to liberty. Come, love, come!

[*Exeunt Mowdrey and Lestelle, hastily*, R. S. E.; *and they all appear on an eminence of the rock*, R. U. E.

Mow. Alas, there is no hope!—Hark, hark! the torrent is rushing down upon us. See! see! Assistance is at hand—help! help! help! [*Waves handkerchief.*

[MUSIC.—*Varnish continues waving his torch, and the agitated waters rush furiously into the cave, entirely covering the stage to the orchestra—the sound of the gong, and loud peals of thunder heard—a pilot, Peter Von Bummell, with a torch, Captain Peppercoal, &c., appear in a sloop from the very back—they come under the rock*, R. U. E., *and receive Lestelle, Mowdrey, and Varnish aboard—sails are hoisted, with British flag, and as the cutter turns round to return, shout*, "Huzza!"—*incessant noise, as on board a vessel, with crash, gong, and thunder, until the Curtain falls.*

THE END.

Index of Actors and Theatre Managers

BANNISTER, John (1760–1836) was originally an art student at the Royal Academy under Rowlandson. Under the sponsorship of Garrick he took to the stage, first at the Haymarket. He became famous for tragedy at Drury Lane, but later showed a natural flair for comedy and specialised in this type of drama. He was the first Don Ferolo Whiskerandos in *The Critic*, and later went on extensive provincial tours. He returned to London and became one of the managers of Drury Lane, retiring in 1815. He maintained his contacts with the art world, especially with Rowlandson, Morland and Gainsborough.

BARRYMORE, William. There were two people in the English theatre at this time having the same name though they were not related neither to each other nor to the American theatrical family bearing the name. The elder (1758–1830) was connected with the Coburg Theatre in its early days and the younger (?–1845) was a general actor who also wrote several plays.

BLANCHARD, William, (1769–1835) is first recorded as having been a member of a travelling company in 1785 when he played under the name Bentley. He remained as an actor and manager in the provinces for many years before making his first London appearance at Covent Garden in 1800. Apart from a short visit to America in 1831 he stayed at Covent Garden until his death. Contemporary accounts give him most credit for heavy comedy and character parts. He had two sons, of which the younger, Edward, became a well-known writer of burlesques and pantomimes, usually appearing under the *nom de plume* of Francisco Frost.

COLMAN, George, the younger (1762–1836) took over the management of the Haymarket from his father, and ran it, although with only partial success, until 1803. He was the writer of many plays revealing great comic talent. Through influential friends he became the examiner of plays in 1824. Those who thought, by inference drawn from his own works, that he would be liberal censor were disappointed and puzzled. When tackled on the subject of his somewhat strict rulings he replied: 'At that time I was a careless immoral author. I am now the Examiner of Plays. I did my business as an author at that time, and I do my business as an Examiner now!' According to Clement Scott, Colman was ever anxious about his fees as examiner, and on one occasion was over zealous in trying to licence an oratorio. He was very disappointed when the authorities ruled that the Bible did not require the Lord Chamberlain's licence!

COOKE, Thomas Potter, (1786–1864) was the archetypical British tar. He was the son of a surgeon, and ran off to join the navy at the age of ten. On board H.M.S. *Raven* he was a sharer in Earl St. Vincent's victory, subsequently wrecked off Cuxhaven and afterwards sailed with the *Prince of Wales*.

Leaving the navy after the peace of Amiens he joined the company at the Royalty in 1804 and played at Astley's and the Lyceum before leaving for Dublin. 1809 saw him back in England and at the Surrey. He played at both Covent Garden and Drury Lane, his long nautical experience obviously fitting him for his most successful role, that of William in Jerrold's *Blackey'd Susan*, a part which he played 785 times. His other famous roles included the Vampire (which he also played in French at the Porte St. Martin, Paris), and Vanderdecken in *The Flying Dutchman*. He also directed some melodramas.

ELLISTON, Robert William, (1774–1831) was born in George Street, Bloomsbury, the son of an eminent watchmaker. His uncle was master of Sydney College, Cambridge, and enrolled the boy at St Paul's School, intending that he should enter the Church.

His first appearance on stage was in a 'private' (amateur) performance of *Pierre* and he subsequently played the various country theatres.

His family disowned him and he began to doubt his choice of career, writing to his uncle, imploring to be allowed home and start afresh. He did return, but it was not long before his passion for the stage returned and through another member of the family, Professor Martyn, he received an introduction to George Stevens, then editing the works of Shakespeare. It was Stevens who arranged for Ellistone to see Kemble at Drury Lane. Due to a misunderstanding, Elliston did not accept the engagement and in 1793 appeared instead as Romeo for Dimond in Bath.

His first professional London appearance was not until 1796 when he appeared at the Haymarket for Colman.

Elliston liked to dabble in management and at one time held the leases of innumerable provincial theatres. He took over the Surrey, and in 1819 managed Drury Lane. He engaged a fine acting company, including Kean, and with Clarkson Stanfield and David Roberts as his painters, the theatre gained a reputation for high-class scenic effects. He was, however, far too extravagant and was declared bankrupt in 1826. Somehow he managed to pay off his debts and in 1827 was back at the Surrey. This time his fortune was made for the play he secured was Jerrold's *Blackey'd Susan*, with T. P. Cooke—an immediate success which ran for over one hundred consecutive performances and was revived many times.

FITZBALL, Edward, (1792–1873) dramatised most of Scott's works, and, though he worked mainly for the minor theatres, wrote for Covent Garden under Osbaldiston's management. He also went to Drury Lane where he provided the libretti for many of Bunn's light operas.

HARLEY, John Pritt, (1790–?) was the son of a silk merchant who carried on business in the neighbourhood of St Martin in the Fields, London. He went against the wishes of his family in 1807 by joining Jerrold's* company at Cranbrook in Kent, eventually appearing in many provincial theatres including Southend, Essex, Rochester, Stamford, York, Worthing and Brighton.

His first London engagement was on 15 July 1815 at the English Opera House. In September of the same year he joined the company at Drury Lane and was trained in comedy parts by Bannister, the senior comedian there. Contemporary critics placed his acting on the same high plane as that of Fawcett and Matthews.

HOLCROFT, Thomas, (1744–1809) was the son of an itinerant shoemaker and in his earlier years trained racehorses at Newmarket.

By the age of twenty-five he had become acquainted with Macklin and Foote and through this association became attracted to the stage. He had a hard time as an actor though he did play at Drury Lane. His first play, *Duplicity*, written in 1781 was received so well that he decided to give up acting and take to writing. While his most famous play may be *The Road to Ruin* he has been credited with introducing melodrama to the English stage in the form of *A Tale of Mystery*. He was self-educated and became a very good French scholar, besides being adept at painting and fond of music. A friend of Lamb, Holcroft was also editor of *The Theatrical Recorder* which was first published as a monthly periodical in 1805 and contained English translations of French and Spanish plays.

He once was charged with High Treason but proceedings were dropped before he stood trial.

JERROLD, Douglas William, (1803–57) was resident dramatist at the Coburg and subsequently at the Surrey. He had served in the navy with the scene painter Clarkson Stanfield, with whom he worked again when Stanfield was scenic artist at the Coburg.

It was Jerrold's *Blackey'd Susan* which turned the tide on bad fortune at the Surrey and he became such an eminently successful writer that his plays were also taken up by the patent theatres. He was also involved with *Punch* from its inception.

JORDAN, Dorothy (Dorothea), (1761–1816) was a great success as a player of comedy, particularly in what were called 'breeches parts' (men's parts, played by women). Her career originated in the Irish Theatres and in 1782 she came to England, first appearing in Leeds on Wilkinson's circuit and later in York where she was seen by Smith of Drury Lane. She was encouraged to come to London and Sheridan engaged her to play second female lead to Mrs Siddons. Her personal life was fraught with disaster—she was herself illegitimate, and she died in France.

* Not the author of the same name.

KEELEY, Robert, (1793–1869) was one of the most famous low comedians of the nineteenth century appearing both at the Olympic and Adelphi.

His wife Mary was trained as a singer and made her début at the English Opera House. She often played 'breeches parts' such as Jack Sheppard in the drama about the highwayman but is acknowledged to have been at her best in sentimental roles. They managed the English Opera House (after it had become known as the Lyceum) for three years and at one time were also in partnership with Charles Kean.

KEMBLE. A famous family of English actors founded by Roger Kemble formerly a hairdresser who became a strolling actor-manager. He married Sarah Ward, the daughter of a provincial manager. Those members of the family paramount during the period in our survey were:
JOHN PHILIP (1757–1823), manager successively of Drury Lane and Covent Garden, and financially unsuccessful at either theatre. In later years he was forced to sell his library, and his collection of old plays went to the Duke of Devonshire. He was often described as a great actor in the grand manner, and certainly his looks were most striking. However, Leigh Hunt, writing in 1807 saw fit to parody his style of speech in the following verse:

Varchue, the happy wisdom's known
in making what we wish our own;
Nay, e'en to wish what wishes thee
imparts the blest reality;
For since the soul that *purses* mine,
Sweet Myra's soul, is full of thine,
In my breast too thy spirit *stares*,
Since all my soul is full of *hairs*.

This does make more sense if for Varchue, one reads Virtue, for the, thy, for purses, pierces, for stares, stirs, and for hairs, hers—but then that was grand acting! Kemble rebuilt Covent Garden, and, in a bid to get back the large amounts expended on this, the prices of admission for the 1809 season were increased. This gave rise to the 'O.P.' riots in which for nearly two months performances were disrupted by those in the pit demanding a return to the old prices (hence O.P.). The management eventually gave way and the price of admission to the pit returned to its previous level, but that for the boxes remained at the new price.

CHARLES (1775–1854) was first a civil servant but left this position for the stage. He made the first attempts to bring historical accuracy to his productions and it was for his 1823 production of *King John* that Planche designed and supervised the costumes. Charles Kemble reigned over the stage for twenty-five years, and was forced in to retirement by increasing deafness. He did not sever all links with his profession however because he continued to give Shakespeare readings and, in 1840, became examiner of plays.

FANNY (Frances, Anne) (1809–93) made her first appearance at Covent Garden in 1829 to save her father Charles from bankruptcy. She was immediately successful and appeared at Covent Garden for three years playing many roles associated with Mrs Siddons.

STEPHEN (1752–1822) was John Philip's younger brother, and was perhaps the least successful of this phenomenal family. He managed a provincial touring company and theatres in Edinburgh and Ireland. He became enormously fat and, it is said, could play Falstaff without padding. He managed Drury Lane in 1818 somewhat unsuccessfully and retired after having presented his son, Henry, as Romeo. Henry, like his father, never achieved the greatness of the other Kembles and, having played at the Coburg for some seasons, eventually sank into oblivion.

KOTZEBUE, August von, (1761–1819) spent his early years as a civil servant, subsequently devoting himself to the theatre in Vienna. He held strong political views, which culminated in his being stabbed in 1819. Without him, it is doubtful if there would have been gothic melodrama at all. Many of his works formed the basis of British plays and in his time he was more popular in his native Germany than even Schiller. Sheridan was not beneath borrowing the text of Kotzebue's *Die Spanier in Peru* as the foundation for his *Pizarro*.

LEWIS, Matthew Gregory, (1775–1818). Most famous for his novel *The Monk*, hence his nickname 'Monk' Lewis. Among his plays are *The Castle Spectre* and the equestrian drama *Timour the Tartar*. He wrote in the style of Kotzebue, the great German dramatist, and translated two of his plays.

MISS LOVE (1801–?). Born in Cheapside, London, the daughter of an army officer. From an early age she was trained in music and engaged by Arnold for the English Opera House where she played many leading parts. At the end of her initial engagement there she was offered better terms by Covent Garden and transferred her services to that theatre.

The indisposition of Miss Tree, the leading singer there, meant that Miss Love was brought forward in a leading role much sooner than would have been usual and, although described as 'a pleasing singer rather than a great one', she became immensely popular.

Her provincial tours were always successful and during the late 1820s she was under contract at Drury Lane.

PALMER, John, (1742–98) was the son of Robert Palmer, pit door keeper at Drury Lane. His first engagements were for Foote at the Haymarket and in 1767 he was taken by Garrick for Drury Lane. He ventured in to management and built the Royalty, Wellclose Square, East London, in 1787. He here attempted a high-class bill of fare, but in 1803 after his death his theatre was the subject of the Reverend Thirlwell's pamphlet on 'A Solemn Protest Against the Revival of Scenic Interludes and Exhibitions at the Royalty, containing remarks on *Pizarro*, *The Stranger* and *John Bull*'. Palmer died on tour at Liverpool, strangely enough, in *The Stranger*. Legend has it that he had just uttered the speech, 'There is another and a better world', when he fell lifeless on the stage. He had been disturbed at the death of his own son and, so a contemporary report says, he 'fell a sacrifice to the poignancy of his own feelings, and the audience were doomed to witness a catastrophe which was truly melancholy'. The coincidence was too much for those who loved to preach against the theatre and his sudden end was used to give point to many a tale of retributive judgement. His theatre in Wellclose Square was eventually burnt down in 1826, re-opening in 1828 as the Royal Brunswick, but collapsed three days after the opening killing fifteen people during rehearsals of *Guy Mannering*. Legend again has it that while the dust was still settling, a sermon against the evil of the playhouses was preached to bystanders among the ruins!

PIXÉRÉCOURT, Guilbert de, (1773–1844) was the father of French melodrama and, by virtue of the fact that at that time there was no international copyright, the father of English melodrama too. He also wrote fairy-tale plots and other types of drama, presenting them at his own Théâtre de la Gaîté in Paris. This was the first of the French theatres not to be State-aided and was open from 1808 until destroyed for a street-rebuilding scheme in 1862.

PLANCHÉ, James Robinson, (1796–1880) was responsible for many innovations on the British stage as well as being a most prolific author of most of the common types of drama. His first play was given at Drury Lane in 1818, and he also wrote the English libretti for many operas, including Weber's *Oberon*, *The Magic Flute* and *William Tell*. He continually pressed for reform in the copyright laws and it was mainly his efforts which led to the passing of 3 William IV c. 15 which gave protection to dramatic authors. Not only was he associated from the earliest days with Madame Vestris at the Olympic and Lyceum, writing, some say, his best works for her, but he was also instrumental in making the closure of the theatres come at a more reasonable hour of the night, eleven o'clock instead of twelve or even one in the morning. In 1834 he published *History of British Costume*, long a standard work on the subject. He became Rouge Croix Pursuivant of Arms and later Somerset Herald at the Herald's College and had in the course of this duty often to go abroad to confer the Order of the Garter on foreign royalty. Together with Charles Kemble he brought historical accuracy to stage costume and settings.

O. SMITH (born 1786 at York). His real name was Richard John Smith but according to legend he gained the initial 'O' from his performances in melodrama of a character called Obi.

He was destined for the legal profession and was articled to a solicitor at Bath. Finding legal life dull he enlisted in the merchant navy and sailed from Bristol for the Guinea Coast in 1803. He was soon in trouble for helping slaves to escape and returned to England to avoid punishment. The attraction of the stage provoked a family feud and he spent some months as a strolling player in Wales before joining Macready as a player and prompter at Sheffield.

After the Sheffield engagement he appeared at Edinburgh and Glasgow returning to Bath in 1807, where he was seen by Elliston and engaged for the Surrey and made his first appearance there in May 1810.

O. Smith excelled in the demonic characters of melodrama—Zamiel in *Der Freischutz*, Vanderdecken in *The Flying Dutchman*, the monster in *Frankenstein* and also as generally villainous characters—Guy Fawkes for example.

He eventually played at the theatres royal though continuing to undertake engagements at the minor theatres.

TERRY, Daniel, (1789–1829) was no relation to the other famous theatrical Terry family. He was not only an actor but a dramatist for Covent Garden too, adapting Scott's works for the stage, and writing opera libretti.

He made his first stage appearance in London in 1815 at the Haymarket playing in *The Clandestine Marriage* and appears to have been at Covent Garden from 1813 to 1822. He supported Mrs Siddons in her farewell performance in Edinburgh in 1815.

Terry was a partner of Frederick Yates for a while at the Adelphi Theatre, but retired when the venture became financially unstable.